Directors of Industry

The British Corporate Network 1904–76

John Scott and Catherine Griff

Polity Press

© John Scott and Catherine Griff 1984

First published 1984 by
Polity Press, Cambridge, in association with Basil Blackwell, Oxford.

Editorial Office: Polity Press, PO Box 202, Cambridge, CB1 2BT, UK.

Basil Blackwell Ltd
108, Cowley Road, Oxford, OX4 1JF, UK.

Basil Blackwell Inc.
432 Park Avenue South, Suite 1505, New York, NY 10016, USA.

British Library Cataloguing in Publication Data

Scott, John
  Directors of industry: the British intercorporate network,
  1904–1976.
  1. Power (Social sciences)—History—20th century
  2. Corporations—Great Britain—History—20th century
  302.3'5   HM131
  ISBN 0 7456 0019 0

Also included in the Library of Congress Cataloging in Publication Lists

Typeset by Katerprint Co Ltd, Oxford
Printed in Great Britain by Bell and Bain Limited, Glasgow

In memory of
William John Scott (1886–1963)
Alice Scott (1891–1984)

Contents

Contents

List of Tables and Figures

TABLES

List of Tables and Figures

FIGURES

Acknowledgements

A number of people were kind enough to read and comment upon parts of the manuscript. Tony Giddens read it in its entirety and made a number of helpful comments, and Howard Aldrich, John Barnes, and Clyde Mitchell gave me detailed comments on the early part. I am grateful to all of them for their help. A number of informal discussions with Mike Useem proved fruitful in the early stages of data analysis. It would be invidious to mention any of the individual members of the international research group with which I have worked, as so many of the ideas emerged out of our many collective discussions. A special mention must be given, however, to the Dutch team – Frans Stokman, Donald Elsas, and Frans Wasseur – who supervised much of the computing which was carried out on the 1976 data. They were unfailingly helpful in this and many other ways, and their help was reinforced by the hospitality and institutional support given by the Sociologisch Instituut of the University of Groningen. Various parts of the project and the analysis have been discussed at seminars at the Universities of Bath, Essex, Leicester, Strathclyde, and York, at the London School of Economics, Kingston Polytechnic, and at Ormskirk and Paisley Colleges. I am grateful to all the participants for their comments.

The research was supported by a grant from the Social Science Research Council before it capitulated to political pressure and dropped the word 'science' from its title. I am grateful to the Council for its support and hope that this book might be a small contribution towards reasserting the scientific claims of social research. The research benefited greatly from being carried out at Leicester University, where a number of my colleagues have been very helpful. Despite facing a climate of financial attrition and political hostility, I am sure that the Department of Sociology will survive the shock of recent years.

Research assistance was received at various stages from Charlotte Kitson, Jill Scott, and Martyn Taylor. I am also grateful to the many companies which responded to my requests for information and provided additional data for the researchers to work on. Betty Jennings did a marvellous job in typing the manuscript quickly and efficiently.

My research associate for two years was Catherine Griff. She was involved in all the data analysis as well as supervising a related investigation into company shareholdings. Her overall contribution is incalculable. Although her return to Australia prevented her from cooperating in the writing of the book, her contribution was so great that it is only fitting that she should be regarded as joint author of the work.

John Scott
April 1984

Introduction

Studies of corporate power structure have begun to proliferate since Zeitlin's (1974) blast against managerial theories of industrial capitalism. Although Marxist writers had long proposed alternative models of corporate power, substantial work was carried out only by isolated scholars such as Mills and Domhoff. The basis of managerialism – that ownership had become separated from control in the large enterprise – was shown by Zeitlin to be a 'pseudo-fact', an assumption with little empirical basis. Zeitlin's critique expressed a growing interest in reopening issues prematurely closed by managerialism, and it presaged a mass of writings over the ensuing ten years. One of the present authors wrote a book in the middle of that period (Scott, 1979) in which an attempt was made to bring some order to the work that was being carried out in Europe, America, and elsewhere. The pace of development since then has been so great that the book has now to be thoroughly revised in order to take account not only of new data but also of new concepts and models. The present book is an attempt to apply some of these new ideas to British data collected in the Company Analysis Project (see Appendix), which began as a study of Scottish companies in 1973 (Scott and Hughes, 1980)[1] and became part of a larger international study (Stokman et al., 1984).

In the works upon which this project has drawn, four major models of corporate power structure have been proposed: resource dependence, class cohesion, finance capital, and bank control.[2] The resource dependence model is closest to the managerial position and holds that the relative power of enterprises depends upon the resources which they have available to them. Enterprises must come to terms with one another through negotiations, cooperation, and alliances aimed at securing the required resources. Differential control over resources produces differentials of power and enables powerful enterprises to force non-competition or preferential trading agreements. The model of class cohesion directs its attention to the ways in which corporate enterprises form part of a pattern of class privilege. Shared business interests are reinforced through a common educational background and through membership of clubs, associations, and political bodies. These bonds lubricate the wheels of commerce and create a high level of cohesion among the dominant stratum of business leaders. The model of finance capital stresses the centrality of capital in corporate power and argues that this is expressed in an organisational fusion of enterprises operating in a variety of economic sectors. This results in the formation of large groups of enterprises within which banks and other financial enterprises are able to ensure a degree of coordination in corporate affairs. This view is taken somewhat further in the model of bank control, which holds that banks are able to use their control over capital to exercise control over other enterprises. The bank control model assumes a conflict of interest between banks and other enterprises, and it depicts banks as building 'interest groups' or 'financial empires' of subordinate enterprises engaged in manufacturing, retailing, transport, and so on.

The common element in these competing models is an awareness of the existence and significance of intercorporate relations. The managerialist assumption of the autonomy of the large enterprise is rejected in favour of viewpoints which stress the ways in which corporate enterprises become involved in power relations with one another. The aim of this book is to explore some of the implications of these models and to show how they might be used to analyse the British corporate power structure. The theoretical basis of these models is explored in chapter 1, which constructs a model of the business enterprise and its intercorporate relations. Chapters 2 and 3 examine the structure of these relations at national and regional levels and within particular sectors in order to map some of the contours of corporate power structure in Britain. Chapters 4 and 5 examine issues of property ownership and class structure, and chapter 6 discusses the role and power of banks. It will be concluded that the valid elements of the managerialist position must be placed in the context of a theoretical scheme which takes account of the valid points of the alternative models. That theoretical scheme centres upon the analysis of intercorporate relations.

Introduction

NOTES

1. Some of the lists of company directors had to be excluded from Scott and Hughes (1980) for reasons of space. These lists, and some corrections to the original data, are printed in a booklet: J. Scott, *Multiple Directors in Top Scottish Companies* (1982). This is available through the national copyright libraries, the British Library (Lending Division), Leicester University Library, and various public libraries. Listings of companies and directors studied in the present project are available from J. Scott for the cost of reproduction.
2. The models discussed here are discussed more fully in Stokman et al. (1984), chapter 1. This discussion runs parallel to the arguments contained in two recent contributions to the *Annual Review of Sociology*, Glasberg and Schwartz (1983) and Useem (1980).

CHAPTER ONE

The Business Enterprise and the Intercorporate Network

Study of the business enterprise and the modes of control to which it is subjected have been one of the growth areas in the social sciences in recent years. Economists have examined the market strategies pursued by various types of enterprise; organisational theorists have studied their internal administrative controls, industrial sociologists have related these concerns to patterns of control over the labour process; and other researchers have examined the connections between the modern corporation and such phenomena as class structure and the state. A particularly important theme in much of this work has been the analysis of intercorporate relations. That is, the traditional focus on the individual enterprise and its market environment has been supplemented by a greater awareness of the ways in which relations between enterprises contribute both to their environments and to their internal processes. Variously termed the 'inter-organisational perspective', 'structural analysis', and 'social network analysis', this involves a stress on investigating the various forms of capital, commercial, and personal relations which enterprises establish among themselves as ways of enhancing their capacities for action.

A major concern of those who have written on the relational features of economic processes has been 'interlocking directorships', the relations between enterprises which are created when one person is a member of two or more company boards. The analysis of interlocking directorships, or more simply interlocks, is a powerful technique of social investigation, but it has frequently been utilised in a naive way. The relative ease with which basic information can be collected has sometimes resulted in crude depictions of the conspiratorial exercise of financial power. But though limitations exist in many previous studies, advances too have been made in recent work. Basic information can, indeed, be garnered with ease, but the checking and 'cleaning' of these data and their utilisation for scientific purposes require a great deal of care, hard work, and, above all, theoretical and methodological sophistication. The purpose of this book is to contribute to the development of a structural analysis of business by showing how this work can be integrated with other traditions of research into business organisation. In particular, the theoretical perspective which has emerged in analyses of intercorporate relations will be used as a framework for presenting the results of an empirical study of major British companies in the twentieth century. This perspective will be outlined in chapter 1, and the following chapters will relate the data on British companies to the concepts introduced here and to some of the important debates that have emerged from investigations of the business enterprise.

THE ENTERPRISE AND CORPORATE STRATEGY

The typical unit of economic activity is the *plant*, the unit which is most familiar to people in their everyday lives. A plant, or an establishment, can be considered as 'a body of persons engaged in production (or distribution) at a given time and place, housed in contiguous buildings, and controlled by a single firm' (Florence, 1953, p. 22). Such plants – factories, offices, and shops – form parts of the localised congregations of plants and houses that we term urban industrial centres. But, as Florence's definition makes clear, control over plants in a capitalist system is typically exercised not by the urban authorities but by a *firm*. A firm is a unit of control over economic affairs which comprises one or more plants operating in one or more industrial centres. The firm may be organised as an individual sole trader (for example, the small shopkeeper), as a partnership, or as any of a number of forms of 'corporate' organisation (Berkowitz, 1982, pp. 105–7).

The characteristic corporate form of economic activity in Britain is the joint stock company, the 'corporation' in American law. A joint stock company is a business undertaking constituted as a distinct legal entity and comprising members who provide the share capital for its activities and officers who act in its name. While a company normally operates through one or more plants, it may at the same time form part of a larger group of companies. When the members of such a group are tied together through the ownership of their shares by another company it is appropriate to speak of an 'enterprise' or 'concern'.

The first true joint stock companies were the chartered companies of the seventeenth century, but the modern form of company dates from the Companies Act (1844). Regulations for joint stock organisation were altered and codified in a series of subsequent Acts and the majority of present-day companies operate under these laws. Some chartered companies survive in Britain and a number of companies are formed as mutual associations, friendly societies, or cooperatives, but their forms of administration follow closely those of the joint stock company. Government enterprises organised as 'public corporations' have an independent legal existence but do not operate with joint stock capital; they do, nevertheless, adopt similar administrative practices. Each nation has a distinct body of company law, and so international comparisons must take account of the resulting variations in the legal form of the business enterprise. The common feature of all systems is that the legal and institutional locus of control over the affairs of an enterprise is the body of directors of the parent company. The directors of the company supervise its operations and execute decisions. Britain and the USA have a single-board system in which supervisory and executive functions are vested in the same board, though these tasks are distributed among board members. Although many companies are now setting up audit or finance committees and management or policy committees, these bodies have no legal status and are subordinate to the main board. By contrast, company law in Germany and the Netherlands defines a split between an executive management board and a non-executive supervisory board. In France, Belgium, and Italy there is a separation between an administrative board, which operates in a similar way to the single British board, and an auditing board with no decision-making powers.

The legally defined role of the director in Britain, therefore, is to see that the company meets it obligations under company law. The directors have fiduciary responsibilities as virtual trustees for the body of shareholders, who legally constitute the owners of the company. The shareholders' annual meeting, where shareholders vote according to the rights attached to the type of shares they hold, elects the board of directors and must approve the decisions of the directors in relation to dividends, changes in capital, and preparation of the accounts. Although a company must have directors to manage its affairs, some or all of their powers can be delegated to subordinate managers. Thus, in addition to setting the broad financial framework of the company, the directors must appoint the executives who are to implement these decisions (Florence, 1953, pp. 174–6; Hadden, 1977; Mace, 1971, p. 7; Bacon and Brown, 1977).

But the social reality of the business enterprise does not correspond perfectly to the legal model. The directors of the parent company may usurp many of the powers ascribed legally to the shareholders' meeting, and so *de facto* power may lie with those who are actually able to determine the composition of the board. The 'election' of directors frequently consists of a process of co-optation by those who are already board members, the main constraint on this being the need to mobilise sufficient votes to counter whatever opposition might emerge. Within the board of directors, also, the relation between internal executives and the 'outside' non-executive directors can take a number of forms. Mace (1971) has argued that the typical American company board has 15 members: 8 outside directors (one of whom may be a retired executive of the company) and 7 insiders, including the chief executive, 1 or 2 executive vice-presidents, and a number of general managers and divisional executives. As will be seen in the rest of this book, British arrangements are now very similar. Legal definitions are thus just one constraint within which a business enterprise operates, and the sociological concept of the enterprise must be studied on the basis of what Florence termed a 'realistic analysis' of its actions.

It is argued here that such an analysis shows that the board of directors is an *arena* in which struggles to determine corporate strategy take place. The board is not necessarily a unified *agency* of control acting in terms of its own or shareholders' interests. Business leaders are recruited from those who have control over the resources required by the enterprise, or from their nominees, and the boardroom is the arena in which these leaders struggle for dominance. To control an enterprise is to determine its corporate strategy by participating in the leadership group, by putting pressure on the active leadership, or by acting as a passive constraint with the potential for intervention (Kotz, 1978, p. 17). The various contenders for control will draw upon the resources available to them in order to protect or enhance their position

(Zald, 1969). This depiction of corporate nature as red in tooth and claw must be qualified by the recognition that the struggle for control may remain latent for much of the time. Company boards are not centres of continuous and deliberate struggles for supremacy; boardroom struggles are a relatively infrequent occurrence. The various contenders do, however, have differing interests and there is the ever present possibility that this latent conflict of interest will erupt into overt conflict over the composition of the board. The normal smooth functioning of the enterprise depends upon the establishment of a *modus vivendi*, a balance of power within the 'dominant coalition' (Child, 1972, p. 14) which minimises the potential for conflict.

The spread of the joint stock company created the possibility of a separation between the legal entitlement to a share in the ownership of corporate capital and the ability to participate in the use of that capital. When the shares of a company become widely dispersed among a large number of shareholders no single 'owner' is in a position to 'control' the affairs of the company, and there are too many separate owners for them to cooperate for the purpose of control. Under these circumstances, internal career managers may be able to usurp the power of control which is nominally held by the legal owners. This possibility is the basis for the controversial thesis of the 'managerial revolution', which has recently come under critical scrutiny (Scott, 1979, 1982a). A major tenet of this thesis is the claim that while inside and outside directors share the same legal responsibilities, those with an inside executive function may have access to resources not available to the outside directors. Theorists of the managerial revolution stress the critical importance of executives in corporate decision-making, arguing that outside directors are the passive subjects of executive manipulation (Pahl and Winkler, 1974). Full-time executives have control over the information received by their fellow board members and are able to structure this information in such a way as to pre-empt decisions. The information and options presented to the board are such that the desired course of action emerges as the only 'realistic' one. Through such non-decision-making processes, argue Pahl and Winkler, the outside directors are effectively manipulated (Pahl and Winkler, 1974, p. 109). From this point of view, the composition of the board is all but irrelevant.

But a number of arguments can be raised against this thesis. Even if it is accepted that many non-executive directors do not

initiate policy proposals or play any crucial role in the choice
between alternatives, it may still be the case that they act as a
passive discipline on the executives. Their presence on the board
forces the executives to sift the various alternatives in the light of
the anticipated reactions of the outside directors. The executives
know that every month or so they will be required to appear
before the board to account for the operations of the enterprise.
The outside director does not want to be involved in the details of
particular decisions, and sees his or her role as simply keeping the
executives 'on their toes'. The appearance of manipulation masks
the reality of passive discipline. As Mace argues:

> The latest possibility that questions might be asked requires that
> the top executives of the company analyse their present situation
> and be prepared to answer all possible questions which might – but
> probably will not – be raised. (Mace, 1971, p. 23)

Indeed, the role of the outside director will often be more active
than this implies. Non-executive directors bring information and
opinions from outside the enterprise and are, therefore, able to
function as advisers on ideas evolved within the executive. Such
advice may be technical, legal, or financial, or may relate to areas
such as politics, public relations, property, and pensions (Mace,
1971, p. 13ff.). Furthermore, because the board holds ultimate
financial responsibility and ensures that all corporate matters are
translated into monetary terms, outside directors can influence
decisions with minimal 'inside' knowledge. They need to know
little about the specific products of the enterprises they direct
when all important decisions can be reduced to a range of
budgetary options. The outside directors can contribute to the
making of financial decisions in terms of financial criteria (Fitch
and Oppenheimer, 1970, p. 85).

The decisions made by the board relate to the general strategy
of the enterprise rather than to its day-to-day operations.
Corporate strategy involves determining the goals of the enterprise and planning the financing and timing of new investments in
relation to such matters as the range and diversity of products.
This requires supervision of the enterprise's investment decisions
and their consequences, and supervision of the management
through an institutionalised system of delegated authority (Barratt Brown, 1968). A corporate strategy evolves through a
continuous monitoring of the actual and predicted actions of

other enterprises, as these actions impose constraints upon the options available to the business leadership (Child, 1972; Chandler, 1962). An enterprise can be said to be continuously 'scanning' its environment, in order to gather information. A major part of the organisational structure is concerned with filtering and processing incoming information. At its most routine level, for example, incoming post and telephone calls have to be directed to the appropriate departments, where they are then directed to the appropriate desk. At a more significant level, the results of meetings with other companies and outside bodies have to be translated into memos and files for direction to particular departments. A corporate 'definition of the situation' – embodied in the standard operating procedures – provides rules for the interpretation of information gathered by the 'external scan', or 'environmental scan', in a way that is meaningful for the officers of the enterprise (Hedberg, 1981, p. 8). One crucial function of outside directors is to enhance the external scan of the enterprise, the information which they bring supplementing that which is processed inside the enterprise and passed up the corporate hierarchy.

The historical stages through which strategic decision-making has developed have been usefully described in the work of Chandler (1962) and his colleagues. Chandler argues that the emergence of the large national enterprise at the turn of the twentieth century involved the creation of either a loose amalgamation of semi-autonomous concerns or centralised 'functional' systems of administration. Only in the functional enterprise was control over corporate strategy and operations significantly transformed. The various administrative functions were subdivided into distinct departments handling finance, purchasing, sales, personnel, and so on. Each enterprise had a head office which acted as the central decision-making body for coordinating and planning the activities of the constituent firms and plants. As enterprises evolved a strategy of continual product innovation – aimed at offsetting the slow market growth experienced with any particular established product – so they became more concerned with the problems of marketing than simply with the management of production. Activities were decentralised into product divisions, each of which operated as a separate profit centre, subject to financial supervision from the general office (Williamson, 1970, chapter 7). Within this 'divisional' structure strategic control was finally separated from operational administration.

The functions of managing day-to-day operations and the executive supervision of this process of management were separated from the ultimate responsibility for determining corporate strategy. The parent board and central office became responsible for strategy while supervision of day-to-day operations was transferred to the divisional level (Chandler and Redlich, 1961). Those enterprises which took the path of multinational operation were involved in a further change. Corporate strategy became 'global strategy': while strategic decisions were taken in the parent company's offices in New York, London, or Frankfurt, operational administration took place at the level of the overseas branch plants and subsidiary companies (Hymer, 1972, pp. 46–7, 50).

The stages in corporate administration, therefore, are related to developments in strategic control. For Chandler the 'managerial revolution' was a crucial precondition for the emergence of modern business organisation. Before such claims can be adequately assessed, however, it is necessary to relate the issues of strategic control and internal administration to the wider context of interorganisational relations. In product markets and capital markets individual enterprises are involved in relations of both competition and cooperation, and Zeitlin and his associates have correctly emphasised that such questions require a consideration of the structure of intercorporate linkages in which each particular enterprise is embedded (see especially Zeitlin, 1974; Zeitlin and Norich, 1979). In order to analyse these relations it is necessary to construct a systematic framework of concepts which can grasp the structure of the social networks formed by business enterprises.

THE MORPHOLOGY OF SOCIAL NETWORKS

The origins of social network analysis are to be found in two branches of social science: in social psychology, where Moreno (1934) initiated a research tradition on the implications of friendship choices for leadership and group performance; and in social anthropology, where Barnes (1954) employed the image of a network to describe community structure. In sociology, Bott (1957) extended Barnes' work on the informal interpersonal relations of friendship and kinship from a rural to an urban context. With the exception of the technical use of network ideas in geography to model traffic flows and similar processes, most work on social networks since the 1950s has used the idea of a social network as an image or a rhetorical device. Rarely has it been used as a central theoretical concept.[1] For example, in the area of 'community studies' Stacey and her co-workers made very effective use of network models in studying the connections between political parties, churches, and voluntary organisations in Banbury. The models were not, however, constructed system-atically and their structural features were not investigated by formal analytical procedures (Stacey, 1960; Stacey et al., 1975). During the past decade, however, this has changed: numerous systematic and formal applications of network concepts have been carried out; a journal, *Social Networks*, is devoted to theoretical and empirical extensions of this work; and the International Network for Social Network Analysis brings together many of the leading exponents. In addition to this, recent work in general social theory by Elias (1970) and Giddens (1979 and 1981) has proposed ideas that facilitate some fruitful developments in social network analysis.

Social network analysis is not simply a method, metaphor, or set of concepts; nor is it a specific theory. Rather, it is a broad perspective on the analysis of social relations (Wellman, 1981; Berkowitz, 1982, p. 150; Blau, 1982). It expresses the structural or relational concerns of sociology, and those who have been described as 'network analysts' have simply concentrated their attention on formalising and clarifying some of the concepts necessary to grasp the structural features of social life. The basic principle of this evolving perspective is that agents are signi-ficantly connected to others, each of whom has similar connec-tions to further agents. As a result, there exists a definite network of relations between agents. A social network has properties irreducible to those of individual agents, even though it is the outcome of the combined actions of those agents. An adequate understanding of social networks, therefore, concerns itself with the features of the network as a whole, rather than simply with the direct contacts of a particular focal agent (Barnes, 1969, p. 57). Social network analysis involves a move away from those approaches which treat social processes as the sum of individual attributes. While it is, for many purposes, perfectly legitimate to focus on agents as the unit of analysis and to treat their social relations as a relatively unproblematic set of background factors, this is far from being an adequate perspective for social science as a whole. The relational focus of social network analysis places the 'dialectic' of action and structure at the heart of the sociological enterprise (Wellman, 1981, pp. 14–17; Berkowitz, 1982, pp. 48–50; Knoke and Kuklinski, 1982, pp. 10–12; see also Layder, 1981).

Social networks are built out of social relations, and social relations involve both orientations and transactions. All social relations involve a cognitive state or an expression of attitude: agents are aware of one another or unaware of one another, they like or dislike one another, and so on. Such orientations become embedded in normatively defined roles (Parsons, 1951). But once agents have orientated themselves they proceed to 'transact' with one another. Mitchell (1973) has argued that transactions can be analysed in terms of the two dimensions of 'information' and 'resources', but an alternative terminology adopted here sees those transactions in which material means and conditions are central as 'instrumental' transactions and those in which the informational content is central as 'symbolic' transactions. When systems of action are composed mainly of instrumental trans-actions the social relations constitute a 'political economy' (Benson, 1975 and 1977; Price, 1981, p. 299); when systems are centred on symbolic transactions they constitute channels of communication. These distinctions, however useful, are always abstractions from the features of concrete social bonds: orienta-tions are complex processes in which social meanings are combined and re-combined, and all transactions have both an instrumental and a symbolic content. But the analysis of concrete social systems does involve breaking them down into the various analytically distinct relations of which they are composed. Any abstraction which is aimed at isolating relations of a particular type (such as kinship, politics, or clientage) will result in what has been termed a 'partial network' (Barnes, 1969, pp. 5–7). Such partial networks are differentiated from one another by the specific meanings embodied in the orientations which define them and by their particular mix of instrumental and symbolic elements (Boissevain, 1974, pp. 28–30). The networks of kinship relations, capital relations, and interlocking directorships are three such partial networks which will figure prominently in this book. Each such network can be studied from the standpoint of the regular patterns which underly their surface features. Having isolated the 'structural principles' or 'generative mechanisms' (Bhaskar, 1975) of partial networks, sociologists must proceed to investigate the ways in which they fit together to form an operative whole. While it is, of course, impossible to grasp concrete reality in all its complexity, it is possible to examine the articulation of partial networks with one another and to discover whether they are mutually reinforcing or antagonistic. This problem – the problem of system integration – is one of the central problems of sociological analysis (Mitchell, 1969a, p. 47; Lockwood, 1964; Mouzelis, 1974; Mishra, 1982; Giddens, 1981).

In the analysis of partial networks, and hence in the analysis of system integration, three major processes are involved: reciprocity, institutionalisation, and reproduction. *Reciprocity* refers to whether or not a transaction or an orientation is mutual or one-sided. As such, the degree of reciprocity in a relation may be seen as defining varying degrees of autonomy and dependence for the agents involved (Gouldner, 1959). To the extent that a relation is not reciprocal, a 'direction' may be assigned to it. If A owes money to B and B owes money to C, then there is a definite inequality and directionality in the relations between the three agents. The *institutionalisation* of social relations refers to their intensity and durability. An intense relation is one in which the obligations or expectations involved in it have a high certainty of being met, and a durable relation is one which persists over time or which is renewed whenever necessary. An institutionalised pattern of relations, therefore, is one in which the relations are both intense and durable. *Reproduction* is perhaps the most fundamental problem to be discussed here. Social relations must be reproduced or transformed over time and so the structure of a social network must be understood as both the condition and the outcome of the actions of agents (Giddens, 1979; Ziegler, 1978; Granovetter, 1979, pp. 504–5; van Poucke, 1979). Actions are determined by the agents' pattern of contacts within the network, these contacts providing opportunities for and setting limits on their freedom of action. The ability of agents to pursue their interests is constrained by the pre-existing structure of the network, and their ability to reproduce that structure, whether or not they consciously intend this, is a consequence of the opportunities available to them for manipulating and mobilising the network links. The intentions of agents, and the extent of their knowledge of network structure, are contingent and not necessary aspects of the reproduction of network structure. An institutionalised relation between lender and borrower, for example, depends upon the ability of the borrower (whether a person or an enterprise) to secure the means to meet its obligations to the lender, and thus the borrower's ability to reproduce or transform the relation of dependence between them is constrained by its access to those who control the means to do so. The contingency involved in social action is the reason why observed patterns in social networks are constantly subject to the possibility of structural transformation. Thom (1975) has described this interplay of reproduction and transformation as the study of morphogenesis, a process in which the dynamics of change in social systems produce a succession of structural forms punctuated by 'catastrophic' discontinuities.

A central aspect of the most recent work on social networks has been the attempt to show that the morphological features of social networks can be translated into mathematical terms. Empirical researchers on topics which appeared particularly ripe for the systematic application of network concepts – especially interlocking directorships and power structure – have drawn on technical advances in mathematics to interpret their data. The growth of computing facilities in the 1960s opened up possibilities for handling networks with large numbers of members and so reinforced the tendency to draw on existing mathematical work. Throughout the 1970s, therefore, social network analyses reached a higher level of technical rigour (Burt, 1980; Mitchell, 1979, p. 435). The particular branch of mathematics which has been applied in the analysis of social networks is 'graph theory', in terms of which social relations can be represented as mathematical relations. The mathematical concept of a graph involves the idea of points (or nodes) connected by lines (sometimes termed 'edges' or 'arcs'), and the formal properties of a graph can be analysed by representing it as a matrix.[2] Graph theory is that body of mathematical theory which analyses the properties of graphs by operating on their matrices. Certain graph theoretical procedures can be implemented by hand or with minimal computing assistance, but this will usually prove tedious for large data sets and is applicable for only the simplest measures. In recent years, therefore, a number of specialised computer programs have been written for handling graph theory. The package of programs on which all the measures in this book are based is GRADAP, which is currently the most flexible and accessible collection of routines suitable for social network analysis.[3]

Some of the main graph theoretical measures must be summarised here in order to illustrate their relevance to social network concepts. If 'point' is taken as the equivalent of 'agent', and 'line' as the equivalent of 'social relation', then graph theory provides a powerful language for the formal description of the morphology of social networks (Barnes, 1972). Two points in a graph are said to be *adjacent* if they are connected by a line, and a continuous sequence of points connected by lines is termed a *path* (Knoke and Kuklinski, 1982). The length of a path is measured by the number of lines of which it is composed and, because there will normally be several paths between any pair of points, the *distance* between two points is measured by the length of the shortest path between them.[4] Identification of paths in a graph, therefore, goes beyond direct contacts between points to indirect connections through intermediate points.[5] The concept of distance has often been extended to take account of the intensity of the lines which make up the path: points are closer to one another as the lines which connect them are more intense. The simplest graph theoretical measure of intensity is the *multiplicity* of the line, though this measure must be used with care. When two adjacent points are connected by a line which represents more than one relation of the same type, then the line representing this relation can be characterised by its 'value': two persons who are each members of the same four associations, for example, can be represented as two points connected by a line of value four. The notion of multiplicity should not, however, be taken as a measure of intensity when relations of a different type are involved. When, for example, two people are related as friends, neighbours, and business partners, their overall relationship is not necessarily any more intense than the relationship between people who are 'only' related as kinsmen and friends. Clearly, in such cases, the quality of the relations makes a separate contribution to intensity. Those points in a graph which are closest might also be expected to have the most durable relations, and it might be expected that such lines would be reinstated quickly if broken (Palmer, 1983). It should not be assumed, however, that intensity (multiplicity) and durability (reinstatement) will necessarily vary in a one-to-one manner. Indeed, sociologically significant variations might be expected to occur.

The *neighbourhood* of a point consists of those other points which are reachable within a specified distance. The *adjacency* of a point is the number of points within the neighbourhood of distance one (direct contacts) and is sometimes referred to as the 'degree of connection' of a point. This concept of adjacency has frequently found a place in analyses of social networks, an agent's distance one neighbourhood being termed its 'primary star' (Barnes, 1969, p. 58). The number of points in the distance two neighbourhood can also be used as a social network measure, being designated the agent's 'second order star'. This measures the number of agents to which a focal agent is directly connected, together with those with which it has a common neighbour. While paths of distance one or two involve social relations of which agents may be subjectively aware, this is not always the case with longer paths. The relevance of longer paths concerns not so much the subjectively meaningful contacts of an agent, though this may be important in such areas as kinship, but its ability to mobilise the links which constitute the network. An agent with a larger neighbourhood at a specified distance will have greater opportunities for mobilising other members of the network in support of its actions. For this reason, neighbourhood concepts have often been taken as measures of the *centrality* of agents in a network.[6] Centrality is an indicator of the extent to which an agent is highly connected to other agents and thus corresponds to its 'popularity' or 'accessibility'.

Graph theory permits an analysis not only of the network position of individual agents, but also of the structural features of the network as a whole. The simplest such measure is *connectivity*, a measure of cohesiveness based upon the probability that any two randomly selected points will be connected by a path: the more fragmented is the network, the lower is the connectivity.[7] Perhaps the single most frequently used measure of cohesiveness is *density*, the ratio of the actual number of lines in the graph to the number which would be present if all points were connected to all others. The density of a network reflects such factors as the size of the network and the ability of agents to accumulate contacts (Barnes, 1979, pp. 416–18) and so must be used with care. Owing to the relative ease with which it can be calculated, it has frequently been used in ways that overlook its limitations. As will be shown in the following chapter, density is most usefully employed in longitudinal comparisons of the same partial network over time and in cross-sectional comparisons of similar partial networks at the same period.

If the cohesiveness of a network can be measured through its connectivity and density, network fragmentation can be measured by the number and type of the subgraphs of which it consists. A subgraph is simply a subset of points together with the lines connecting them. Any graph can, of course, be fragmented into a large number of subgraphs according to arbitrary criteria for selecting subsets. More useful procedures attempt to identify the 'natural' divisions within a network as the basis for analysing subgraphs. A *cluster* is a subgroup of closely linked agents, and the need to decide on the degree of closeness that will be taken as defining cluster membership means that the definition of clusters is always somewhat arbitrary (Mitchell, 1979, pp. 435–6). Clusters have a relatively low ratio of external to internal connections, and the concept of centrifugality has been developed as a measure of the proportion of lines carried by cluster members which run within the cluster. Points can be clustered in terms of the path distance of their members to one another or in terms of their density, and having loosely defined boundaries they are 'fuzzy sets' which may overlap to a greater or lesser extent (Berkowitz and Heil, 1980, pp. 5–7; Lankford, 1974; Everitt, 1974).[8] Other important concepts for measuring fragmentation are component and clique. A *component* is a subset of connected points within a graph in which not all the possible lines are present. Within a component any point can be reached from any other through a continuous path, but no paths exist to points outide the component. Typically social networks consist of a number of distinct components and a number of isolated agents.[9] A *clique* is a group within which all agents are connected to one another by paths of a specified maximum distance. Cliques with a maximum distance between members of one (one-cliques) and two (two-cliques) are readily interpretable: all members are directly connected in a one-clique, and all have either a direct connection or a common neighbour in a two-clique. But cliques with a greater maximum distance do not seem so meaningful (it should also be noted that the number of cliques in a network tends to increase rapidly as the maximum path length is increased).[10] The sociological importance of identifying clusters, components, and cliques lies in the fact that their members may engage in preferential transactions with one another and may become aware of their existence as a social group. If the latter occurs, members may orientate themselves towards one another as an organised group capable of acting in concert (Barnes, 1954, p. 238; Mitchell, 1973, pp. 31–3.)

Centralisation is a feature of the whole network, by contrast with the centrality of particular agents, and fragmentation and centralisation must be considered as independent aspects of structural morphology. The simplest measure of centralisation is based upon the adjacencies of the points in the graph: the 'degree' of the network as a whole is the average number of lines running to any point. This measure varies directly with the density and inversely with the size of the graph.[11] Various measures of centralisation are reviewed in Bavelas (1950) and Freeman (1978). A particularly useful measure of centralisation is simply the proportion of points falling into the structural centre of the graph. The *centre* is the largest two-clique of locally central points, a group of central points which are mutually reachable at distance two. This measure of centralisation is related to the density: less dense graphs tend to be less centralised because both measures are dependent upon the extent to which the agents represented by the points are able to sustain large numbers of lines to other agents (Snijders, 1981).[12]

It should be clear that graph theory provides a number of readily interpretable concepts for social network analysis. Although some of the terminology may seem obscure, the sociological relevance of the concepts is generally obvious. It must not be assumed, however, that the sociologist can simply turn to graph theory and mechanistically apply it to social network data. The choice of particular measures can never be a purely technical matter. The researcher has to decide which measures are theoretically and empirically appropriate for the data in question. The choice between alternative measures of centrality, for example, is inevitably a theoretical decision based upon how realistic the researcher judges the assumptions of the various measures to be. Mathematics can be an extremely powerful aid to social network analysis, but it can never obviate the need to make theoretical and empirical decisions about the sociological properties of social networks.

THE ENTERPRISE AND STRATEGIES OF SOCIAL TRANSFORMATION

It was argued above, following Zeitlin (1974), that a central concern of research on business organisation should be the interorganisational relations in which it is involved. The previous section outlined the most general concepts required for this purpose, and it is now necessary to show how these concepts can be employed to describe the features of the intercorporate network. This description will demonstrate the specific form taken by the 'duality of structure' (Giddens, 1979) in business affairs: from the standpoint of each individual enterprise, the rest of the intercorporate network constitutes its 'environment', the situation within which it is constrained to act; from the standpoint of the network as a whole, the individual enterprises are only of importance in so far as they contribute to the reproduction or transformation of the network.

The network of intercorporate relations is a partial network which combines various social relations together to form its characteristic 'multiplex' bonds. These bonds combine, in varying mixes, capital relations, commercial relations, and personal relations. *Capital relations* are links of shareholding and credit created when one company participates in another's share capital, when families have holdings in two or more enterprises, when banks grant overdrafts and long-term credit, and so on. *Commercial relations* are trading and servicing links which exist by virtue of the fact that enterprises are buyers and sellers of one another's products, participate in joint ventures and consortiums, and employ the services of firms of lawyers, accountants, registrars, and consultants. The market in conventional economic terminology is a particular view of the network of commercial relations. *Personal relations* are links between firms, often at board level, which derive from the sharing or linking of their personnel: interlocking directorships and relations of friendship, kinship, and political association between officers all tie enterprises together. Such personal relations may, up to a point, be taken as indicators of other less easily observable intercorporate relations. It is important, however, not to underestimate the autonomy of personal relations and their independent significance in the nexus of business connections.

It was argued in the previous section that network transactions may be instrumental or symbolic, and each type of intercorporate relation may be involved in both of these types of transaction. It is through such transactions that enterprises are able to obtain the resources they require to carry out their activities. Resources are obtained through the appropriation and conversion of what may be termed 'social media' – money, materials, and information – which flow through the intercorporate network. The access of individual enterprises to the media they require for conversion into resources is determined by their structural location in the network. Instrumental transactions between enterprises involve the media of money and raw materials which can be put to work in the process of production and so converted into money capital and commodity capital resources. In symbolic transactions the basic medium is information: knowledge, expectations, implicit understandings, and so on (for a related view, see Lockwood, 1956). This information flows through the network and may be appropriated by environmental scanning and converted into intelligence, an important resource for corporate action. Intelligence is not a resource which can itself function as capital in the process of production, but it is important as a determinant of the ways in which capital can be obtained and used. The distribution of resources (capital and intelligence) within a network may be more or less concentrated, and particular enterprises will be more or less favourably placed in relation to the flow of the money, materials, and information they require. Those enterprises which are able to monopolise a particular resource will be able to restrict its flow to other enterprises. Location in the inter-corporate network – of which the 'market situation' is only one aspect – is a constraint upon the business leadership because it is the determinant of access to the social media of money, materials, and information.[13]

It is through the network of intercorporate relations that money, materials, and information can flow from one enterprise to another. The quality and quantity of these media depend upon the number of lines in the network and on their intensity, durability, and directionality. The pattern of the flow through the network depends upon its cohesiveness, fragmentation, and centralisation. The ecology of the network comprises the constraints under which each enterprise operates. These constraints are defined by the location and relative centrality of each enterprise within the network. The network itself is the result of the actions of agents (both people and enterprises) and is a condition of their further actions. Various models have been proposed for understanding how enterprises operate within such a network. The two most important, perhaps, are the complementary models of 'resource dependence' and 'uncertainty reduction' (Aldrich and Mindlin, 1977; Aldrich, 1982).

The distribution of resources among enterprises creates a pattern of dependencies among them; and differences in the pattern of distribution will generate variations in the structure of interdependence. Some structures will involve greater reciprocity than others. Dependence is a basis of power, and imbalances in the pattern of interdependencies will tend to be associated with differentials in the balance of power. The possibilities of exercising power are a function of the structural opportunities available to agents. Because agents operate within structurally determined constraints, their power consists of the structured possibilities of action which are available to them. This power varies with the opportunities opened up by the structure of the system (Lukes, 1977, p. 29; Hoerning, 1971, p. 10; see also Lukes, 1974). Although power must be seen as an aspect of personal or corporate agency, it would be wrong to adopt the position which Levine and Roy (1979) criticise as 'social vitalism'. Agents do not possess power independently of their social positions. An agent's position within a social network determines its access to or control over resources, and such resources can be transformed, reproduced, or accumulated (Baumgartner et al., 1977, p. 14). Power can only be maximised by mobilising the connections which constitute the network (Perrucci and Pilisuk, 1970, pp. 1042–3).[14]

Power is always an aspect of an agent's strategic use of resources, and, as enterprises may be assumed to attempt to maximise their autonomy by minimising their dependence on others, an enterprise which seeks to exercise power over others will do so through a strategy aimed at making them dependent on itself. Strategies in relation to the distribution of resources, therefore, will be concerned with the autonomy, and hence the power, of one enterprise relative to others (Aldrich, 1979, pp. 111–15, 118–22). Those agents which are most central in the network have the greatest potential for power (Cook, 1977, p. 71; Cook, 1982, p. 185; Benton, 1981, pp. 175–6), though the precise scale of their power potential may be related to the directionality of the relations in which they are involved. Centrality to the flow of resources may be reflected in centrality in relation to any or all of the three types of intercorporate relation – capital, commercial, personal – and an enterprise which can optimise its autonomy by centrality in terms of one relation may not need to achieve a high centrality in terms of others. A large multinational subsidiary which has access to the funds of its parent company and occupies a dominant market position may not need to enter into personal relations with other enterprises, while a smaller, regional enterprise with limited capital may be highly dependent upon the contacts it can mobilise through the non-executive directors who sit on its board.

The resource dependence model is applicable to all corporate resources, though the priority accorded to capital over intelligence means that dependence on sources of money and materials is likely to have a greater salience for an enterprise than its dependence on sources of information. Intelligence does, however, have a further significance for business enterprise, and this has been grasped by the uncertainty reduction model. Intelligence, it will be recalled, is information which has been accumulated and processed by an enterprise. The intelligence possessed by an enterprise determines the degree of 'uncertainty' it faces in its environment. The standard operating procedures of the enterprise process incoming information so as to generate the intelligence on which business leaders base their decisions. A perceived lack of intelligence results in uncertainty in decision-making, while a perceived abundance results in greater apparent predictability. The intelligence available to enterprises is determined by the principles which structure the intercorporate network. Depending on the flow of information and the manner in which an enterprise responds to this flow, parts of the environment may be regarded as entirely predictable while others are perceived as areas of considerable uncertainty. Predictability and uncertainty are understood here as they are perceived by the business leaders. Corporate executives may perceive that the behaviour of another enterprise is predictable even if this belief is objectively unfounded. Enterprises may be assumed to attempt to minimise the perceived uncertainty by maximising their access to desired information. Corporate strategies must, therefore, be concerned with the quality and quantity of information available to the business leadership (Aldrich, 1979, pp. 122–32).

Natural selection models of the enterprise have stressed that the environment may make it possible for firms to survive even when they fail to adopt 'rational' procedures of decision-making. So long as the consequences of their actions are compatible with the environmental constraints, they will survive. Corporate success and failure is not, therefore, dependent in any straightforward way upon the quality of the strategy evolved by business leaders. A clear and coherent corporate strategy which is premised upon inadequate intelligence may result in business failure, even if the strategy accords with the logic of the situation as it appears to the leadership. While corporate strategies can be explained in terms of the orientations of the business leadership, the success or failure of those strategies must be explained in terms of the actual structure of the intercorporate network.

The corporate strategy pursued by an enterprise is concerned with the levels of dependence and uncertainty to be found in its environment, the existing network of intercorporate relations. In pursuing its strategy the corporate leadership may operate within the constraints of the existing structure of the network, or it may seek to transform the environmental distribution of money, materials, and information in order to optimise its long-term capacities for action (Baumgartner et al., 1977). When an enterprise pursues a strategy of transformation it will attempt to alter its relations to other enterprises. Figure 1.1 sets out a classification of such strategies, which can be bilateral or multilateral and

Figure 1.1   Strategies of Transformation

Level of integration	Bilateral strategy	Multilateral strategy
A. Personal relations	Personal union	Community of interest
B. Capital participations	Liaison scheme	Holding system
C. Coalition of interests	Joint venture	Combine
D. Fusion of interests	Merger	Amalgamation

may involve a greater or lesser degree of integration between enterprises (for similar views see Aldrich, 1979, pp. 295ff.; Florence, 1953, pp. 126–7).

Figure 1.1 shows the interplay of capital, commercial, and personal relations in strategies of transformation. A *personal union* is a straightforward dyadic interlocking directorship or an equivalent personal relation. Two enterprises may establish such relations as a minimal way of attempting to exercise some control over their environment. In a *community of interest* there is a similar minimal organisation of a larger number of enterprises which may involve the establishment of commercial relations in the form of loose-knit cartels or price rings based on informal 'gentlemen's agreements' or on more formal arrangements. A *liaison scheme* exists where an interlock between two enterprises is supplemented by small capital participations in order to give the association a stronger and more formalised expression. The multilateral *holding system* exists where there is a mutual exchange of shares and directorships among a number of enterprises and where these enterprises tend to engage in preferential trading. A particularly strong form of this strategy is to be found among the numerous Belgian holding companies (Cuyvers and Meeusen, 1976). In *joint ventures* two enterprises, which may already operate a liaison scheme, set up one or more jointly owned subsidiaries. This is taken further in the *combine*, where a number of enterprises set up one or more joint ventures or central selling agencies. In the USA, monopolistic alliances involving holding systems, joint ventures, or combines have frequently been termed 'trusts', and political concern over monopoly has spawned anti-trust legislation. In a *merger* two enterprises become fused into a single unit through complete or majority ownership, though a substantial stake of less than 50 per cent may approximate to this.[15] An *amalgamation* is a large-scale fusion of enterprises into a single unit, within which their trading relations may be internalised. If the amalgamated companies formerly had interlocking directorships among themselves (forming a community of interest, a holding system, or a combine), then these interlocks too will become 'internalised' and the tight knot in the network of interlocks will be condensed into a single point: what were formerly interlocks between separate enterprises become hierarchical relations between the officers of a single enterprise. Interlocking, from this latter standpoint, is a stage in the transformation of market relations into authority relations, of the 'invisible hand' into the 'visible hand'. Interlocks are 'between market and hierarchy' (Williamson, 1975; Chandler, 1977; Fennema, 1982, p. 43; Francis et al., 1983).

The relationships between some of the categories in Figure 1.1 can perhaps be clarified by the typology presented in Figure 1.2,

Figure 1.2   Forms of Immediate Control

| | Degree of control | |
Level of ownership	Exclusive	Shared
Majority	Subsidiary	Joint venture
Minority	Associate	Joint associate

which classifies some of the ways in which one enterprise may be controlled by another.[16] The typology does not concern itself with the control status of the ultimate parent, but only with the forms of control it may exert over its subordinates. It is, therefore, a typology of those forms of 'immediate' control which emerge in the strategies of transformation discussed above. The level of ownership may involve the parent holding either a majority of the shares in another company or else a substantial minority holding (Scott, 1979, chapter 2). This holding may be held exclusively by one company or shared by two or more. Mergers and amalgamations will always involve the formation of one or more 'subsidiaries', whereas combines will tend to rely mainly on forms of minority control.

The extent of the control which one company exercises over others in the relations outlined in figures 1.1 and 1.2 has been documented in the classification of administrative structures presented by Chandler (1962). As was shown in the first section of this chapter, the various administrative forms have been associated with alterations in the exercise of strategic control and with changes in the organisation and role of the board of directors. The typology from dyadic interlock to multidivisional amalgamation is not, however, a strict monotonic scale; there is no uniform increase in the 'strength' of the relations. Although each level of integration in figure 1.1 may be regarded as stronger than the preceding one, there are various discontinuities between levels. Capital participations, where an enterprise is a substantial participant in the capital of another, will frequently be associated with interlocking directorships, but this is not necessarily the case; and an increase in the number of interlocks between two enterprises may increase the intensity of the line to the point at which it is equal or greater in strength to a capital participation (Berkowitz et al., 1978). Lines of multiplicity two or more in the partial network of interlocks may be stronger than lines of multiplicity one in the partial network of capital participations.[17] It should also be noted that the strategies of transformation need not, and rarely will, involve equal partners. Enterprises enter into such relations in order to enhance their network position relative to others and so it is realistic to expect one of the partners to dominate the relations which are created. Strategies of transformation may further be classified as vertical or horizontal. *Vertical* strategies exist where enterprises located in adjacent stages of production or service come together (Williamson, 1975, chapters 5, 6, 7). A particularly important type of vertical strategy is that between providers and users of credit. *Horizontal* strategies occur where new relations are formed between enterprises which compete with one another for supplies or markets. Such strategies will occur within particular economic sectors.

THE NETWORK OF INTERLOCKING DIRECTORSHIPS

The main concern of this book is to present the results of some research on the network of interlocking directorships in Britain, and it is necessary to give a more systematic account of this partial network and of its articulation with the other strands of the intercorporate network. In Britain there have been few studies of interlocks, and there has been almost no attempt to map out the structure of the network in a systematic way. Some British researchers have constructed ad hoc network diagrams for small groups of enterprises (Stanworth and Giddens, 1975; Whitley, 1973 and 1974; Scott and Hughes, 1975), and a few have attempted to tabulate numbers of interlocks and network densities (Johnson and Apps, 1979; Scott and Hughes, 1980). A major reason for the lack of a research tradition on interlocks in Britain has perhaps been the absence both of a strong Marxist movement and of a strong anti-trust movement. Early research on bank interlocks in Germany by Otto Jeidels was taken up by Lenin, Hilferding, and other Marxists as the basis for their analyses of economic power in the era of 'finance capitalism'. In the United States liberal political ideology saw interlocks as one aspect of the concentration of power, and writers such as Brandeis and Moody expressed concern about the 'Money Trust' of big bankers, which stimulated anti-trust legislation.[18] Both research traditions, therefore, owed much to the consequences of the rapid and late industrialisation of Germany and the United States, both economies becoming highly concentrated under the aegis of banks. National variations in intercorporate structure are a major source of national variations in research traditions. The American debates were the basis of a long tradition of academic research into interlocks which eventuated in the perspective of structural analysis (Berkowitz, 1980 and 1982; Burt, 1978b; Friedmann, 1979), the perspective employed in this book.

An interlock is created when two companies have a director in common, and a director who sits on two or more boards has been termed a 'multiple director'. As critics of interlock research have emphasised, however, not all interlocks have equal significance, and for this reason the present research attempts to discriminate between different types of interlock. Figure 1.3 presents a typology of interlocks based on the intensity of the interlock between any two companies. The most intense interlock is the

Figure 1.3   Intensity of Interlocking Directorships

| Position in company B | Position in company A | |
	Inside	*Outside*
Inside	Tight interlock	Primary interlock
Outside	Primary interlock	Loose interlock

tight interlock, which exists when a person holds an executive directorship in both company A and company B. Tight interlocks, therefore, normally occur within enterprises and are typically found between a parent company and its operating subsidiaries. Such interlocks are of limited importance for the present study, which focuses on the relations between enterprises, though tight interlocks may occur within holding systems and combines. A *primary interlock* occurs when an inside, executive director of one enterprise (company A) holds an outside, non-executive directorship in another (company B). The interlock is termed 'primary' because it involves the base company of the person involved, but it should not be assumed that this relation is stronger in any one direction. In some circumstances it is possible to treat the line between A and B as being directed from the inside to the outside position, and this is assumed for convenience in the definitions presented in this section; but the imputation of a direction must always draw on evidence other than the interlock itself. Some of the problems in imputing directionality will be discussed in later chapters. A *loose interlock* is the least intense type of interlock, and results when a person holds an outside position on two boards. There are two main types of loose interlock: induced and secondary.

An *induced interlock* (see figure 1.4) exists simply as a consequence of the prior existence of two primary interlocks

Figure 1.4   Types of Interlocks and Connections

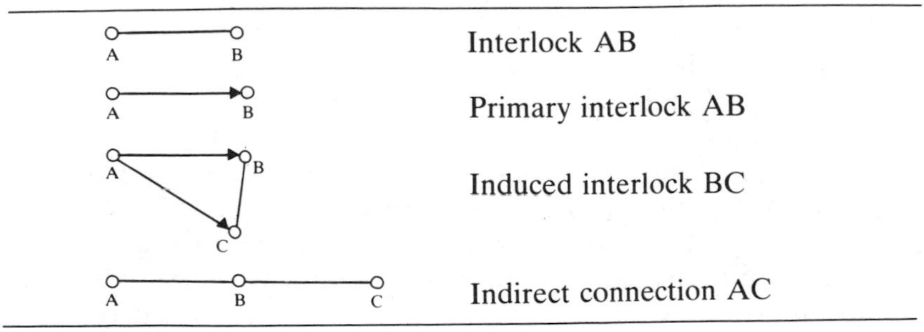

Interlock AB

Primary interlock AB

Induced interlock BC

Indirect connection AC

carried by one director. If an executive of company A holds
outside directorships in companies B and C, then the primary
interlocks AB and AC induce a loose interlock between companies B and C.[19] It is important to emphasise, however, that it is
possible that interlock BC was responsible for the creation of
either AB or AC; that is, the executive of A who sat on C's board
may have subsequently been recruited to B's board as a representative of C and not as a representative of A. The definitions
proposed do not attempt to prejudge these questions of timing
and causation: it is simply claimed that, once established,
interlocks can be classified by their intensity. A *secondary
interlock* is totally unconnected with primary interlocks and exists
because a person with a base outside the companies being
investigated (for example, a politician) sits on two or more boards
as an outside director.[20] It is important to distinguish interlocks
per se, which are always lines in the network, from those paths of
distance two or more which create indirect connections between
companies. Such paths may be built up from interlocks of a
number of distinct types and are important structural features of
the network. A number of writers, however, have misleadingly
called indirect connections of distance two 'interlocks' (for
example, Bunting, 1976b, p. 28; Pennings, 1980, p. 3; Herman,
1981, p. 198; Johnson and Apps, 1979, pp. 361–3). Although
paths of distance two may be of considerable importance in
networks of interlocking directorships, they must be sharply
distinguished from the interlocks themselves.

The measure of 'strength' that has initially been used in these
definitions is the same as that employed by Bearden et al. (1975):
it is assumed that interlocks involving executives are more
'intimate' and therefore stronger than those which do not. This
assumption is supported by the work of Ornstein (1982) in
Canada and Palmer (1983) in the USA, who have discovered that
primary interlocks were more likely to be reinstated on the death
or retirement of their incumbents than were loose interlocks.
Ornstein also discovered that lines of multiplicity two or more
had a high probability of reinstatement, suggesting that a multiple
line composed of loose interlocks may be as strong as a primary
line. Intimacy and multiplicity may make independent contributions to the strength of intercorporate relations. Granovetter
(1973 and 1982) has done much to highlight the nature of strong
and weak relations, arguing that strong relations tend to be most
important for the structuring of activities within clusters and
other subsystems. By contrast, he argues, weak relations tend to

be 'boundary spanning' or bridging relations between sub-systems. Although information, for example, may flow less freely through weak relations, a cluster which has a large number of weak relations with other parts of the network may receive a considerable amount of information about distant parts of the network (see also Friedkin, 1982, p. 281). Both strong and weak ties are important features of social networks.

Interlocks, especially primary interlocks, will often come into being as an expression of such institutional links as capital and commercial relations between enterprises. For this reason, they may be used as traces or indicators to map these underlying institutional links. Similarly, interlocks may be created for the purpose of control. One enterprise may attempt to exercise control over another in order to maximise its own advantage, and writers on 'bank control' have generally stressed this type of interlock (Fitch and Oppenheimer, 1970a, 1970b, 1970c). But bank interlocks need not result from attempts at control. Enterprises seek vertical interlocks with banks and other credit organisations so as to ensure easier access to capital; and even where this is not the deliberate intent, those enterprises which are well-placed in relation to banks tend to find themselves better able to obtain capital (Ratcliff, 1980). In addition to interlocks associated with capital or commercial relations or with the exercise of control are those created for purposes of loose coordination. Writers using the resource dependence model, for example, have argued that recruiting directors from specific other enterprises can be a way of securing some control over resources through the collective action of the interlocked firms. In this way, interlocking may provide an 'opportunity to evolve a stable collective structure of coordinated action through which interdependence is managed' (Pfeffer and Salancik, 1978, p. 161; Burt et al., 1980). The composition of the board of directors can be used to create a community of interest within which some degree of coordination can be achieved. Although interlocking is a more flexible and less durable relation than is complete fusion, it always involves the danger that the person co-opted by an enterprise may begin to have a substantial influence over its affairs and so reduce its autonomy (Mizruchi, 1982, pp. 41–4).

But some interlocks are due to none of these reasons. They are, rather, accidental or contingent features of business activity. In recruiting a director to its board, the leaders of an enterprise may regard whatever other directorships he or she holds as being irrelevant or unimportant (Craven, 1978). These 'contingent' interlocks are created when a person is recruited because of one particular directorship held (say, on a bank), because of the prestige that he or she can bring to the enterprise, or because of a breadth of general business expertise. Of particular importance is the attempt to bring in sources of expertise to an enterprise board in order to enhance its external scan, and this is often justified in terms of maxims of good managerial practice. Business leaders hold theories of competent board membership, theories which refer to the characteristics required of directors if they are to perform their role effectively. These theories, generally implicit, are routinely applied in recruitment and promotion, and if embodied in managerial ideologies may be taken as formal axioms of business practice (Spencer and McAuley, 1980). They generally refer to the possession of managerial or administrative talent, or to specific technical expertise. Sometimes these qualities can be brought to the board by the appointment of insiders, but often the recruitment of experts from outside is involved – especially when the expert can also supply prestige and contacts or can perform a public relations role. Mace (1971, p. 87) found that leaders of large enterprises held very strict ideas about the 'acceptability' of outside directors. It was important that the person be a chairman or chief executive, the particular company with which the person was associated being far less important. Such people, possessing prestige and expertise, are in high demand and tend to be recruited to many boards, and so create a great many interlocks (Hirsch, 1975; Poensgen, 1980, p. 29).

The external scan of an enterprise is a process of selective information-gathering and becomes more important as environments become more 'turbulent' (with greater interdependence and more rapid change). Useem argues that interlocks enhance the external scan: the large enterprise has to monitor government, labour relations, markets, technology, finance, and so on, and this can be achieved by recruiting directors who are likely to enhance the amount of information to which the enterprise has access. Interlocks, therefore, supplement the activities of the departments formally engaged in external scanning. Current intelligence can be garnered by sitting on the board of another enterprise and by having outside directors on one's own board. This is generally summed up as bringing in an 'outside view' or 'someone with contacts' (Useem, 1982, p. 209).

Although many interlocks may originate for a number of more

or less contingent reasons, through processes which introduce a random element of 'noise' into the pattern of relations, the accumulation of interlocks into a definite structure will have important consequences for the flow of resources and for future executive and director recruitment. The recruitment of officers to an enterprise inevitably takes place within a pre-existing structure and so will be constrained by the position of that enterprise within the intercorporate network. Put simply, enterprises tend to recruit from those other enterprises which are close to them in the network. Recruitment practices, therefore, tend to reproduce the existing structure of the network, regardless of whether the network contains a significant random element. Once a network structure emerges, therefore, it will tend to be reproduced through its own internal dynamics. Of course, structural transformation can occur in the same way. The structural constraints facing an enterprise may cause it to engage in actions which have a cumulative disruptive effect on the rest of the network. While enterprises may be unconscious agents of social reproduction, they are also unconscious agents of social transformation.

A number of hypotheses about corporate behaviour and its implications for network structure have been drawn in this chapter. The strategies pursued by those who lead business enterprises are aimed at enhancing the position of the enterprise within its environment and have, as their unintended consequence, an impact on the wider intercorporate network which determines the environmental location of each individual enterprise. The various participants in business leadership stand in definite relations to the internal administration of the enterprise and to the web of capital, commercial, and personal relations in which it is embedded, and the dynamics of their actions can be grasped through the concepts and techniques of social network analysis. The chapters which follow will employ this perspective to study corporate behaviour and the intercorporate network in Britain, using data collected in the Company Analysis Project.[21] Chapter 2 examines some of the major properties of the network as a whole and investigates how they have altered over time, while chapter 3 relates those properties to a more detailed investigation of the characteristics of particular sectors and regions within the overall network. Chapter 4 takes up the debate on the managerial revolution and examines evidence on family enterprise and kinship networks. In chapter 5 the 'inner circle' of multiple directors are examined in relation to evidence on their social background and political connections, and in chapter 6 the relations between banks and industry is the central theme.

NOTES

1. For general reviews of social network analysis, see Mitchell (1969 and 1974), Barnes (1972), Berkowitz (1982), and Boissevain (1980).
2. If the points in the graph represent only one type of unit, say people, then the relations between the people may be represented as entries in an 'adjacency matrix' in which the presence or absence of a line between two points is indicated by the content of the appropriate cell in the matrix. In an adjacency matrix each element appears as both a row and a column, and so the presence of a line or its intensity can be represented by an entry in the cell where the point row and point column intersect. An everyday example of an adjacency matrix is an atlas mileage chart in which the row and column elements are towns and the cells contain the distances between pairs of towns. Where two sets of elements are analysed, one represented by the rows and the other by columns, the matrix is termed an 'incidence matrix'. Unless otherwise stated, the analyses contained in this book relate to adjacency matrices.
3. Some of the main specialized programs are reviewed in Sonquist (1980) and Mitchell (1981). Particular programs are discussed in Levine and Roy (1979) and in Berkowitz et al. (1979). GRADAP is outlined in *Connections*, 1:2, 1978, pp. 21–5, and is fully documented in Stokman and van Veen (1981). The GRADAP procedures are based in part on Anthonisse (1973).
4. Isolated points or points in unconnected sections of the network have an infinite distance from one another as there are no paths connecting them. For this reason it is usual to calculate distances only within sets of connected points.
5. Distance has frequently been expressed in spatial terms through the use of procedures for multidimensional scaling. See Coxon (1979, pp. 490–2).
6. For general reviews of concepts and measures of centrality, see Freeman (1978 and 1980), Mizruchi and Bunting (1981), and Mariolis and Jones (1982).
7. Mizruchi (1982) misleadingly uses 'connectivity' as a generic term for density and a variety of other measures of network cohesiveness.
8. Barnes (1969, pp. 64–6) has suggested that clusters should have a minimum of five members and a minimum density of 0.8. This is, of course, an arbitrary specification, but it is perhaps a realistic assessment of the sociological reality of clustering. It should be noted, however, that an increase in cluster size will, other things being

equal, tend to lead to lower cluster densities. Lattin and Wong (1982) propose a method of clustering based on density measures and appropriate to large, sparse networks. See the comment in Carrington (1982).

9. A component, naturally, has a minimum size of two, otherwise isolated points would qualify as components.

10. In some measures cliques are identified not only on the basis of distance but also on the basis of the multiplicities of the lines making up the paths. It is important to emphasise that it is not necessary that the members of a clique should be connected only through other members of the clique. A 'clan' is a clique within which the connections between members pass only through other members. See Mokken (1979).

11. For this reason it is possible to estimate network density from a random sample of agents, on the assumption that the sample can be used to estimate the average degree for the network as a whole (Niemeijer, 1973, p. 8; Boissevain, 1974, p. 40).

12. In a network divided into components, each component may have its own structural centre.

13. The arguments of this section draw heavily on discussions with Christopher Dandeker, though he should not be held responsible for the conclusions drawn.

14. This position involves a rejection of the arguments of Wrong (1968) and Hamilton (1976 and 1977) that power must involve intentional acts. Similarly, power has no necessary link to wants, interests, or preferences.

15. On joint ventures and mergers, see Pfeffer and Salancik (1978), chapter 6; Pfeffer (1972a); Phillips (1960). On the general issue of the origins of new organisational forms, see Aldrich and Fish (1982).

16. This typology is extended and discussed further in chapter 4.

17. Berkowitz et al. (1978) have tried to calculate equivalencies between number of interlocks and size of minority participations.

18. For overviews of the history of research on interlocks, see Fennema and Schijf (1978), Andrews (1982), Sofef (1979), and Useem (1979).

19. Note that if the primary interlocks AB and AC are held by different people then there is no interlock at all between B and C.

20. The definition of a primary interlock was introduced in Sweezy (1939, p. 162). However, Sweezy uses the term secondary interlock in a broader sense to encompass what have been termed induced interlocks. General discussions of the measurement of interlocks can be found in Bunting (1976b) and in Smith and Desfosses (1972).

21. The organisation of the project is described in the Introduction and in the Appendix.

CHAPTER TWO

Network Structure and the Concentration of Capital

Social network analysis has great potential for illuminating the question of economic concentration. Existing studies of concentration have all too often ignored this potential and have, therefore, employed an impoverished method of analysis. At the same time, empirical studies of concentration have rarely related their investigations to the conceptual schemes developed by theoretical economists. Abstract discussions of oligopoly and monopoly power have remained separate from the empirical data which could be used to exemplify those concepts. It is beyond the scope of this book to rectify this failure of economic analysis, but some indications can be given of the direction in which to proceed. The potential of the theoretical framework presented in the previous chapter will be illustrated by reinterpreting certain existing studies of concentration and by relating to them the data collected in the Company Analysis Project.

In order to achieve this theoretically informed account of economic power in Britain it is necessary to make some initial points of clarification. Monopolisation, understood as an increase in the level of economic concentration, has conventionally been measured by the extent to which the economy as a whole or its various sectors are dominated by a small number of units of production. This focus on 'unit concentration' has led to a general disregard of all intercorporate relations except those capital relations which fuse economic units through merger or amalgamation into unified enterprises. Even the attempt of Marx to distinguish the 'concentration' of capital through internal growth from 'centralisation' of capital through amalgamation failed to recognise the variety of processes through which economic units can be allied. The conventional focus on unit concentration must be complemented by an analysis of what may be called 'network concentration', understood as the concentration of control over enterprises through commercial, capital, and personal relations.

Whether the analyst is concerned with unit concentration or network concentration, a number of definitional problems arise (Utton, 1970). Initially it is necessary to define the unit of analysis – plant, firm, or enterprise – and the attribute in terms of which it is to be analysed. The decision on whether to measure assets, turnover (sales), employment, share capital, or value added, for example, is never clear-cut, the choice of yardstick depending on a mixture of theoretical, empirical, and practical decisions. The units and their attributes may then be studied in relation to the particular markets in which they compete, the sector of economic activity in which they operate, or the economy as a whole. Typically, studies of unit concentration have investigated the output or employment position of large enterprises in specific markets or in the manufacturing sector. Unit concentration has normally been measured by the concentration ratio, the proportion of activity accounted for by the largest enterprises in the relevant market or sector. The number of enterprises taken as the basis of the ratio will be small when narrowly defined markets are examined, the three-firm ratio is particularly widely used, but will be much larger when whole sectors are studied. Studies of the manufacturing sector, for example, have investigated the dominance of the 'top' 50, 100 or 200 manufacturing enterprises. Use of the concentration ratio involves the choice of an arbitrary number of top enterprises, and alternative measures based on the size distribution of all enterprises have been the Lorenz curve, and its associated Gini coefficient, and the log normal curve, in which the variance in the logarithms of firm size is taken as a measure of the inequality of the distribution.

The present study is based upon a selection of the largest 200 non-financial enterprises and 50 large financial enterprises for 1904, 1938, and 1976. Although the choice of the 'top 200' is based on an arbitrary cut-off, an interest in 'big business' precluded any attempt at analysing all enterprises, small, medium, and large, involved in manufacturing and distribution. The choice of 200 as the cut-off point for non-financial enterprises was made to facilitate comparability with other data sets. Numerous American studies of unit concentration, ownership and control, and interlocking directorships have studied the top 200 enterprises for the relevant date, and the British data set for 1976 was part of an international investigation in which the top

200 in each of ten participating countries was selected for comparative study.[1] It is in the light of this selection procedure, with all its advantages and limitations, that the results of the research must be interpreted. In particular, the measures of concentration employed will be influenced by this procedure. If a study is concerned with unit concentration, then it can be said that the proportion of output accounted for by the top 200 enterprises has increased from x per cent to y per cent over a specified period, but difficulties arise if this is combined with statements about network concentration. It would, of course, be possible to say that the level of concentration in the network of top companies had increased or decreased over the same period, assuming an adequate measure of network concentration can be decided upon; but network concentration cannot necessarily be treated as a monotonic variable. That is, it may not vary uniformly along a one-dimensional scale.

Consider the example of capital relations. The concentration of capital relations occurs when separate enterprises are brought closer together through shareholding participations and banking relations to form the kinds of groups depicted in figure 1.1. The highest level of concentration exists when groups of companies are amalgamated into unified enterprises, with the constituent elements ceasing to be autonomous. A drift towards merger and amalgamation among a particular selection of enterprises will, over time, result in a fall in the number of autonomous enterprises contained in the selection, as independent enterprises become subsidiary firms of the leading enterprises. A selection procedure which is not longitudinal (following the history of an initial selection of top enterprises) but cross-sectional (selecting a new top 200 for each period studied) will distort this process. In the cross-sectional research design, the concentration of the network through merger and amalgamation will be masked by the constant inclusion of new enterprises for study. It is for this reason that unit concentration and network concentration must be taken together if meaningful comparisons are to be made. While it is perfectly legitimate to say that the network of the top 200 enterprises of 1976 was more or less concentrated than the network of the top 200 of 1904, it is also important to know whether the proportion of economic activity accounted for by the 1976 top 200 was greater or lesser than was the case for its predecessor. Monopolisation may only be said to have occurred if a constant proportion of activity is accounted for by progressively more concentrated networks of companies, or if an increasing proportion of activity is accounted for by sets of companies with similar levels of network concentration.

Those few studies of network concentration which have been carried out in Britain have, like the present study, investigated interlocking directorships, treating these personal relations as proxies for commercial and capital relations as well as regarding them as important intercorporate relations in their own right. These studies have generally taken one measure of network concentration as the basis for their arguments, most usually the number or density of interlocks (Johnson and Apps, 1979; Stanworth and Giddens, 1975). The density measure is itself based on the number of interlocks and is influenced by the number of enterprises selected for study. Owing to the arbitrary nature of the cut-off point chosen in the concentration ratio approach, the boundaries of the data set will not necessarily reflect 'the actual configuration of the social space' (Barnes, 1979, p. 408). That is to say, the boundaries of the graph studied may correspond neither to whatever boundaries there may be in the actual size distribution of enterprises nor to the boundaries of the social relations among the enterprises. To clarify the latter point, enterprises within the top 200 may have numerous interlocks with enterprises outside the top 200, and the investigator makes an arbitrary decision to ignore these in measuring network concentration. But density is also influenced in a very direct way by the size of the graph. Friedkin (1981) constructed random graphs, in which the distribution of lines was the outcome of a random process, and found that the connectivity of the graphs increased dramatically at relatively low levels of density and that the larger the graph the lower was the level of density at which high levels of connectivity occurred. Friedkin suggests that if it is assumed that there are limits to the maximum number of direct links which an agent can sustain – a reasonable assumption for interlocking directorships – then the maximum figure for network density would decline with network size: the larger number of enterprises chosen for study, the lower will be the maximum density (see also Snijders, 1981). These problems must be taken into account in discussions of network density. But even then, density alone cannot serve as a measure of network concentration, for it is unrelated to many other features of network morphology, notably the intensity of the lines and the existence of components, clusters, and cliques (Mitchell, 1969; Boissevain, 1974, pp. 39–40; Niemeijer, 1973, p. 46 see also Mizruchi, 1982, p. 69; Barnes, 1979; Aldrich, 1982; Knoke and Kuklinski, 1982, pp. 22–6). An adequate analysis of network concentration must, therefore, draw upon the whole battery of social network concepts introduced in chapter 1.

Any attempt to assess trends in concentration on the basis of cross-sectional data must begin with a discussion of the 'survival'

Table 2.1   Company Continuity, 1904–76

Fate of 1904 companies	No.	Fate of 1938 companies	No.
On 1938 list	56	On 1976 list	52
Acquired by companies on 1938 list	53	Acquired by companies on 1976 list	69
Outside 1938 list	63	Outside 1976 list	26
Acquired by companies outside 1938 list	8	Acquired by companies outside 1976 list	16
Liquidated	20	Liquidated or otherwise dissolved	37
Totals	200		200

of particular enterprises from one period to the next and so of continuity in the coverage of the successive data sets. Table 2.1 shows the general patterns of continuity and discontinuity between the data sets used in the present study. A company is regarded as continuing in existence if it qualifies for selection in two successive periods. This criterion, of course, is based upon the legal continuity of a particular company and does not necessarily reflect any changes in the social organisation of that company over the period. Thus, companies which merged with others on the list might be regarded as having some degree of continuity over the period as subordinate parts of larger enterprises. It can be seen that 56 of the parent companies of 1904 were also present on the 1938 list, and that a further 53 companies had become subsidiaries of 1938 parents. Of the companies going into liquidation, eight were reconstructed as new companies which survived into 1938 as subsidiaries or parents. In these various ways more than a half of the 1904 companies survived in some form or another to be represented on the 1938 list, though only 28 per cent of the 1904 companies survived in their original legal form as parent companies. Merger and amalgamation resulted in the loss of almost a third of the 1904 companies, these companies disappearing at an average rate of 1.8 per year over the period. Using similar criteria, the survival rate between 1938 and 1976 was somewhat higher, though only 26 per cent survived as parent companies. Only 13 companies appeared in the same form in each of the three periods. Merger and amalgamation resulted in the loss of 1938 companies at an average annual rate of 2.2 companies. The large number of liquidations by 1976 was accounted for mainly by the postwar extension of the public sector: 2 public boards were dissolved and reconstructed, and 29 companies were liquidated because their assets had been nationalised or following their acquisition by new public boards.

TRENDS IN ECONOMIC CONCENTRATION

Existing studies of unit concentration in Britain show a clear picture of the major trends during the period under investigation. In manufacturing, mining, and distribution, there is evidence of a rise in concentration from 1885 to 1939, followed by a fallback to a level in 1950 equal to that reached in 1924 (Utton, 1970, p. 87, based on Hart and Prais, 1956). A moderate increase between 1951 and 1958 was followed by a more rapid increase up to 1968 and then a slight levelling off at a high level through the 1970s (Hart and Clarke, 1980, pp. 6–7; Prais, 1976, p. 3ff.; Hannah, 1976a, p. 102ff.). The British manufacturing sector had become the most highly concentrated in the world (Utton, 1982, p. 22).[2] Large companies came to account for a major part of the output of the manufacturing sector as a whole, and this increase has been due mainly to their diversification, through internal growth and through merger, into related and unrelated industries. By the 1970s the top 100 manufacturers were a group of very large enterprises responsible for more than two-fifths of manufacturing sales, having almost doubled their share in the postwar years. Through their operating subsidiaries, which increasingly dominated particular markets, these enterprises encountered one another in numerous industrial sectors (Utton, 1982, p. 27).

An important aspect of this increase in unit concentration at the level of the enterprise is that it has not been directly associated with increased concentration at the plant level. More than a half of all people working in factories employing more than ten people in 1935 were working for very large enterprises, though they were not necessarily working in large plants. Leak and Maizels (1945) have shown that 35.4 per cent of these factory employees were in 'plants' with 500 or more workers, 44.5 per cent were in 'firms' with 500 or more workers, and 50.0 per cent were in 'enterprises' with 500 or more workers. That is, most workers were, by the 1930s, working in the 'big business' sector, though they might still have been employed in relatively small plants or in small subsidiaries of a large parent. This dominance of large enterprises was especially marked in railways, coal-mining, iron and steel, and electrical engineering, in each of which sectors more than three-quarters of the employees were in large enterprises. In cars and cycles, cotton spinning and doub-ling, mechanical engineering, and chemicals, between a half and two-thirds of workers were employed in large enterprises (Florence, 1953, p. 128). There seems to have been little change in the period up to the 1950s. Evely and Little (1960) used concentration ratios to show that in 1951 some 23 per cent of trades were high in concentration and that these were generally trades with very large capital requirements: chemicals, engineer-ing, vehicles, shipbuilding, drink, tobacco, and mining (Utton, 1970, p. 75; Prais, 1976, pp. 8–9).

The data collected in the Company Analysis Project depict the particular enterprises involved in this growth in unit concentra-tion. The majority of the largest non-financial enterprises in 1904 were railway companies, all the top ten being found in this sector.

Table 2.2   The Largest Non-Railway Enterprises, 1904

Manufacturing	*Capital (£m)*	*Non-manufacturing*	*Capital (£m)*
1. Imperial Tobacco	15.5	1. Gas Light & Coke	21.6
2. J & P Coats	10.0	2. London & India Docks	11.1
3. Watney, Combe, Reid	8.7	3. Manchester Ship Canal	8.0
4. United Alkali	5.7	4. Anglo-American	
5. Vickers, Sons & Maxim	5.2	Telegraph	7.0
6. Calico Printers	5.0	5. South Metropolitan	
7. Bleachers Association	4.6	Gas	6.3
8. Fine Cotton Spinners	4.5	6. British South Africa	6.0
9. Arthur Guinness	4.5	7. Eastern Telegraph	6.0
10. Associated Portland		8. National Telephone	5.5
Cement	4.1	9. Dalgety	4.0
		10. Imperial Continental	
		Gas	3.8

Table 2.3   The Largest Non-Financial Enterprises, 1938

Manufacturing	*Capital (£m)*	*Non-manufacturing*	*Capital (£m)*
1. Imperial Chemical Industries	74.2	1. London, Midland & Scottish Railway	304.6
2. Lever Brothers & Unilever	67.4	2. London & North Eastern Railway	257.4
3. Imperial Tobacco	50.4	3. Southern Railway	114.1
4. British-American Tobacco	34.2	4. Great Western Railway	109.8
5. Courtaulds	32.0	5. Anglo-Saxon Petroleum	49.5
6. J & P Coats	20.2	6. 'Shell' Transport & Trading	40.9
7. Vickers	14.5	7. Anglo-Iranian Oil	32.8
8. Guest, Keen & Nettlefolds	13.0	8. Asiatic Petroleum	31.3
9. Distillers	12.9	9. Gas Light & Coke	29.3
10. Dunlop Robber	12.7	10. Cable & Wireless	23.6

The ten largest manufacturing enterprises of 1904, as shown in table 2.2, comprised 4 textile producers, 2 brewers, and 1 each in chemicals, engineering, tobacco, and construction materials.[3] By 1938, as shown in table 2.3, the ten largest manufacturers consisted of 2 textile-producers, 2 in food and drink, 2 in tobacco, 2 in engineering, and 1 each in chemicals and rubber. Three of

Table 2.4   The Largest Non-Financial Enterprises, 1976

Manufacturing	*Turnover (£m)*	*Non-manufacturing*	*Turnover (£m)*
1. BAT Industries	5.6	1. British Petroleum	12.9
2. Imperial Chemical Industries	4.1	2. 'Shell' Transport & Trading	10.0
3. Unilever	3.8	3. Electricity Council	4.1
4. British Steel	3.1	4. Post Office	3.8
5. Imperial Group	2.9	5. National Enterprise Board[a]	2.8
6. British Leyland	2.3	6. National Coal Board	2.4
7. General Electric	1.8	7. Esso Petroleum	2.0
8. Cavenham	1.7	8. British Gas	2.0
9. Ford	1.6	9. Rio Tinto Zinc	1.7
10. Bowater	1.5	10. Grand Metropolitan	1.5

Note: [a] The turnover of the NEB included that of its subsidiary, British Leyland, for most of the financial year.

these were in the top ten manufacturers in both periods.[4] By 1976, as shown in table 2.4, textile producers had completely disappeared from the top ten and the whole list was more diverse. Three enterprises were in the top ten of both 1938 and 1976,[5] and Imperial Group (formerly Imperial Tobacco) was one of the top ten manufacturers in each of the three periods. A similar trend towards diversification was evident among the top ten non-manufacturing enterprises, and by 1976 the distinction between manufacturing and non-manufacturing enterprises had become rather artificial. The top ten non-manufacturers of 1904 were mainly 'utilities': 3 gas, 3 telecommunications, 1 docks, 1 canal, and 2 overseas trading enterprises. In 1938 the 4 biggest non-manufacturers were railways (excluded from the 1904 list), and the remaining 6 members of the top ten comprised 4 oil and 2 utility enterprises.[6] Gas Light & Coke was in the top ten of both 1904 and 1938, and Shell was in the top ten of both 1938 and 1976.[7]

Having reviewed the evidence on unit concentration and the rise of 'big business', it is now possible to turn to evidence on network concentration. Table 2.5 presents some basic measures drawn from the data sets of the Company Analysis Project, and a number of initial conclusions can be drawn from a comparison

Table 2.5　The Top 250: Cohesiveness and Fragmentation, 1904–76

Measure	1904	1938	1976
Inclusiveness[a]	197	201	189
Connectivity (%)[b]	50.3%	60.1%	54.7%
Network density	0.013	0.019	0.017
No. of components	9	4	3
No. of companies in large component	177	194	185
Density of largest component	0.025	0.031	0.032

Notes: [a] Inclusiveness refers to the number of companies which were inter-locked.
[b] Connectivity refers to the proportion of pairs of companies which are mutually reachable through unbroken paths.

between 1904 and 1976. In both years the great majority of companies were interlocked, but the number of isolated companies increased from 53 in 1904 to 61 in 1976. The overall density of the network, however, also increased: from 0.013 to 0.017.[8] The value of the density measure may vary from 0 to 1, a density figure of 0.017 indicating that 1.7 per cent of the possible lines were actually present. This figure is, of course, low, but it has already been argued that maximum density declines with network size. Friedkin (1981) suggests that networks with more than 140 agents and with a maximum of 30 lines per agent will have a maximum density in the region of 0.2. This is likely to be the order of magnitude for the maximum density in any large network of enterprises in which no company is interlocked with more than 30 other companies, and so the levels discovered for 1904 and 1976 should be compared with this effective maximum.[9] As both density and connectivity increased between 1904 and 1976 it can be concluded that there was an overall increase in the cohesiveness of the network. The fragmentation of the network declined between 1904 and 1976, owing to an increase in the number of companies falling within the large component and a reduction in the number of smaller components. The number of components, subsets of connected enterprises, fell from 9 to 3, with the largest component in 1976 containing virtually all the interlocked companies.[10]

These changes in cohesiveness and fragmentation were consequences of changes in the number and distribution of lines. Table 2.6 shows that the number of lines among the top 250

Table 2.6   Distribution of Lines and Interlocks, 1904–76

Multi-plicity of line	1904		1938		1976	
	No. of lines	No. of interlocks	No. of lines	No. of interlocks	No. of lines	No. of interlocks
1	331	331	445	445	507	507
2	52	104	85	170	25	50
3	8	24	26	78	9	27
4	5	20	8	32	—	—
5	3	15	6	30	—	—
6	1	6	5	30	—	—
7	1	10	2	14	1	7
10	—	—	1	10	—	—
Totals	401	510	578	809	542	591

Note: The number of interlocks is the product of the multiplicity and the number of lines. The totals of interlocks in table 2.7 are equal to those in table 2.6. It should be noted that the sum of the adjacencies in a network is equal to twice the number of lines.

companies increased from 401 in 1904 to 542 in 1976, an increase of over one-third. The number of interlocks, however, did not increase at such a rate, because the number of lines with high multiplicity fell by a half over the period: in 1904 there were 10 lines with a value of 4 or more, but in 1976 only 1 line reached this value. The network was becoming less fragmented and more cohesive, but the relations making up the network were becoming less intense. The early period had a relatively large number of structural divisions and a relatively high number of multiple lines; in the later period virtually all interlocked companies were linked through lines of value one into a large component.

The changes in the number and distribution of lines were in turn consequences of changes in the number and distribution of directorships among people. Table 2.7 shows that the total number of directors increased substantially from 2204 in 1904 to

Table 2.7   Distribution of Directorships, 1904–76

No. of directorships per person	1904			1938			1976		
	A	B	C	A	B	C	A	B	C
1	1901	1901	—	1844	1844	—	2400	2400	—
2	234	468	234	218	436	218	195	390	195
3	57	171	171	70	210	210	60	180	180
4	5	20	30	23	92	138	16	64	96
5	6	30	60	9	45	90	9	45	90
6	1	6	15	6	36	90	2	12	30
7	—	—	—	3	21	63	—	—	—
Totals	2204	2596	510	2173	2684	809	2682	3091	591

Note: A = Number of people; B = Number of directorships held by the people in A; C = Number of interlocks generated by the people in A.
A person with N directorships generates $N(N-1)/2$ interlocks.
Thus, $B = AN$ and $C = B(N-1)/2$.

2682 in 1976, an increase of 21.7 per cent, which reflects an increase in mean board size from 8.7 members to 10.7 members. By contrast, the number of multiple directors fell by 6.9 per cent over the whole period: from 303 in 1904 to 282 in 1976. The net result was that the multiple directors came to represent a smaller proportion of the total number of directors, perhaps reflecting a greater segregation between the roles of multiple and single director. It would also appear that this smaller number of multiple directors were directing their activities more efficiently, as the multiple directors of 1904 generated only three-quarters of the lines generated by those of 1976. Multiple directors in 1976 were likely to hold more directorships, but they spread their activities widely and so produced a more dense network.

The network produced by these directors has gradually become more centralised. The simplest measure of network centralisation is based upon the adjacency, or degree, of the points. The degree of the interlock network as a whole is the average number of lines carried by an enterprise, and therefore its value varies directly with density.[11] Between 1904 and 1976 the network degree increased from 3.21 to 4.34. In view of the predominance of the large component in each period and the increased centralisation of the network around the component, it is perhaps important to assess the level of centralisation within that component. The increase in the degree of the large component from 4.36 to 5.84 reflects its increasing density, and a more useful measure is the extent to which the component contains a structural centre. The centre, as defined in chapter 1, is a set of individually central enterprises which are all mutually connected by paths of distance two or less. In 1904 the centre comprised just 2 enterprises, while in 1976 it contained 9 enterprises. The centre of the British intercorporate network increased in size, but it remained remarkably small in international terms. In 1976 the centre of the Dutch network contained 38 enterprises, and the German centre contained 34; only in the USA and France, with 12 and 15 respectively, did the network centre seem to be as small as in Britain (Stokman et al., 1984). It would appear that the small British centre was not a significant structural feature of the network.

If a number of enterprises were located at the centre of the network, many more were isolated or peripheral. An enterprise is isolated if it has no interlocks within the top 250, and the number of such isolates increased from 50 to 61 between 1904 and 1976. The 1904 isolates were distinct in terms of their ownership, size, and industry. They tended to be small, family-owned enterprises, and more than half of them came from four industrial sectors: 5 from railways, 6 from finance, 10 from food and drink, and 6 from textiles and allied industries. The 1976 isolates were heavily drawn from food, retailing, oil, and trading, reflecting the importance of family and foreign ownership in these sectors,[12] but isolation was less closely associated with size than in 1904. There were 12 isolates in the top 50 non-financials, and the remaining ranks of the top 200 showed a constant rate of about 1 in 3 uninterlocked.

Two meanings of peripherality must be distinguished. An enterprise is 'locally peripheral' if it has only one interlock; such an enterprise has minimum adjacency. An enterprise can be said to be 'globally peripheral' if it interlocks with few enterprises which themselves have a low adjacency. In 1904 there were 50 enterprises with 1 interlock, of which 12 were formed into isolated pairs, 1 was a member of a small component, and 37 were locally peripheral in the large component. Many of the latter, however, interlocked with banks, railways, or assurance companies, which themselves tended to have many interlocks. Only a small proportion of the locally peripheral enterprises were globally peripheral. In 1976 there were 34 enterprises with 1 interlock, of which 4 were formed into isolated pairs and 30 were locally peripheral in the large component. These tended to be smaller than the isolates, suggesting that if a large company interlocked at all it was unlikely to be peripheral. Table 2.8 shows the globally peripheral companies of 1976, where global peripherality is measured by the total distance between an enterprise and all other enterprises in the large component.[13] Seven of these enterprises were also locally peripheral, the remaining three owing their position to interlocks among themselves. Guinness Peat and Linfood had 3 common directors but had only 1 'external' interlock (with Land Securities Investment Trust), while 1 of Wimpey's 2 interlocks was with Petrofina.

Table 2.8   The Ten Most Peripheral Enterprises, 1976

Rank in large component		Sum distance[a]
185	Petrofina UK	1016
184	Croda International	924
183	C. T. Bowring	838
182	Brooke Bond Liebig	837
181	George Wimpey	833
180	J. Lyons	827
179	{ Guinness Peat	826
	{ Linfood Holdings	826
177	Ciba-Geigy	819
176	Fitch Lovell	817

Note: [a] Sum distance is the total distance between the enterprise and all other enterprises in the large component.

Although the number of isolates increased between 1904 and 1976, the number of locally peripheral companies fell substantially, resulting in a small fall in the number of marginal enterprises. The small increase in the size of the centre was associated with an increased concentration of enterprises around it.

Certain trends are apparent from this comparison of data for 1904 and 1976, but these changes did not constitute a smooth transformation over time. The data for 1938 show that a number of variables which had increased their value after 1904 subsequently fell to their 1976 level. The measures of inclusiveness, connectivity, and density in table 2.5 suggest that the overall level of interlocking increased markedly between 1904 and 1938, and then fell back somewhat in the postwar period.[14] The period 1904 to 1976, therefore, falls into two distinct phases punctuated by the Second World War. The figures for 1938 suggest that the interwar period was a stage of transition between the situation prior to the First World War and that of the 1970s. It can be seen from table 2.6 that the number of interlocks increased from 510 in 1904 to a massive 809 in 1938. This increase was due to the fact that the number of multiple lines more than doubled between 1904 and 1938. In 1904 the network of multiple lines alone (disregarding all lines of value one) consisted of 24 components, the largest of which was a 17-member City of London core. By 1938 this City core had grown and extended its links to incorporate many of the regionally based companies, forming a tightly integrated component of 63 companies containing three-quarters of all the multiple lines. The decline in the intensity of interlocking between 1938 and 1976 led to the emergence of a more diffuse pattern: the 1976 network of multiple lines contained 17 components, the largest of which included 13 companies centred on the Midland Bank. The number of isolated pairs in the network of multiple lines decreased consistently from 15 to 14 to 12, and the number of components with 3 or more members decreased from 8 to 7 to 5. The network of multiple lines in 1976, although containing fewer enterprises than that of 1904, was less fragmented internally. The more diffuse nature of the 1976 network can also be seen from the fact that there was a 22 per cent increase between 1904 and 1976 in the number of companies which were interlocked only through lines of value one.

THE DEVELOPMENT OF A NATIONAL NETWORK

The various explanations of economic concentration have concerned themselves almost exclusively with unit concentration; network concentration and unit concentration have rarely been considered together as inseparable aspects of the development of British capital. A particularly influential explanation of unit concentration is that of Prais (1976), who argues that simple probability assumptions about enterprise performance can be used to explain the 'spontaneous drift' through which some enterprises increase in size and so produce higher levels of concentration in the economy as a whole. Prais claims that his argument need not assume that large enterprises grow more rapidly than small ones: assuming a random distribution of growth chances, there will be a long-term tendency for the size distribution of enterprises to approximate to the pattern observed in the various empirical studies.[15] The drift towards concentration, argues Prais (1976, p. 166), began with the disruption of the stable, competitive manufacturing economy of the nineteenth century by the introduction of limited liability in the 1890s. This legal innovation opened up growth opportunities and liberated the long-term dynamic of concentration which was inherent in the configuration of relations between enterprises.

The basic problem with this explanation is that its central assumption – that the probability of growth or decline is unrelated to the initial size of an enterprise – seems unrealistic (Hannah and Kay, 1977, p. 99). The assumption can be made more plausible by assuming that a history of growth is, other things being equal, likely to be associated with enhanced prospects for growth in the present, and that large size is associated with slower growth, but that the predicted size distribution of enterprises would then no longer correspond to that observed (Hannah and Kay, 1977, p. 101). Critics of the model of spontaneous drift have argued that a realistic model must take account of the role of mergers and amalgamations in producing higher levels of concentration, and even Prais recognised that the model fits only the period before the merger wave of the 1950s and 1960s. He concludes that a full explanation of concentration has to recognise mergers, financial intermediaries, and government policy as independent causal mechanisms. These mechanisms, however, were incorporated in his argument only as ad hoc explanatory 'factors', and the inadequate assumptions of the model of spontaneous drift were not altered. It is argued here that an adequate explanation must be cast in historical terms and must be based on realistic assumptions about corporate behaviour. Only on such a basis can unit and network concentration be encompassed within the same explanatory framework.

The model proposed here is based on the gradual extension of a national intercorporate network within which unit and network concentrations have combined to generate increasing levels of monopolisation. An 'unfolding' model has been employed by Roy (1983) in his analysis of interlocks in the USA. Roy argues that the period from 1886 to 1905 saw the unfolding of a core of large-scale capitalist concerns and resulted in the creation of an inclusive and well-connected network. Large capital-intensive enterprises in railways, coal, and telegraphs were formed by and in association with the major investment banks and comprised the economic core inside a periphery of relatively isolated sectors. The influence of the core gradually expanded as its capital and commercial relations spread out into the periphery and were expressed in personal relations. By the turn of the century most economic sectors were interlocked with the core, some of them heavily, and a number of interlocks had begun to appear among the peripheral enterprises. By 1905 a national network had emerged, within which core and periphery could not so easily be distinguished; the concentrated, capital-intensive, banker-oriented sector of the economy had enlarged itself to the point where it encompassed most of large-scale industry:

> As entrepreneurial enterprises were merged and incorporated, the participating businessmen became integrated into the corporate class organisation. Businesses restructured their internal organization in conformity to and in conjunction with the centralized structure of corporate capital, forming proprietary relationships and becoming 'spheres' in the interlocking structure. (Roy, 1983, p. 256)

A similar process has occurred in the British economy, but the process of unfolding was much slower than in the USA. The core of the economy in Britain was a City of London core which had come into being in the late nineteenth century. From the industrial revolution until the middle of the nineteenth century a close relationship existed between manufacturing industry and the small country bankers. Long-term capital for industrial growth was not available from the London banks, and industrial expansion was financed by the entrepreneurial families themselves and by the country banks, which provided effective long-term capital by the continuous renewal of short-term credit. As the capital requirements of the manufacturers grew, however, the country banks were unable to continue in this role. Attempts to continue the practice of long-term industrial finance on the new, larger scale led to an overstretching of bank resources and to a rash of banking failures, culminating in that of the City of Glasgow Bank in 1878:

> A point had been reached where the entire system had either to be re-organised to withstand the greater risks of steadily enlarging industrial requirements or the system had to withdraw from long-term industrial involvement. The system withdrew. (Kennedy, 1976, p. 160)

The form of this withdrawal was the incorporation of many provincial banks into a national banking system run by City financiers and centred on the Bank of England. Joint stock banks dominated by the merchants and private bankers gobbled up the country banks. In this new environment the manufacturers had themselves to turn to joint stock organisation in order to raise the capital they required, and this often involved the amalgamation of firms into units large enough for stock exchange flotation. Those provincial manufacturers which were trying to draw on larger pools of capital were rejected by the dominant London banks and had to resort to the services of smaller merchant and private banks involved in share-issuing business and to company promoters. Although some promoters simply floated over capitalised companies in order to make a quick profit for themselves, others took a more active role in the companies with which they were associated. Terah Hooley was the epitome of the former, while David Chadwick of Manchester, George White of Bristol, and Osborne O'Hagan of London (O'Hagan, 1929) were among the more active promoters. Most of these promoters, however, were small and had little long-term impact on the capital market (Hannah, 1976a; Kennedy, 1976; Cottrell, 1980), the central feature of the economy being an institutional separation of banking from manufacturing. The split between the City and industry was a product of the economic developments of the late nineteenth century, as many provincial banks were forced to adopt the accepted practices of the City financiers.

The 1904 intercorporate network illustrates very clearly the consequences of these developments (see table 2.9). Although most of the 24 components in the network of multiple lines[16] had a regional base or were associated with a particular entrepreneur or promoter, the largest component was a City core based around the joint stock banks and the major assurance

Table 2.9   City and Industry Links, 1904–76

	Number of companies connected to[a]		
	13 London banks[b] *(1904)*	*6 London banks*[b] *(1938)*	*5 London banks*[b] *(1976)*
Railways and canals	15	4	1
Shipping and docks	5	7	1
Other transport	3	1	1
Utilities[c]	5	7	0
Oil	2	5	2
Overseas[d]	5	11	4
Manufacturing and heavy industry	11	29	41
Distribution and services[e]	0	5	6
Insurance	6	9	6
Other financial	5	14	21
Totals	57	92	83
Total financial	11	23	27
Total non-financial	46	69	56

Notes: [a] Where two or more banks were connected to the same company, that company is counted once only.
[b] The London banks are the Bank of England and the clearing banks based in London.
[c] Utilities are water, gas, electricity, telephone, and telegraph services based in Britain.
[d] Overseas refers to overseas electricity, tramway, mining, and trading companies.
[e] Distribution and services includes diversified conglomerates having no significant manufacturing base.

companies. One-third of the members of this City core were clearing banks, while just 2 of the other 8 non-pair components contained clearing banks. Table 2.9 shows that the 13 London clearing banks of 1904 were collectively interlocked with 46 non-financial enterprises. Less than one-fifth of these enterprises were manufacturers, and four of those were old-established breweries.[17] The London banks preferred to interlock with railways and the older commercial sectors; the banks were interlocked with 15 railway and canal companies, 5 shippers, 5 utilities, 4 transport companies, 3 traders, and 3 overseas mines. The key carriers of these interlocks were the City merchants who dominated the bank boards. Outside the City core were a large number of isolated and peripheral enterprises and a few regional or personal communities of interest. Regional groupings included the Glasgow Tennant group, a Newcastle group based around the Armstrong enterprise, a Liverpool group, and an Aberdeen group, while the personal groups included those associated with Marcus Samuel, Osborne O'Hagan, and John Ellerman. The main structural feature of the network was a split between the City and provincial business, with the latter being fragmented into a number of district regional components and clusters.

The City of London core 'unfolded' into the smaller components and the peripheral and isolated enterprises as a result of the economic transformations which began with the First World War. The war saw an increased level of government intervention in the economy as the magnitude of its military requirements became apparent. The main focus of government controls was the Ministry of Munitions, which regulated all the main armaments, transport, and equipment enterprises. Under Lloyd George many prominent industrialists were brought into the emerging corporatist structures, but the postwar period was marked only by a loose 'corporate bias' as the wartime structures were dismantled (Middlemas, 1979). Most of the machinery of economic controls was dismantled after the postwar boom of 1919–20, and although the railways were reorganised into four major groups before being returned to private hands, the coalmines were handed back with little of no restructuring (Pollard, 1962). In the short-lived boom and subsequently promoters such as Clarence Hatry, Philip Hill, Sir Edgar Sperling, and Frederick Szarvasy were active in a series of successful and unsuccessful mergers and amalgamations – even the notorious Hooley made a brief reappearance (Hooley, 1929). Many of the promoters had short careers before their businesses tumbled, but Hatry stumbled on until he was brought down in the midst of his attempt to float United Steel in 1929 (Hatry, 1939; Deeson, 1971); Szarvasy's influence persisted despite the failure of his master company; and Philip Hill built a substantial group based on property.[18] The main factor generating economic change was the changing balance between the old heavy industries of the North and the new industries of the Midlands and the South. The main growth areas of the interwar economy were to be found in such sectors as artificial textiles, electricity supply, electrical engineering, motor vehicles, aircraft, chemicals, rubber, glass and retail distribution. In each of these sectors a number of large enterprises grew through internal expansion, and mergers and amalgamations became especially important in the late 1920s: artificial fibres came under the dominance of Courtaulds and British Celanese; motor cars were dominated by Austin and Morris; in chemicals ICI and Lever prevailed; Pilkingtons had a virtual monopoly of quality glass production; and retail groups such as Boots and Marks & Spencer were building up large national chains.

It was during the late 1920s that the most dramatic changes in unit and network concentration took place. The economic collapse of 1920–21 threatened to cause great losses for those banks which had granted overdrafts to the firms now in trouble. In order to avoid massive defaults on those overdrafts they had little alternative but to participate substantially in the share and debenture capital of the troubled enterprises and to become actively involved in plans for industrial reconstruction. The separation of banks and industry which had emerged in the late nineteenth century could not be sustained under such circumstances. A current of 'corporatist' thought turned many bankers, industrialists, and politicians towards deliberate policies of 'rationalisation', using the large bank shareholdings and capital involvements as the material base for implementing such policies (Hannah, 1976a, chapter 3; Booth, 1982). Although governments generally supported such moves, they were not interested in any state-directed intervention; and the banks themselves were widely regarded as the most appropriate vehicles for industrial reconstruction. The Bank of England, under the leadership of Montagu Norman and still privately owned, became the organising focus of bank intervention, and involved some of the larger insurance companies. Securities Management Trust and Bankers' Industrial Development were set up as agencies through which the Bank could direct the funds subscribed by the banks and insurance companies, and their role was especially important in cotton, shipbuilding, and iron and steel. In cotton, banking interests inspired the creation of the Lancashire Cotton Corporation to amalgamate the companies with which they were associated, and they formed the Spindles Board to close down excess

C

capacity. National Shipbuilders Security was set up to purchase and close surplus yards; its most notorious closure was the yard at Jarrow (Wilkinson, 1939). Such a high level of rationalisation was not achieved in iron and steel, though the banks created the Iron and Steel Federation to engage in price fixing and to exercise some control over investments.[19]

Although the partial recovery of the 1930s enabled the banks to begin to withdraw from a number of their industrial participations, the intercorporate network of 1938 reflected the period of industrial collapse and bank-sponsored rationalisation. Unit concentration, overall and within major sectors, had increased to a high level. Equally important, however, was the changing relationship between banks and industry. The 'unfolding' of the City core as banks and insurance companies extended their capital and commercial relations throughout the economy had transformed the fragmented interlock network of 1904 into a significantly more cohesive structure. The network of multiple lines now contained 21 components – compared with 24 in 1904 – but the largest component included 63 enterprises and most other components were isolated pairs. The network of interlocks was forged into a unified system under the aegis of the banking system: the large component in the network of multiple lines included all but one of the London clearing banks (the exception was Barclays). This large component, the heart of the overall interlock network, was organised at a national level, and the continued strength of family control and regionalism resulted in a number of distinct clusters in the 1938 network: the South Wales coal and steel combine, Oppenheimer's South African and Rhodesian mining interests, and communities of interests such as the Shell/Anglo-Iranian oil group and a Liverpool shipping group. Many interlocks were associated with vertical or horizontal integration, often on a regional basis, or were associated with financial participations by investment companies and banks. As can be seen from table 2.9, 32 per cent of the enterprises with which the banks were interlocked were in manufacturing and heavy industry, and the banks were now interlocked with electrical utilities, South African mining enterprises, and retail chains. By 1938, therefore, the interlock evidence is strongly suggestive of a growing fusion of interests between banking and industry: of a drift towards 'finance capital'.

This pattern of relations between the financial and non-financial sectors affected the form of business enterprise which dominated Britain's interwar economy. In Britain the large national enterprise emerged not as the 'functional' organisation which prevailed in the USA, but in the form of the loose 'holding company'.[20] The main explanation for this is the differential role played by families and bankers in the two countries. Chandler (1962) argues that the New York investment banks played a key role in the USA in creating the conditions under which multi-divisional administration could emerge. These financiers created large amalgamations of firms which they then ruthlessly re-organised into the centralised, functional enterprises that were dominant by the end of the First World War. Such a close association between banking and industry developed in Britain only hesitantly during the 1930s, and the banks were reluctant partners in this association. Amalgamations of family firms, therefore, tended to remain as loosely federated holding companies. Channon (1973) argues that family firms were unwilling to diversify and to adopt the multidivisional organisation. Large holding-company amalgamations developed in response to severe price competition, but these amalgamations tended to occur under the leadership of a particular family or group of families. The parent board was often an arena for struggles between families, each of which was defending its part of the enterprise; and attempts by families to maintain their control precluded any reorganisation of the amalgamated enterprises along functional lines (Hannah, 1974).

The development of finance capital was much accelerated in the period after the Second World War. Although the clearing banks withdrew from the high levels of industrial participation which had been thrust upon them in the interwar period, insurance companies and pension funds became increasingly important purchasers of company shares. Declining levels of family shareholding created a constant supply of shares for the financial intermediaries to buy. At the same time, the merchant banks developed their role in corporate finance. 'Institutional' funds had, in real terms, remained relatively stable from 1938 until the early 1950s, but had almost doubled by 1962, and had more than trebled by 1972 (Prais, 1976, p. 116, table 5.5). The bulk of these increased funds had been placed in company securities, especially ordinary shares, with the main switch to these investments beginning in the late 1950s. Table 2.10 shows the consequences of this trend for a particular large enterprise. In 1938 Peninsular and Oriental Steam Navigation (P & O) had no

Table 2.10　The Top 20 Stockholders in P & O, 1938–76

	% of stock controlled		
	1938	*1957*	*1976*
Individuals[a]	4.95	2.71	—
Insurance companies	1.15	5.22	8.64
Pension funds	—	1.10	4.01
Other financial companies[b]	2.08	2.32	7.13
Other non-financial companies	2.30	0.34	—
Other[c]	2.44	2.70	0.45
Total controlled by top 20	12.92	14.39	20.23

Notes:　[a] Individuals includes private investment companies.
　　　　[b] The total controlled by merchant banks and investment trusts (included under 'Other financial companies') was 0.89 per cent in 1938, 1.60 per cent in 1957, and 5.00 per cent in 1976.
　　　　[c] Other comprises the P & O Colonial Stock Trust in 1938 and 1957, and the Church Commissioners in 1957 and 1976.
Sources: 1938: *Fairplay's Annual Summary of British Shipping Finance*, London, Fairplay magazine; 1957: *The 'Syren' Financial Yearbook*, London, the Syren and Shiping magazine; 1976: share registers at Companies House.

dominant shareholder. Although its shares had become fairly widely dispersed, its 20 largest shareholders held 12.92 per cent of the shares; and individuals were the biggest group of shareholders among these 20. By 1957 its stock had become less dispersed, and the insurance companies and pension funds had increased their holdings at the expense of individuals and non-financial companies. The figures for 1976 show that the 20 largest shareholders held 20.23 per cent, that no individuals were to be found among them, and that insurance companies, pension funds, and other financial companies had all increased their holdings. P & O is typical of those large enterprises with no single dominant shareholder and illustrates clearly the increased role that financial intermediaries came to play in particular enterprises and in the economy as a whole. This growth in shareholding by financial intermediaries enhanced the availability of share and loan capital for expansion and became an important impetus to the takeover boom of the 1950s and 1960s.

The studies of unit concentration showed evidence of an upward trend from 1904 to 1938, followed by a slight decline and then a massive increase in the 1960s. The evidence on interlocking shows a similar rise in the first part of the period but a fall during the postwar period. It would seem that network concentration reinforced the drive towards unit concentration in the first half of the century. Bilateral relations between banks and non-financial companies became particularly important in facilitating unit concentration, and these bilateral relations often involved interlocks as well as financial participations. The growth in interlocking was a precondition for, and an expression of, the growth in unit concentration. Since the 1950s the large number of mergers and amalgamations has reduced the need for interlocking between separate enterprises. As horizontally linked enterprises have merged, pre-existing interlocks have, in many cases, been converted into relations of full fusion: interlocks have become transformed into hierarchical personal relations between executives. This trend is associated with the diversification of individual enterprises and the nationalisation of many large enterprises. Diversification through merger has meant that those interlocks which previously expressed commercial relations of vertical integration have frequently become hierarchical executive relations within diversified enterprises. Nationalisation of enterprises operating in heavy industry, energy, and transport has led to the amalgamation of enterprises which had previously formed regionally based communities of interest and combines. Domestic mergers and nationalisation, therefore, have resulted in a lower level of interlocking. This has been associated with an increase in the number of isolated enterprises, which is largely to be explained by the greater number of foreign subsidiaries and by the takeover of British companies by foreign enterprises.

At the level of the individual business enterprise these trends have resulted in enterprises moving directly from the holding company organisation to the decentralised multidivisional structure, but this occurred mainly during the 1950s and often only when family control had been undermined. In 1950 just 13 per cent of the 100 largest manufacturing enterprises studied by Channon had adopted the multidivisional organisation; by 1960 this figure had risen to 30 per cent, and by 1970 to 72 per cent (Channon, 1973, p. 67). The main impetus towards diversification and a multidivisional structure was the growth of American competition, and American subsidiaries led the way in administrative reform.

The growth of a national intercorporate network, in which financial and non-financial enterprises were fully integrated, was complete by 1976, when the remaining isolated and peripheral

enterprises consisted mainly of family firms and foreign subsidiaries. The form taken by this fusion of bank and industrial
capital can be seen in table 2.9. The five London banks were
interlocked with 83 of the top 250 enterprises, slightly fewer than
in 1938, but almost half of all these interlocks were with
enterprises in manufacturing and heavy industry. Equally important was an alteration in the structure of the financial sector itself:
the proportion of bank interlocks with other financials increased
between 1904 and 1938, and increased again between 1938 and
1976. Whereas most of the financial interlocks of the 13 banks of
1938 were with the large insurance companies, those of the 5
banks of 1976 were mostly with enterprises involved in property,
investment management, consumer credit, and other areas of
specialist lending. The banks were no longer part of a City core[21]
but were diversified financial conglomerates which had developed
interlocks with specialist financials, manufacturers, and service
enterprises. A particularly important feature of this situation is
the fact that the banks were among the major organising pivots of
the interlock network: 4 of the 5 non-pair components in the
network of multiple lines contained a clearing bank.[22]

The British intercorporate network can be described as having
evolved towards the fusion of all sectors of capital, which
Hilferding (1910) defined as 'finance capital'. Banks, insurers,
large manufacturers, and other large enterprises may be regarded
as units of finance capital: regardless of the areas of production
and service in which their branch plants and subsidiaries may
operate, they combine within themselves both money capital and
its 'productive' use. Hilferding's analysis, however, pointed
beyond this fusion *within* major enterprises to the characteristic
forms of association *between* them. Finance capital must be
understood as involving distinct forms of intercorporate relation.
Hilferding claimed that so long as banks are merely intermediaries in the system of payments they are concerned only with
the current solvency of their customer enterprises. But as soon as
they lend investment funds they must become concerned with the
long-term prospects of enterprises; and the greater such lending is
in relation to the enterprise's total capital, the deeper that
concern will become. The reason for this is that investment loans
can only be repaid over the long term and so the interests of the
bank and its customer become entwined. The interdependence of
banker and customer increases, and the position of the bank in
relation to the flow of money makes it the dominant partner in

the relationship (Hilferding, 1910, pp. 94–5). When a large enterprise operates in this way, the position of banker becomes assimilated to that of shareholder and the bank seeks to safeguard its interests by spreading its investments across a large number of companies and through board-level representation. Spreading investments reduces bank dependence on any particular enterprise and, incidentally, precludes the formation of tight bank-centred combines or 'interest groups'. Board representation leads to a larger number of interlocks between banks and other enterprises, many of which will be associated with institutionalised capital or commercial relations (Hilferding, 1910, p. 121). Finance capital is capital which is used in any or all sectors of the economy and which is channelled through the banks and other credit-giving enterprises to those sectors in which it is to be employed; finance capital, therefore, involves the institutional dominance, or 'hegemony' (Mintz and Schwartz, 1984), of the intermediaries which control the capital market.[23] The role of multiple directors in this process has been summed up in Hilferding's concept of the 'personal union':

> A circle of people emerges who, thanks to their own capital resources or to the concentrated power of outside capital which they represent (in the case of bank directors), become members of the boards of directors of numerous corporations. There develops in this way a kind of personal union, on one side among the various corporations themselves, and on the other, between the corporations and the bank; and the common ownership interest which is thus formed among the various corporations must necessarily exert a powerful influence upon their policies. (Hilferding, 1910, pp. 119–20)

As oligopoly has come to characterise most of the major product markets, so the oligopolistic enterprises have come to monopolise the flow of capital through the economy and the financial intermediaries have achieved key positions in this flow. Monopoly capital is the basis upon which large enterprises are able to determine the limits of action available to the small and medium-sized businesses which operate outside the monopolised areas of the economy. The conditions of action in these 'competitive' sectors are therefore structured by the same processes which structure monopoly capital itself. Small businesses and medium-sized enterprises have become increasingly dependent upon big business, this dependence being rooted in the supply of raw materials or finished goods, control over technology, and access to capital. An understanding of the structure of power within big business is the key to understanding power in the economy as a whole.

This chapter has examined some of the properties of the inter-corporate network as a whole, density and fragmentation being the most important. It has been shown that an extensive national network had emerged in Britain by 1976 and that this resulted from a gradual extension of the City core to cover other sectors of the network, and from a transformation of the City core itself. The intense interlocking which characterised many of the larger enterprises in 1938 had, by 1976, given way to less intensive interlocks among a more diverse group of enterprises. At the heart of this network, though not constituting a structural centre, were the enterprises which dominated the capital market, and the whole system could be regarded as epitomising a model of finance capital. The location of these enterprises in the flow of money and their ability to monopolise capital would clearly enable them to use their position to maximise their own autonomy and to make other enterprises dependent upon them. This is the key to the 'hegemonic' structure of the 1976 network. Many of these same enterprises were able to use their interlocks to enhance their access to the intelligence they required to formulate and pursue their corporate strategies. The patterns of interlocking discovered at the aggregate level must be taken as indicators of changes in the structural flow of money, raw materials, and information and therefore of changes in the relative power of different enter-prises. Such issues will be pursued in chapters 5 and 6, where interlocks are broken down into their various subtypes and are related in more detail to intercorporate transactions and to the structures of the various partial networks. The following chapter explores some of the trends in interlocking within particular sectors of the economy and examines the impact made on these sectors by the development of finance capital.

NOTES

1. The data selection is discussed more fully in the Appendix. See also Stokman et al. (1984, chapter 1).
2. On unit concentration in the USA, see Blumberg (1975, chapters 2, 3, 4); Herman (1981).

3. A contemporary discussion of concentration is Macrosty (1907).
4. United Alkali from the 1904 top ten had become a subsidiary of ICI, and British-American Tobacco was, in part, a continuation of the original Imperial Tobacco.
5. Some of the steel-making assets of Vickers and GKN were eventually incorporated into British Steel. See Scott (1962 and 1978), Trebilcock (1977), and Beynon and Wainwright (1979).
6. If the 1938 railways had been excluded, the top ten would have included 2 more oil companies (Burmah Oil and Iraq Petroleum), 1 more utility (City of London Electric), and a distributor (Co-operative Wholesale).
7. Eastern Telegraph became a major constituent of Cable & Wireless, Anglo Saxon Petroleum was acquired by Shell, and the assets of Gas Light & Coke were transferred to British Gas.
8. Density is calculated by the formula

$$d = \frac{L}{N(N-1)/2}$$

where L is the number of lines and N is the number of points. In a graph with directed lines, however, the density is simply $L/N(N-1)$, where L is the number of directed lines. These definitions disregard the 'values' of the lines in the network.
9. The 1976 figure of 0.017 should be compared with the international results presented in Stokman et al. (1984): for example, Netherlands 0.031, France 0.034, USA 0.035, Germany 0.041.
10. Where no account is taken of the directionality of the lines, the analysis is concerned with 'weak' components. 'Strong' components are found in a directed graph when a subset of points is connected by lines which run in the same direction: a strong component permits a continuous 'flow' from one point to the next. Components are 'maximally connected' in the sense that every pair of points is connected by a path. In graph-theoretical terminology, a weak component contains not paths but 'semi-paths', as the directionality of the lines varies. In undirected graphs, weak and strong components cannot be distinguished. Stokman and van Veen (1981) relate components to 'blocks', but this usage must be distinguished from the 'block' concept used by White and his colleagues at Harvard. See Levine and Mullins (1978).
11. In undirected graphs this is measured by the formula $2L/N$. As noted in chapter 1, footnote 11, it is possible to use this formula to estimate network density from a random sample of enterprises. If the network degree is estimated from the sample, then

$$density = \frac{network\ degree}{(N-1)}$$

12. Only three came from the financial sector, all from mass savings enterprises: Pearl Assurance, Alliance Building Society, and Leeds Building Society.
13. This measure is the 'sum distance'. It has sometimes been proposed that 'eccentricity' is a measure of global peripherality, where the eccentricity of a point is the distance at which it stands from the point which is furthest removed from it in the graph. This is, however, difficult to use as a measure of peripherality, as a point with high eccentricity may nevertheless be very close to the majority of other points.
14. Similarly, the number of multiple directors increased from 303 to 329 and then fell back to 282, and the network degree increased from 3.21 to 4.62 and then fell back to 4.34. The degree of the large component in 1938 was 5.92.
15. This pattern is described in the sigmoid shape of the log-normal distribution. The probability assumptions constitute the 'Gibrat effect'.
16. The network of multiple lines is the network created when lines of value one are disregarded.
17. The others were British Westinghouse, Linotype and Machinery, British Oil and Cake Mills, GKN, Bolckow Vaughan, Wigan Coal, and Swan Hunter.
18. Philip Hill's interests survived throughout the period under investigation and were represented in the 1976 network by the merchant bank Hill Samuel and its associates.
19. On this period, see Pollard (1962); Hannah (1976a, chapters 4, 5). See also Rees (1922).
20. The concept of 'holding company' used here – a parent company which holds all the shares in a number of semi-autonomous subsidiaries – should be distinguished from the usage in Belgium and France, where it refers to the holding system defined in figure 1.1.
21. This contradicts the argument of Aaronovitch (1955 and 1961).
22. The fifth component contained a major merchant bank. This feature of the network is fully discussed in chapter 6.
23. Hilferding's own account was too dependent on the particular characteristics of the German case, where the banks were 'universal banks' combining commercial and investment banking. His emphasis on bank dominance (and his neglect of other credit intermediaries) has become even more exaggerated in some American discussions of 'bank control'. This view will be critically examined in chapter 6.

CHAPTER THREE

Regional and Sectoral Structuring

Four major processes in the development of the modern business enterprise have been especially important for the structuring of the intercorporate network: diversification, national integration, internationalisation, and nationalisation. Chandler (1962) has shown that the first three of these are closely intertwined. He argues that the prevailing form of enterprise prior to the 1890s was the individual family firm operating a single factory under the personal management of the owner and subject to the conditions of a competitive economy. Such firms were typically limited to particular products and localities within the economy. Over the following years, mergers and amalgamations led to the consolidation of many of these small enterprises into large, nationally integrated units as businesses responded to the problems of organising mass production at low cost. In the centralised, 'functional' systems of management which were established in these national enterprises the various functions of business administration were subdivided into specialist departments: finance, purchasing, sales, personnel, and so on. A head office became the central decision-making body for coordinating and planning the activities of the enterprise as a whole. As their product ranges were diversified and they ceased to be limited to particular industrial sectors, these enterprises began to decentralise production into separate product divisions. Each such division operated as an autonomous profit centre but was coordinated with the others through a general office at the level of the enterprise as a whole.

These internal developments had definite consequences for the external relations of enterprises. Diversification of individual enterprises resulted in a breaking down of barriers between sectors, as enterprises were no longer restricted to particular markets, and it became increasingly difficult to distinguish one sector from another. Food producers became involved in hotels, leisure, and insurance; cigarette producers became involved in brewing, chemicals, and office machinery; and armaments manufacturers became involved in television, computers, and publishing. Each particular market became the meeting place not of specialist producers but of diversified conglomerates, and such broad labels as 'food and drink', 'engineering', and 'chemicals' began to lose their relevance. No longer could a particular enterprise be allocated unambiguously to a particular sector. The emergence of integrated 'national' concerns initially involved the strengthening of a distinctly national economy, leading to a lessening of regional differentiation. Like the economic 'sector', the 'region' became of less importance as a structural principle in the economy. But national integration has increasingly been undermined by internationalisation. The move towards multinational operations, which was particularly rapid after the Second World War, involved the emergence of a 'global' corporate strategy. Within the global strategies of multinational enterprises, strategic decisions were made in the major metropolitan centres and operational administration was handled by subordinate executives in the branch plants and subsidiaries.[1] In consequence, chains of dependence emerged between and within national economies. The more dependent areas experienced a 'disarticulation' of their interindustry linkages, as a higher proportion of capital and commercial relations ran from periphery to centre rather than around the periphery. In those areas most subject to foreign penetration the capital, commercial, and personal relations of subsidiaries to their parents became more important than those between subsidiaries and local enterprises. The network of intercorporate relations within the area became fragmented, and the number of isolated enterprises increased.

Nationalisation and the extension of the public sector do not figure as a central theme in the Chandler thesis, but are undoubtedly of general importance outside the USA. Especially since the interwar years, the state has become increasingly important in the regulation and planning of economic activity and in direct ownership and control of business enterprises. Public enterprise has come to play an increasingly important role alongside privately owned businesses and has a number of possible implications for network structure. The creation of a state sector may result in the isolation of state from private enterprises as the major public concerns become closely tied to their sponsoring ministries. On the other hand, state enterprises may engage in mutual cpaital, commercial, and personal relations and so become forged into a distinct section of the intercorporate network. The growth of the public sector has the potential to counteract any disarticulation of the economy by creating a cohesive cluster of leading enterprises in which the interests of the national economy and the national state can be fused.

These four processes can be analysed in network terms by focusing on the trends of interlocking in a number of sections of the network. Regions and economic sectors can be depicted as 'subgraphs', subsets of points drawn from the whole graph, and thus can be analysed on the basis of the whole gamut of social network concepts. Because a sector forms a subgraph it is possible also to regard it as a cluster within the network as a whole. As such, its centrifugality is measured by the proportion of all the lines connecting its members that run within the sector. An 'internal line' is one which connects enterprises operating in the same sector or region, while an 'external line' connects them with outsiders. The cohesiveness of a sector or region, and therefore the potential for preferential transactions within it can be measured by its density (measured by internal lines) and its centrifugality (the proportion of lines which are internal). Cohesiveness, therefore, is an important indicator of the extent to which distinctive sectors and regions can be identified.

THE INTERNATIONALISATION OF CAPITAL

The implications of the growth of multinational enterprise for the British business system can be seen in two dimensions: the activities of British investors overseas, and the activities of foreign investors in Britain. For 1904 it is difficult to make a sharp distinction between foreign-controlled enterprises with substantial British participations (such as British Westinghouse) and British-controlled enterprises with substantial foreign participations (such as Nobel-Dynamite). Although the top 200 non-financials of 1904 included 1 almost wholly-owned American subsidiary and 1 company owned by a foreign family, there were also a number of enterprises which were registered in Britain, operated overseas, and had foreign interests on their boards.

Many of the overseas investment and holding companies were in such a 'mixed' state: numerous gas, traction, and metal mining companies were solidly British, a number of American and South African brewers had substantial foreign ownership. This mixed character is reflected also in personal relations: the boards and shareholders of many of the colonial traders, overseas banks, and shippers included expatriates living in the colonial territories.[2]

The broad trends of internationalisation can be obtained by focusing initially on those British non-financial parents subject to majority foreign ownership.[3] Table 3.1 shows that the foreign sector of 1904 included just 4 parents, of which 3 were interlocked within the top 200. There was only one internal line, connecting British Westinghouse with Linotype & Machinery,[4] and the carrier of this interlock was the British chairman of Linotype. The

Table 3.1   Internationalisation and Interlocking in the
Top 200 Non-Financials, 1904–76

	No. of foreign-controlled companies			No. of lines	
	Inter-locked	Uninter-locked	Total	Internal	External
1904	3	1	4	1	10[a]
1938	3	2	5	0	14
1976	13	24	37	1	28

Note: [a] Three external lines running between UERL (Underground Electric Railways of London) and its associates are not included in this total.

use of a British chairman to connect the two enterprises reflects a strategy on the part of their parents aimed at integrating their foreign operations into the British intercorporate network. This strategy was reinforced by bank interlocks connecting them to the City core.[5] UERL (Underground Electric Railways of London, the parent of the Underground combine), was itself a part of this core, and had been set up to consolidate the control of an American banking syndicate over the Metropolitan District Railway. The combine included a tramway and the Piccadilly line railway, and it went on to acquire other London railways, tramways, and bus operators, which were welded together through cross-shareholdings and interlocks.[6]

British overseas investments tended to originate in the activities of financiers, promoters, and syndicates, and many took the form of 'portfolio' investment rather than 'direct' investment

(Cottrell, 1975). Not infrequently the affairs of the enterprises involved were overseen on the spot by expatriate Britons, often Scotsmen, who were employed by the enterprises or acted as their agents. Investment trusts were particularly active in overseas investment (Lenman and Donaldson, 1971; Jackson, 1968; Macmillan, 1967), and other companies also adopted an investment orientation as holding companies for overseas assets, rather than operating as parent companies with wholly owned subsidiaries. The 1904 network showed a concentration of British overseas investment in certain industrial sectors: trading, oil, and mining, together with lesser interests in food, drink, and transport. The leading interests in most of these enterprises were drawn from the City and provincial merchants, whose main area of involvement was of course the trading sector itself. Joint stock trading companies were often formed by a particular merchant partnership to undertake one aspect of its activities or by a merchant syndicate to operate as a joint venture in one part of the world. Many of the trading enterprises had manufacturing, ranching, or plantation interests, and the merchants themselves were frequently involved in oil and mining. The Gladstone and Hubbard families of Russian merchants joined with V. H. Smith of Morgan Grenfell and two of the Philipps brothers[7] to control two oil producers in southern Russia; Burmah Oil was run by the Glasgow East India merchants Cargill & King (Anon., n.d.; Colverd, 1972); and Shell was run by the Far Eastern merchant Marcus Samuel. Similarly, the largest mining enterprises operating in Western Australia, South Africa, South America, and the USA were all controlled by City merchants who handled the gold, diamonds, and chemicals produced. By contrast, some oil and mining enterprises were outside mercantile influence: European Petroleum was run by the Pease coalmining family; Schibaieff Petroleum had substantial Dutch participation; and the Spanish and Norwegian mines operated by Tharsis Sulphur and Dunderland Iron drew their directors and principal shareholders from industrial concerns.

Table 3.1 shows that there were five foreign-controlled enterprises in the top 200 of 1938. Three of these were interlocked within the top 250, two falling within the large component of the network.[8] Ford Motor, in particular, was well-integrated into the network, having an interlock with the Bank of England and two interlocks with National Provincial Bank. There were no internal lines within the foreign sector, and the bulk of the 14 external lines involved interlocks between Edmundson's Electricity and other utilities. Foreign influence extended beyond these majority-owned enterprises to those in which foreign interests held minority participations. The General Electric Company and Associated Electrical Industries had minority stakes held by General Electric of America;[9] Babcock & Wilcox and Electric & Musical Industries both had American minority participations; Associated British Pictures was jointly controlled by British interests and by Warner Brothers; Shell and Unilever were Anglo-Dutch enterprises; and a mixture of foreign and British participations were to be found in Iraq Petroleum, International Sleeping Car, Anglo-Dutch Plantations, and Amalgamated Metal.[10]

The growth of American and other foreign ownership in the postwar period is reflected in the inclusion of 37 foreign-controlled subsidiaries in the top 200 of 1976. At the same time, most large British enterprises themselves had overseas interests and so the whole economy had become more thoroughly inter-nationalised. The foreign multinational, multidivisional enter-prises with British operations might be expected to retain strategic control at their headquarters, delegating only oper-ational management to the British executives, especially in the case of simple branch plants. However, an enterprise may have a number of reasons for delegating at least some aspects of strategic control to its overseas subsidiaries, and where this happens, the parent may also seek to integrate its subsidiary into the local network by recruiting outside directors to its board and encourag-ing its executives to take outside appointments. Thus, variations in interlocking among foreign subsidiaries may be regarded as pointers to variations in the parent–subsidiary relationship (see Francko, 1976; Granick, 1962).

Table 3.1 shows that the increase in the number of foreign-controlled subsidiaries over the period 1904–76 was associated with an increase in the proportion which were isolates. Neverthe-less, a third of the foreign subsidiaries were interlocked, and these enterprises generated 28 lines to 'British' enterprises. Table 3.2 extends this analysis. While European subsidiaries were equally as likely to be interlocked as uninterlocked, North American subsidiaries were far more likely to be isolates. The United States and Canadian subsidiaries were strongly tied into the global organisation of their parents, while European sub-sidiaries were more likely to enter into alliance with British

Table 3.2   Interlocks and Foreign Ownership in the
Top 200 Non-Financials, 1976

	North American subsidiaries		Other subsidiaries[a]		Totals
	Inter-locked	Uninter-locked	Inter-locked	Uninter-locked	
Wholly owned	6	14	4	4	28
Other majority	1	4	2	2	9
Totals	7	18	6	6	37

Note: [a] Mainly West European (including the Netherlands Antilles tax haven),
but including one Soviet subsidiary.

enterprises. However, European interlockers tended to be peripheral while United States interlockers were much closer to the central enterprises in the network. It can be concluded that European parents pursued a strategy aimed at the peripheral integration of their subsidiaries into the British network, and North American parents made their subsidiaries either isolated or central to this network.

Further insight into foreign interlocks can be gained from an examination of their distance two connections. Ten of the 13 interlocked subsidiaries were formed into a single component at distance two, and 4 of the 5 United States subsidiaries in this component were linked through their interlocks with British financials. IBM and Standard Telephones & Cables both had multiple interlocks with a financial.[11] Particularly interesting is the fact that 3 of Prudential Assurance's 5 interlocks were with American subsidiaries. The majority of the interlocks between British financials and United States subsidiaries were induced or secondary and just one was primary. Apart from the bi-national Shell and Unilever groups, the 1976 network included a number of international joint ventures and liaison schemes: Rank Organisation and Tube Investments were each interlocked with joint ventures they had formed with American firms, and both BPB Industries and BICC had United States liaisons.[12]

The general trend over the period from 1904 to 1976 was away from part-ownership of enterprises by foreign individuals, companies, and syndicates and towards wholly owned subsidiaries and branch plants locked into the global strategies of their parents. This drift towards external control, the 'branch plant economy', and the consequent disarticulation of the British economy was countered by interlocking between British and foreign enterprises and by the embedding of the majority of British enterprises in an extensive national network.

THE PUBLIC SECTOR

A public sector was slow to emerge in Britain, the state having taken a back seat throughout Britain's early industrial development. Prior to 1904 the only public enterprises as such were a number of municipal undertakings in transport, gas, water, and electricity supply which rivalled private enterprise in some localities. At a national level the Post Office comprised a major area of state business activity, but this was organised as an office of state rather than as a business enterprise.[13] This meant that the 1904 network contained no wholly public-sector enterprises, though the Manchester Ship Canal had a portion of its capital held by Manchester Corporation. The earliest forms of public enterprise *per se* were the municipal port 'trusts', formed in the middle of the nineteenth century and regulated by statute. Both the Metropolitan Water Board (formed 1903–5) and the Port of London Authority (formed 1909) were designed as large enterprises on the model of the early municipal port 'trusts', with appointed boards drawn from local authorities and private interests,[14] but had no successors until after the First World War. During the war government became extensively involved in transport, heavy industry, and food supply, but its controls were soon relaxed and involved no real expansion of the public sector. The first organisation to be formed as a distinctly modern form of public enterprise was the relatively marginal Forestry Commission (1919), which was, in law, an autonomous corporate body subject to the general supervision of a government department (L. Gordon, 1938). As the state expanded its role in economic activity during the interwar years, this form became typical of the public 'boards' and 'corporations' created on the basis of pre-existing private bodies: the British Broadcasting Corporation in 1927, Central Electricity Board in 1926, and London Passenger Transport Board in 1933.[15] In addition, the state began to take minority share participations in a number of private enterprises:

Imperial Airways in 1923, British Sugar in 1936, and Cable & Wireless in 1938.[16]

Public enterprises are subject to a form of 'ownership' which separates them from private ownership interests: those who provide capital directly to a public corporation are not voting 'members' of that enterprise, and its board of directors are responsible to a political body rather than a meeting of share-holders. It might be expected, therefore, that these different capital relations would be reflected in distinct patterns of interlocking. There is, in fact, some evidence that the growth of the public sector has led to the creation of a group of enterprises which do not interlock in the same way as privately owned enter-prises. The 1938 network shows some of the early signs of this development. The top 200 of that year included 4 public enter-prises and 2 in which public bodies held minority participations. There were no internal lines within this subgraph, but all six enterprises were connected into a 'chain' through intermediate links to other enterprises. Inclusion of distance two connections, therefore, tied all the enterprises into a single component, indicating that public enterprises were less likely to be isolated or peripheral than were private enterprises.[17] Three public boards (the Metropolitan Water Board, London Passenger Transport Board, and Central Electricity Board) were particularly close to the Bank of England, and most were close to central enterprises.

The postwar nationalisations considerably extended the public sector, condensing numerous companies in coal, electricity, gas, transport, and, later, steel into monopolistic state enterprises. The new public enterprises were rather more likely to be isolated than their predecessors, but those which did interlock showed a marked tendency to interlock with other public enterprises. The top 250 included 14 enterprises subject to direct public control, 2 in which there was indirect state majority participation, and 4 with indirect state minority participation. Ten of these 20 enter-prises were connected through 11 internal lines, the density of the subgraph being 0.058. The electric and coal enterprises (but not gas) were isolated from this group, as were the bus companies (but not air and rail transport), and the Post Office.[18] Although the public sector enterprises showed a propensity to interlock with one another, this did not result in their separation from the rest of the network. Indeed, the connections of the nationalised Bank of England to private sector enterprises and the numerous interlocks of the Hill Samuel merchant bank were of decisive importance in connecting the public enterprises. It would appear, therefore, that the relatively dense public sector was embedded in the intercorporate network rather than being separated from it. Public enterprise was an integral part of private enterprise.

INTERLOCKING WITHIN INDUSTRIAL SECTORS

Stimulated by the antitrust concerns of American legislators, a central theme in debates over interlocking has been whether it is associated with horizontal commercial relations between customers or vertical commercial relations between customers and suppliers. Horizontal relations have been analysed in terms of environmental 'turbulence'. In oligopolistic markets the ability of an enterprise to counter the actions of others is minimised, and the environment becomes turbulent as predictability and uncertainty increase (Terreberry, 1968; see also Emery and Trist, 1965). Under these market conditions the creation of interlocks may enable enterprises to secure some control over their turbulent environments. Carrington (1981) has shown that horizontal interlocking in Canada was associated with high levels of market concentration, and that this interlocking contributed to the higher levels of profit earned by oligopolistic enterprises: interlocking between competitors, and indirect horizontal connections mediated by banks, explained the causal effect of market concentration on profitability. The distance two connections, whether intentionally created for this purpose or not, were particularly important, with the banks playing a coordinating role and so limiting damaging competition. By contrast, Burt found that interlocks in the USA did not occur between competitors, and he suggests that the American antitrust laws account for this difference between the USA and Canada (Burt, 1978a; Ziegler et al., 1981).

Pennings (1980, pp. 11–12) has argued that the extent of horizontal interdependence between enterprises is a function of the number of enterprises in the market and the similarity of their products or suppliers. The level of interdependence, therefore, is reflected in the concentration ratio. Pennings argues that interdependence is greatest at intermediate levels of concentration. Under conditions of oligopoly enterprises have relatively large amounts of information about one another, while conditions of intermediate concentration make it more difficult for enterprises to predict one another's responses. Pennings hypothesises that there will be a great need for interfirm coordination at these intermediate levels. Horizontal interlocks alert competing enterprises to one another's otherwise unforeseeable and possibly disruptive actions, and so interlocked firms can reduce the uncertainty of turbulent environments.

Burt (1978a) has argued that vertical interlocking between enterprises in different industrial sectors[19] reflects the degree to which one sector is a constraint upon the profitability of the other. Similarly, Pennings (1980, p. 13) argues that the extent of vertical interdependence depends upon the substitutability of products and services and the criticality of transactions for an enterprise's operations. Where an enterprise in one sector is problematic for an enterprise in another sector, the two might be expected to interlock. The market structure and the interlock structure parallel one another: 'market structure patterning interlock structure and interlocking structure repatterning market structure' (Burt, 1978a, p. 433). This expectation was confirmed for the USA in Burt et al. (1980), suggesting that large enterprises which do much of their business with other large enterprises tend to have more interlocks than do enterprises with many smaller customers. Pfeffer (1972b) has focused on vertical capital relations between the suppliers and consumers of credit, seeing capital as both critical and non-substitutable. Interlocking and the interfirm career mobility of executives are hypothesised to reflect the needs of enterprises for capital (Pfeffer and Leblebici, 1973). The relatively frequent career movement of executives creates the conditions for more intense and durable personal relations such as interlocking. That is, the career mobility of executives fosters interorganisational cohesion in the network as a whole, and this is an important precondition for the forms of interfirm cooperation which arise as enterprises evolve strategies of environmental transformation. In these ways, argues Pfeffer, interlocking ensures that the environment is 'mapped' into the composition of the board (Pfeffer, 1974, p. 336; see also Bunting, 1976c).

British research for 1975 by Johnson and Apps (1979) discovered a relatively small number of interlocks within economic sectors. Examining a total of 235 enterprises they discovered no interlocks within construction, none within services, and only two within distribution. A larger number of interlocks were discovered within 'manufacturing' and 'finance' only because of the size and diversity of those sectors. Johnson and Apps found the only 7 of the 76 manufacturing interlocks were between enterprises operating in the same (Standard Industrial Classification order (SIC)). Data collected in the Company Analysis Project confirms this impression of low levels of horizontal interlocking, though differences were apparent among the periods studied. In addition, variations in horizontal and vertical interlocking were discovered when more narrowly defined economic sectors were analysed.

A number of sectors were examined so as to highlight any patterns of horizontal and vertical interlocking. Taking five illustrative sectors – heavy industry, utilities, food and drink, transport, and mass media – a number of general patterns were discovered.[20] In the majority of cases, as shown in table 3.3, the number of internal lines in 1938 was higher than in either 1904 or

Table 3.3   Interlocks Within Economic Sectors, 1904–76

	No. of companies			No. of internal lines		
	1904	1938	1976	1904	1938	1976
Heavy industry	17	28	6	9	31	1
Utilities	19	25	4	9	17	0
Food and drink	26	22	28	5	8	1
Transport	63	18	9	48	22	3
Mass media	2	9	8	0	2	0

1976, and in all cases the 1976 figure was lower or equal to that for 1904. A common pattern, therefore, seems to be a sharp rise between 1904 and 1938, followed by an equally sharp fallback between 1938 and 1976. This is not, of course, precisely the same trend that was found for the number of lines within the network as a whole; as shown in chapter 2, the rise in this figure between 1904 and 1938 was followed by a subsequent fall to a 1976 level above that for 1904. A provisional conclusion must be that the 1976 network contained a relatively much higher proportion of lines running between sectors than was the case in 1904. Enterprises were becoming less likely to interlock with others in the same sector. While there is some justification for this conclusion, it must be treated with caution. The long-term trend towards diversification characterising large enterprises made it far more difficult in 1976 to allocate enterprises to particular economic sectors.

Both heavy industry and the utility sector exemplify the general trend in within-sector interlocking: rising sharply between 1904 and 1938 and then falling sharply to a negligible level.[21] In each of these sectors two-thirds of the enterprises had interlocks within their own sector in 1904, and in each case nine internal lines were generated. In heavy industry the 9 lines created 3 components: 1 of size 6, a north-eastern component of size 3, and a component comprising the liaison interlock betrween Vickers and Beardmore.[22] The large component was based on a group of enterprises linked to Sir Charles McLaren (later Lord Aberconway) and his associates. The main McLaren enterprises – John Brown, Bolckow Vaughan, Tredegar Iron, Staveley Coal, and Cammell Laird – were interlocked with one another and were also interlocked with Guest, Keen & Nettlefolds. The combine arose from enterprises originally promoted by David Chadwick and in 1904 was headed by Sir Charles and his brother Walter, with the constituent enterprises linked through cross-share-holdings, mutual shareholders, interlocks, and other personal relations. The interests of the combine extended to a number of smaller coal and steel firms and, outside the sector, to enterprises such as the Metropolitan Railway.

In the utilities sector the internal lines created five components. The large component (the others consisted of two members each[23]) was formed around the Pender telegraph combine, which had been built up through the investment activities of John Pender and which extended outside the sector to investment trusts, foreign telegraphs, and cable manufacturers. Trading under the name Associated Telegraph Group, the combine was welded together through multiple lines, cross-shareholdings, and mutual shareholders.[24] In 1904, therefore, both sectors were characterised by a moderate number of internal lines which mainly reflected the personal and regional character of the whole network at that time.

In heavy industry and utilities the number of enterprises and the number of internal lines increased sharply up to 1938, and in both sectors a number of the 1904 components had grown and had intensified their internal relations. Twenty-four of the 28 heavy industrials were formed into 5 components, the second largest of which was the Aberconway (formerly McLaren) group. this group appeared as 4 horizontally interlocked collieries, 2 of which were vertically interlocked with John Brown. The largest component, which included 13 of the heavy industrials, was centred on GKN which, together with Powell Duffryn, was at the heart of a horizontally interlocked South Wales coal combine.[25] This combine was allied with steel through vertical interlocks with the horizontal joint ventures between GKN, Vickers, and Baldwins and the liaison scheme between Tube Investments and Stewards & Lloyds.[26] The large component, therefore, was an extensive community of interest embracing a substantial number of the big enterprises operating in heavy industry.[27]

The interwar years in the utility sector were marked by the growth of the holding system, an especially marked feature of the electricity supply industry. The internal lines created three components, the largest being the 11-member community of interest based on the Balfour-Touche combine. One overseas and four regional power enterprises controlled by George Balfour's master-company Power Securities (itself outside the data set) were maximally interlocked with one another,[28] and were linked through their directors and shareholders to one of its backers from the electrical manufacturing sector (AEI) and to the Touche investment trust Atlas Electric & General. The combine involved numerous capital and commercial relations, as Power Securities acted as manager and shareholder to the power companies, Balfour Beatty was a contractor for building power stations, and AEI supplied much of the equipment.[29] Apart from the electricity suppliers from the Balfour-Touche combine, the large component included the Central Electricity Board, North Eastern Electricity Supply, Calcutta Electricity, and the huge American-controlled holding company Edmundsons Electricity.[30] Electrical enterprises outside this community of interest included regional power companies from Yorkshire and the west of Scotland, a joint venture of British Electric Traction (BET) and the London Passenger Transport Board (LPTB), two London holding companies, and the British Power & Light holding company which operated as an investment arm of the Robert Benson and Edward de Stein merchant banks.[31] The large component also included 2 gas companies, but other utilities had no interlocks within the sector; the 2 telegraphs were not interlocked, as the various Pender companies had been amalgamated into Cable & Wireless, and the 2 water companies too had no interlocks within the sector.

In heavy industry the interwar groups survived until the Second World War; the restructuring initiated by the Bank of England and the commercial banks led to an intensification of group formation and an increased number of internal lines. By contrast, the electricity supply industry was restructured through private holding companies and so the increase in the number of internal lines was not so marked (see table 3.3). By 1976 both sectors had been radically transformed by the extension of the public sector. The postwar nationalisation of coal and the reorganisation of steel[32] significantly reduced the number of enterprises in the sector. The formerly independent enterprises were amalgamated into unified public corporations, which affected the whole pattern of interlocking. There were 6 heavy industrials in the top 200 of 1976 – British Steel, National Coal Board, GKN, Tube Investments, Vickers, and Johnson and Firth Brown, all of which were recognisable descendants of the interwar community of interest. There was only one line among these enterprises, a line expressing the vertical liaison scheme between British Steel and TI. British Steel had a number of primary interlocks expressing functional capital and commercial relations with customers and associates in related sectors: in addition to its interlock with TI, British Steel interlocked with the wire-producers Bridon and the engineers Clarke Chapman. Nationalisation of electricity and gas had been thorough and systematic, and all the utilities in the top 200 of 1976 were public corporations.[33] Reflecting the paucity of interlocks between the various branches of the utility sector in 1938, the 1976 utilities had no interlocks among themselves.[34]

Table 3.3 shows that the food and drink sector followed a similar trend to that found in the sectors already considered, though the rise in the number of internal lines between 1904 and 1938 was far less sharp. The number of enterprises in the sector in 1938 was comparable to that for each of the other sectors, but the number of internal lines was half that found in utilities and about one-quarter of that found in heavy industry. The food and drink sector of 1904 was dominated by the brewers: the 26 enterprises comprised 20 brewers, 1 distiller, 1 soft-drink producer, and 4 food producers. The brewers were the result of an early history of concentration, beginning with the expansion of the eighteenth-century 'porter' breweries which spearheaded the mass production of beer.[35] The growing scale of the industry was reflected in a flush of stock exchange flotations in the 1880s and the creation of the 'beerage', as many of the large brewers became important donors to Conservative Party funds. In the period 1880–91 four brewing peers were created among the market leaders: Lords Ardilaun and Iveagh (Guinness), Lord Hindlip (Allsopp), and

Lord Burton (Bass). Four of the five internal lines connected breweries to one another, though this reflected capital participations and overseas investment rather than horizontal integration. Most of the breweries were family-owned and so remained separate from the heart of the business network, though four brewers (Bass, Watney, Guinness, and Whitbread) were connected at distance two through the Bank of England and the South Eastern Railway. The only other internal line joined Bovril to the Apollinaris & Johannis soft-drinks firm, but this seems to have been part of a vertically integrated community of interest linking food, drink, and hotel enterprises; Bass was interlocked with Gordon Hotels through a line carried by Bass's chairman, and the hotel company had multiple interlocks with Bovril and Apollinaris.[36] No other hotel enterprise in the top 200 had any interlocks with food or drink concerns.

Following the reconstruction of a number of the overcapitalised brewery flotations and a spate of mergers and amalgamations, the top 200 of 1938 included just 7 brewers. The food and drink sector also included 1 distiller and 14 food producers, the continuity in numbers (see table 3.3) masking a radical change in the composition of the sector. The eight internal lines involved one horizontal brewing interlock between Charrington and Britain's largest brewer, Ind Coope,[37] and seven lines forming a community of interest among sugar producers and users. The latter expressed capital and commercial relations among Distillers, United Molasses, Tate & Lyle, and British Sugar. The food and drink sector, therefore, contained a community of interest and a personal union, but there was no marked tendency for the many family-controlled food producers to enter into bilateral or multilateral alliances with one another.

The amalgamation and merger of food and drink enterprises in the postwar period were associated with the strategies of diversification pursued by these enterprises and by those in related sectors: brewers branched out into the 'leisure' industries, and hotel and tobacco enterprises acquired beer and food producers. Allied Breweries and Bass Charrington emerged as national brewing groups, while Imperial Group and Grand Metropolitan moved into brewing from outside.[38] Diversification among food producers was epitomised in Unilever, but was also strong in Reckitt & Colman, Cadbury Schweppes, Rowntree Mackintosh, and Ranks Hovis McDougall.[39] The subsidiaries of the diversified enterprises gained tigher control over particular markets and developed monopolies in bread, margarine, frozen foods, jam, biscuits, tea, and other grocery products (Evely and Little, 1960; Hart et al., 1973). As in previous periods, in 1976 individual entrepreneurs and families were important, but they were now joined by a number of foreign subsidiaries. Indeed, some of the large mergers had been direct responses to the inroads made by American enterprises. The predominance of family and foreign ownership led to a low level of interlocking, reflected in the existence of just one internal line – a vertical interlock between British Sugar and Allied Breweries.

The transport sector shows a major departure from the general patterns so far described, in so far as the number of internal lines fell consistently over the period 1904–76. The peak figure occurred in 1904, rather than 1938, because the heavily-represented railways of that year were drastically reduced in number by the interwar railway amalgamations. Thus, the number of transport enterprises fell by almost three-quarters between 1904 and 1938. Despite the dominance of railways, the transport sector of 1904 was very diverse in composition. It included enterprises involved in shipping, docks, canals, road transport, and railways, with each undertaking tending to remain within the confines of its own branch of transport.[40] Table 3.3 shows the distribution of enterprises and lines within the sector. Both shipping and docks (Pudney, 1975) were dominated by merchants, but there were no interlocks between the two – a consequence of the fact that the docks were London-based while the big liner shipping fleets operated on the Atlantic routes from Liverpool.[41] Two internal lines among shippers ran between non-competing enterprises,[42] but there were no lines among dock companies. The railways and canals were compelled to enter into closer relations as a result of the direct competition between them. The problems of running canals profitably forced the canal companies into a *modus vivendi* with the railways (Hadfield, 1974). Six of the 7 canals in the top 200 of 1904 were interlocked with railways; 2 were also involved in railway liaison schemes and 2 had cooperative agreements with railways.[43] The exception was the Manchester Ship Canal, promoted in the late nineteenth century to enable Manchester to rival the port facilities of Liverpool.[44] The 1904 transport sector included 34 main-line railways, dominated by the 'big four' of London and North Western (LNWR), Midland, Great Western (GWR), and North Eastern (see Bonavia, 1980, Simmons, 1978). Nineteen of these enterprises were interlocked among one another, and a particularly important role in allying them was played by two consortium companies operated as joint ventures by the major enterprises.[45] These consortiums tied the 19 railways into 3 components; without the consortiums the railway network consisted of 5 components. The railways are best seen as forming a number of partly overlapping communities of interest which together formed an extended community of interest at the heart of the British railway system. Indeed, 25 of the railways were connected at either distance one or distance two. In addition to these main-line railways the sector included 8 London railways and tramways, which were connected through 5 internal lines. Four of these lines linked members of the Underground combine, and one joined British Electric traction with an associated tramway.[46]

The discussion of the 1904 transport sector has so far been concerned with the overall structure of interlocking within the sector, but it is worthwhile discussing separately those interlocks which were not associated with capital relations and which did not involve any direct control relationships. Figure 3.1 shows the resulting pattern of 'purely' personal relations. Twenty enterprises were linked through 18 lines into 4 components, the 2 largest of which were extensive communities of interest. One

Figure 3.1   Transport Interlocks Without Participations, 1904

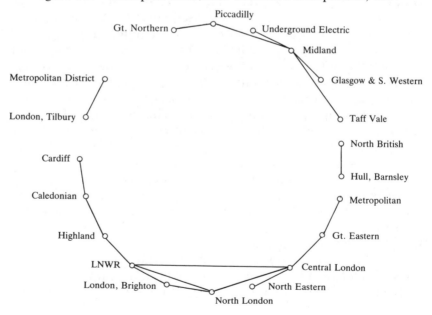

community was centred on the LNWR and the Central London Railway, while the other was centred on the Midland Railway and the Underground combine.[47] Just 1 of these 18 lines was primary, and though 1 of the remainder was carried by a retired executive, most of the others were secondary interlocks carried by peers and gentry who had connections with the localities through which the railways ran. None of the interlocks was strictly horizontal, as they did not occur between railways competing on the same route, but a number expressed relations of cooperation between adjacent or complementary routes and were aimed at securing through routes to further competition with other railways.

The interwar years were marked by amalgamation and reconstruction throughout the transport sector, which in 1938 included 8 shippers, 4 railways, 4 bus operators, and 2 dock and canal companies. The number of railway companies was reduced by the amalgamation of 31 of the main-line companies into 4 giant enterprises and by the transfer of the Irish railways to Eire. The pattern of amalgamation did not correspond to the pre-existing pattern of interlocks but to a government-instigated regional structure.[48] The docks and virtually all London transport were amalgamated into two large public enterprises: the three docks of 1904 were amalgamated with the Royal Docks in 1909 to form the Port of London Authority, and the main London tramways and buses were amalgamated into LPTB in 1933. Much of the restructuring in shipping was due to the growth and subsequent collapse of the Kylsant combine, which had been built up after 1902 and had to be rescued by the Bank of England in 1931.[49] The 1938 transport sector, therefore, was radically different from that of 1904. All but 1 (LPTB) of the 18 enterprises were interlocked within the sector through 22 internal lines. The high number of internal lines reflects the state- and bank-sponsored reconstructions of the sector, which transformed the highly clustered sector of the interwar years into a more diffusely connected one. In fact the network contained just two components. The larger component included 8 shippers, all 4 main-line railways, the PLA, and the Manchester Ship Canal. The small component consisted of the two bus holding companies (BET and Thomas Tilling) and their joint venture, a combine which was allied with the main-line railways through numerous smaller joint ventures in regional bus services (Plummer, 1937; Fulford, 1946 and 1956; and Tilling, 1957).

In the postwar years transport, like many other industries, was affected by both nationalisation and diversification, though foreign ownership was not a significant feature of the sector. Many formerly separate enterprises were amalgamated into unified public enterprises, while others became parts of enterprises involved in other industries. Technological change played a role in enhancing the position of the airlines.[50] During the interwar years the railways had tried to dominate the emerging domestic airlines, but shippers failed to anticipate the eventual impact of overseas air transport. By the 1950s Cunard still had a monopoly on the North Atlantic routes and P & O dominated the Far East, though air transport had become a major competitor to them both. Although having a legal monopoly of scheduled air services for many years, the public airlines met with some competition from smaller airlines and the larger shippers began to take shareholdings in these enterprises.

The extent to which transport had been subject to the pressures of diversification makes it difficult to distinguish a transport sector as such in 1976, but 9 of the top 200 enterprises had substantial transport interests, constituting a major part of their business. All of these enterprises were interlocked, but only 3 lines ran within the sector, and 2 of these reflected the recruitment policies of the sponsoring ministry rather than capital or commercial relations.[51] The major oil companies had become large shippers in their own right, and three of the transport enterprises were linked to the BP and Shell oil companies, both of these having large tanker fleets (Sampson, 1975). Horizontal interlocking was limited to that between British Rail and National Freight, and vertical interlocking to that of P & O with oil companies and the Inchcape trading concern. The 1976 network, therefore, showed a radical decline in the number and salience of internal lines, and showed no evidence of group formation beyond the level of personal unions.

Analysis of the centrifugality of the various sectors has shown a common pattern: their cohesiveness as clusters increased rapidly between 1904 and 1938 and then fell sharply between 1938 and 1976. This common pattern reflects the trend towards diversification among the enterprises operating in these sectors: as they became involved in a wider range of product markets, so they tended to interlock with a wider range of other enterprises rather than simply within a particular sector. Industrial sectors had become less salient as sources of division among Britain's largest enterprises. Particularly important in the interlocks of the diversified enterprises were those with the financial intermediaries which tied the national network together. Interlocking is important not simply for whatever relations of horizontal and vertical integration it expresses, but also for the opportunities it offers to enterprises to accumulate capital and intelligence. The significance of this fact has been discussed especially in studies of the mass media.

The relationship of mass media enterprises to financial intermediaries and to other non-financials has been raised on a number of occasions in the work of Marxists who wish to demonstrate the dominance of bankers over the contents of newspapers and television. In the United States the Labour Research Association drew on Rochester's (1936) model of finance capital to argue that concentration in the mass media and the resulting decline in competition have led to the dominance of a small number of publishing chains, film producers, and broadcasting systems. The interlocks and the capital and commercial relations which exist among these monopolistic media enterprises, and those in other sectors, result in the presentation of a uniform 'Wall St line' in their products: they promote free enterprise and denigrate socialism, they are prejudiced against workers and ethnic minorities, and they reflect militaristic attitudes, including war-mongering (Labour Research Association, 1950, p. 86).

A particularly sophisticated and compelling variant of this argument is that formulated by Mattelart (1976), who attempts to trace in greater detail the precise mechanisms through which intercorporate connections are translated into media content. Mattelart argues that definite stages of 'cultural hegemony' correspond to stages of capital accumulation. He sees the 1960s as the beginning of a period of industrial concentration and diversification which led to a convergence of enterprises producing communications hardware, those involved in military production, and those producing the cultural 'messages' themselves. A closer association of enterprises in electronics, the aerospace industry, and the mass media, and their tendency to become large diversified conglomerates, is reflected in the internationalisation of their sphere of activity – as depicted in Lenin's model of the imperialist division of the world. At the same time, their military entanglements as defence contractors involve them in the military and security use of computer and satellite communications and in the civil application of these same technologies. Newer and more systematic forms of communication and surveillance (satellite and cable television, electronic data processing, information technology, etc.) are developed alongside the older technologies of films, books, and newspapers. These dominent enterprises exist within a structure of competing 'financial empires' (centred on Rockefeller, Mellon, and other business dynasties), which determines the conditions under which other media enterprises must operate. Mass communications becomes one aspect of the global strategies they pursue, and American mass culture itself becomes internationalised. The argument is extended to the claim that European and Japanese enterprises are subject to the same processes and are increasingly involved in the expansion into the Third World spearheaded by American capital.

A full assessment of Mattelart's thesis is beyond the scope of this book, but it is relevant to consider whether the broad trends which he identifies in the USA – the increasing alliance between the media, electronics, and the aerospace industry – can be discerned in Britain.[52] The top 200 of 1904 included just two enterprises involved in the mass media: Amalgamated Press (the Harmsworth magazine-publisher) and Moss Empires. Magazines and theatres were based in traditional technology, and electrical technology was relatively unimportant in the mass media generally: gramophone records relied on mechanical players, and commercial film and radio did not exist. Electric communication was employed by National Telephone and the numerous telegraph companies, but these were not mass 'broadcast' media. As shown in table 3.4, neither of the large media enterprises of 1904 had any interlocks.

Table 3.4   Interlocking and the Mass Media, 1904–76

| | No. of media enterprises | | |
	Interlocked	Uninterlocked	Total
1904	0	2	2
1938	5	4	9
1976	7	1	8

The interwar years were years of concentration in the mass media. By 1937 the national and provincial press was dominated by the Harmsworth and Berry groups, though this duopoly was altered during 1938 when the Berry brothers divided their interests between themselves.[53] Other important groups, among the provincial press, were Westminster Press and United Newspapers. The top 200 of 1938, however, reflected the Harmsworth and Berry dominance: only 1 of the 5 publishers in the top 200 was not controlled by these 2 families.[54] The new technology of film and sound recording had spread from the USA, and American capital was important in producing a duopoly in the British cinema. Gaumont and Associated British Cinemas (ABC) dominated the film industry and, together with an associate of ABC, were to be found in the top 200 of 1938. Gaumont owned 300 cinemas and cafés, while ABC owned almost as many and had its own production studios at Elstree.[55] The remaining media enterprise in the top 200 of 1938 was Electric & Musical Industries, a major producer of gramophones and records which had been controlled by the American giant, RCA, until 1935. Table 3.4 shows that five of the largest media enterprises were interlocked. Shareholdings between the Harmsworth newspaper companies and between ABC and Union Cinemas were, as might be expected, reflected in interlocks, but the other media interlocks were indicative also of capital relations: the Harmsworth companies interlocked with Dunlop and Amalgamated Anthracite Collieries (AAC) because of their common association with the financier F. A. Szarvasy; ABC interlocked with United Molasses because of a common connection to a Scottish investment group; and EMI interlocked with British Power & Light through the merchant banker Edward de Stein. The mass media, therefore, had become larger and more concentrated, and had come to be connected with some of the smaller financial interests in the City and Edinburgh.

The 1940s saw a continuation of the trend towards concentration, though there was some turnover among the controllers of the major enterprises. Continued monopolisation of the cinema was largely the work of J. Arthur Rank, who diversified his family wealth from flour-milling to film-making. Rank acquired Odeon in 1939 and used this as the basis of a massive cinema group based on the Gaumont chain and later renamed Rank Organisation.[56] ABC was jointly owned by the Maxwell family and Warner Brothers until acquired by EMI in the 1960s.[57]

D

The major trend of the postwar period was diversification. By 1976 virtually all the major mass media enterprises had diversified or had become parts of larger conglomerates. New technologies such as television were incorporated into this evolving pattern. Electrical manufacturers, often with television rental interests, became involved in cincmas, broadcasting, and other areas of entertainment (bingo, theatres, bowling); paper manufacturers became entwined with publishing; wholesale and retail distributors, such as W. H. Smith, moved vertically up stream; and numerous companies acquired marginal communications interests. These trends make it difficult to identify a communications sector in 1976, but 8 of the top 200 had substantial mass media involvements and 4 of these were based on or incorporated media enterprises from the 1938 top 200. All but one of the media enterprises were interlocked. There were no internal lines, but 5 of the 8 were connected into two components at distance two. The general feature of the sector, therefore, was the sparsity of interlocks and indirect connections between media enterprises. It did, however, provide considerable support for the Mattelart model of the mass media. EMI and BBC were connected via their common interlock with the aerospace and electrical company Hawker Siddeley (EMI at multiplicity two), and EMI had other interlocks with Lucas Industries and Smiths Industries. Three other media enterprises had electrical and aerospace interlocks: S. Pearson with GEC and Chloride Group, BET with British Aircraft and Vickers, and Thomas Tilling with Rolls-Royce. A later chapter will show that Mattelart's view of competing financial empires cannot be applied to Britain, but it should be noted that many of the links between media, electrical, and aerospace enterprises were created by merchant bankers or by those whom they appointed to company boards.

The broader implications of the Mattelart thesis relate to the existence of a so-called 'media elite'. In his study of Canada, Clement (1975) claims that interlocking can restrict the autonomy of media enterprises in public communication so that the controllers of the mass media become the 'gatekeepers of ideas'. Members of the media elite are drawn from the corporate elite, have business connections with the latter, or come from a similar social background. He concludes that

> The pattern of ownership and selection of personnel to fill key
> decision-making positions within the media in Canada is heavily

biased in favour of the upper class. Given that existential position effects the ideology of people, the content of the mass media as screened by these gatekeepers is also biased in favour of the existing arrangements of power. (Clement, 1975, p. 341)[58]

Clement's central claim is that the directors and executives of the mass communications enterprises exercise a definite control over content. The discussion of interlocking in Britain has shown that the level of interlocking within the sector has been consistently low and that the number of external lines has consistently increased. Mass communications enterprises became more closely tied to other companies in the top 200, and had a large number of financial interlocks. As a result, those who sat on the boards of these companies in 1976 – Clement's media elite – had become less distinct as a group. The press barons had all but disappeared, and the mass communications enterprises were headed by a subset of the corporate directorate as a whole. Does this mean, however, that there was less owner-intervention in matters of content? And does it mean that the mass media were 'biased in favour of the existing arrangements of power'?

Murdock (1977) suggests that strategic control in communications enterprises has implications for operational administration, which in these enterprises includes the programme controllers and editors who decide the content of the papers, films, books, and broadcasts. The pattern of ownership and interlocks within which the exercise of strategic control takes place sets limits on professional autonomy and gives a *potential* for intervention in operational matters. Just as the board of directors of a pharmaceutical or toy firm may step in and withdraw a particular product line, so the directors of a mass communications enterprise may step in to prevent a broadcast or to challenge an editorial. However, research suggests that editorial and other operational decisions in the mass media are determined by a routine system of implicit and explicit criteria of 'newsworthyness' and 'entertainment value' – part of the standard operating procedures of the enterprises – and not by regular and direct owner intervention (see Schlesinger, 1978, and Tracy, 1978). Directors influence content indirectly via the constraints of profitability and audience maximisation. The criteria embodied in operational decisions are those which are consonant with the criterion of profitability (Murdock, 1977; Murdock and Golding, 1973). A newspaper, for example, is a commodity. The differences between 'right-wing' and 'liberal' newpapers, between 'quality' and 'tabloid', are simply reflections of the ability of enterprises to produce for specific differentiated markets. Brewers and distillers produce for different markets, and the political characteristics of newspapers must be seen as no more, and no less, due to proprietorial preferences than are the varying characteristics of beer and whisky, margarine and butter, soap and detergent, or any other alternative consumer goods. It is through such processes that the range of leisure choice is restricted and the range of information is limited: TV sitcoms and populist newspapers are profitable.

REGIONALISM AND NATIONAL INTEGRATION

Economic sectors, it would seem, have become less significant as sources of division between the enterprises which make up the top 200. Diversified enterprises have developed links with one another along lines of vertical and horizontal integration which have little relevance to sectoral divisions, and they have become linked in a national intercorporate network through interlocks with financials. The drive towards national integration of the economy, which was a precondition for diversification, might be expected to have had similar consequences for regional divisions.

Regional structuring was, in the nineteenth century, an important characteristic of economic activity, though numerous studies have debated whether it has become more or less salient (Mandel, 1963; Carney et al., 1976; Hudson, 1981; Watts, 1981; Harrigan, 1982). The uneven spatial distribution of industries across territories can be seen as originating in such 'geographical' factors as the distribution of natural resources, and the resulting concentration of particular industries in a regional pattern might, therefore, seem to be merely a consequence of the 'natural' evolution of these industries. Regional economic development, however, is due to factors other than simply the constraints of the physical environment and the pre-existing industrial mix. That is to say, a region may have certain characteristics which lead its business leaders to pursue courses of action which would not be pursued in other regions. Welsh businessmen, for example, may act as *Welsh* businessmen rather than Welsh *businessmen*. Such characteristics are difficult to grasp without resorting to unrealistic notions of national or regional culture, but an attempt must be made to discover whether a distinct regional factor or process exists. Only then is it possible to assess those arguments which decry the loss of regional 'autonomy'. Inroads by domestic and foreign enterprises from outside the region tie regional enterprises to an external head office rather than to other regional enterprises, and so it is argued that decision-making powers are transferred to the national or international level: regional economies become transformed into 'branch plant economies' (Firn, 1975). Such questions can be approached only through an examination of trends in capital, commercial, and personal relations in particular regions.

Undoubtedly the main claimant as a distinct and continuing regional economy within Britain is the Scottish economy. From the very earliest stages of industrialisation in Scotland, economic development was associated with the expansion of a strong financial sector. Textiles and heavy industry, the core of Scottish industry, provided the basis for the emergence of a number of wealthy business dynasties, and the existence of an autonomous system of banking, insurance, and investment companies created a unified and distinctively 'Scottish' economy (Campbell, 1980; Scott and Hughes, 1980). This is apparent in the data for 1904 (see table 3.5 below). There were 27 Scottish-registered companies in the top 250 of 1904, 3 of these (Burmah, Distillers, Moss Empires) having no interlocks. The interlocked companies generated a total of 83 lines, but further analysis was restricted to the 68 lines left after deleting those generated by the London board of an Anglo-Scottish insurance company.[59] A total of 36 of the 68 lines were between Scottish companies, and 32 ran between Scotland and the rest of Britain. Scottish enterprises accounted for 11 per cent of the top 250 but carried 17 per cent of all lines in the network. Thus, Scottish enterprises had a higher propensity to interlock than their counterparts in other parts of Britain. This would seem to account for their ability to interlock at a high level both with other Scottish companies and with companies outside Scotland. This is apparent from the fact that the interlocked Scottish companies comprised 14 per cent of all interlocked companies, but over half of their 68 lines were among themselves. The Scottish companies of 1904 showed a high propensity to interlock within Scotland. The pattern of interlocks within Scotland involved 36 internal lines joining the companies into 1 large component and 1 pair. The integration of the financial and non-financial sectors was much closer than was the case in Britain as a whole: 10 lines were within the financial sector, 10 were within the non-financial sector, and 16 ran between the 2. Links between Scotland and England were carried mainly by railways, clearing banks, and an insurance company, but a particularly important group of such 'external lines' were carried by directors associated with Sir Charles Tennant. These interlocks involved the London-registered Nobel-Dynamite and British South African Explosives and the Edinburgh-registered Tharsis Sulphur and Union Bank of Scotland.[60] The Nobel trust had been set up to control the international operations of the whole Nobel group, with Tennant and other of the original Scottish backers taking a large stake in the trust. Much of the finance for the British operating company had come from the Union Bank, and a major customer for Nobel explosives was the Tharsis mining company. Sir Charles Tennant was a main-board director of Nobel, chairman of the British operating subsidiary, chairman of the Union Bank, and chairman of Tharsis. The Tennant interlocks, therefore, were associated with a mixture of capital relations and horizontal and vertical commercial relations, the whole complex being rooted in Tennant's Glasgow base (Crathorne, 1973).

By 1938 the number of Scottish companies in the top 250 had fallen to 18, the number of lines they carried had fallen to 54, and just 11 ran within Scotland. Over half of the lines carried by Scottish companies in 1904 had been internal to Scotland; in 1938 this proportion had fallen to one-fifth. All 11 Scottish lines involved financials: 5 linked insurance companies to banks, and 6 linked these financials to non-financials. Almost half of the external lines (lines to English companies) involved Scottish financials, and a number of others involved English financials. However, one-third of the external lines involved relations of horizontal or vertical integration or financial participations. These features of interlocking reflect some of the central features of the interwar economy in Scotland, especially amalgamations and mergers aimed at the restructuring of traditional Scottish industry. The Tennant group, for example, was broken up by the creation of ICI, and Colville became part of an extended steel, shipbuilding, and shipping combine.[61] This period saw a drift of control to the south and increasing inroads by English enterprises north of the border: Stewards & Lloyds moved its main base to Corby in Northamptonshire, the Scottish railways were amalgamated into the four national concerns, and English clearing banks had bought participations or control in a number of Scottish banks.

These trends continued into the postwar period, with the state playing an increasingly important role: coal and steel were nationalised, shipbuilding was restructured, and English and American enterprises set up many manufacturing subsidiaries in Scotland. Branch plants were concentrated in fast-growing sectors such as chemicals, vehicles, and electronics, and the diversification of the industrial structure together with its increased external dependence weakened the integration of the Scottish economy (Scott, 1983; Hood and Young, 1976). The 1976 intercorporate network shows the consequences of these trends. The top 250 included 14 Scottish companies, of which 2 had no interlocks. The remaining 12 enterprises generated 45 lines, of which 11 were internal to Scotland: the latter comprised 4 primary, 2 induced, and 5 secondary lines.[62] As in 1938 most of the internal Scottish lines involved financials, but the network had become less fragmented. While the 1938 Scottish network was formed into 3 components, the 1976 network contained only 1. The Scottish region had become more inclusive and connected internally, and its density was actually higher than in 1904. These figures are summarised in table 3.5.

These trends in Scotland can be compared with interlocking in other regions. The north-east and north-west of England have

Table 3.5   Regional Interlocks, 1904–76

	No. of companies in the top 250	*% of lines within region[a] (internal lines)*	*Density of region[b]*
Scotland			
1904	27	53	0.103
1938	18	20	0.064
1976	14	24	0.121
North-west			
1904	24	43	0.054
1938	19	14	0.058
1976	7	4	0.048
North-east			
1904	8	16	0.179
1938	5	6	0.100
1976	1	—	—

Notes: [a] The base for these percentages is always less than 100.
[b] Note the dependence of density on size, which was discussed in chapter 2.

been chosen for comparison, as both areas were recognisably distinct economic regions in 1904. Industrial development in the north-east was centred on coalmining, and the mine-owners' cartel created conditions under which accumulated surplus funds could be invested in railways, iron, engineering, and ship building (Carney et al., 1976; Carney et al., 1977; Dougan, 1968; McCord, 1979). The north-west, at the very heart of the industrial revolution, was dominated by the textile manufacturers of the Manchester region and the shippers of Liverpool.

Table 3.5 shows that only 5 of the 31 lines (16%) generated by the 8 companies registered in the north-east ran within the region. Three of these internal lines connected Armstrong Whitworth with the Newcastle water and gas companies, and the other two joined Swan Hunter, Consett Iron, and Pease & Partners. Most of the external lines ran through Bolckow Vaughan to the McLaren group and through Armstrong Whitworth to a variety of enterprises. The level of interregional linkages approaches the Scottish level only if the Dunderland Iron consortium and the North Eastern Railway, both registered in London, are included within the regional economy. It seems to have been the absence of large local banking and investment companies in the north-east which led to a low level of integration and to an early drift of control to the south.[63] This is clear when compared with the north-west network. Five of the 24 companies registered in the north-west in 1904 were uninterlocked and the remainder generated 35 lines, of which 15 were internal to the region. These 15 lines connected 15 companies: a Liverpool component of 6, a Manchester component of 7, and an isolated pair.[64] The Liverpool component was centred on the Bank of Liverpool and Royal Insurance, with 5 of its 20 external lines being carried by Cunard. The Manchester component was centred on Williams Deacons Bank and the Manchester and County Bank, and most of its members operated in textiles. Clearly, the relatively high level of regional interlocking in the north-west was due to the existence of financial companies with strong local connections in the region.

By 1938 the number of companies in the north-east and the proportion of lines internal to the region had fallen. The 5 companies generated only 1 line within the region, but 15 external lines. The north-west retained a slightly stronger regional character, with its 19 companies generating 10 internal and 61 external lines. The internal lines connected Liverpool and

Manchester enterprises into a single component centred on Martins Bank (formerly the Bank of Liverpool) and Royal Insurance.[65] Nine of the ten internal lines connected financial with non-financial companies, the remaining line joining Cunard to its associate Cunard White Star. By 1976 the last vestiges of regional distinctiveness in England had disappeared. Only 1 of the top 250 was registered in the north-east and so no regional network could be identified. In the north-west there were 7 companies generating 29 lines, of which only 1 was internal to the region.[66] Of crucial importance in this decline in regional interlocking was the transfer of much financial decision-making to the south, especially the takeover of Martins Bank by Barclays in 1968. If Royal Insurance had also loosened its links with Liverpool, no internal lines would have remained in the north-west. By contrast, Scotland was able to maintain a high proportion of internal lines because of the survival of an autonomous Scottish financial sector.

It would seem that regional economies are not simply the unintended consequences of the spatial distribution of industries. Central to the determination and survival of a regional economy are regionally based financial intermediaries. The north-east and the north-west have both been affected by a drift of decision-making to the south. Financial enterprises based on these regions have gradually been absorbed into London-based financials or have, like many industrials, moved their own head offices to London. Commercial relations tend to run from regional plants to plants outside the region, following the dictates of a London-based parent. In consequence, intraregional flows within industrial input–output tables become fewer in number, and interregional flows become correspondingly greater (Watts, 1981, chapter 4). It is undoubtedly the case that regionalism is a more marked feature of small and medium-sized businesses than it is of the top 200, but the smaller regional enterprises must operate in an environment which is structured by the larger ones. The regionalism, or lack of it, in the top 200 is a crucial condition for the regional orientation of the smaller companies which depend on them. Where regionalism survives, this is reflected in the regionalisation of interlocks; but where regional economies have become 'disarticulated', interlocks run mainly from local enterprises to those based in London. The British corporate network of 1976 was not regionally structured to any great extent, in contrast with the pattern found in the USA (Bearden et al., 1975;

Bearden and Mintz, 1984). The regional pattern of the USA correspond to the regional organisation of American banking, and Scottish distinctiveness was found to depend upon the survival of a strong Scottish financial sector. Whether Scotland follows the path taken by the English regions depends upon the future of its financial enterprises.

NOTES

1. The general features of the Chandler thesis are discussed in chapter 1 above. See Chandler (1962) and Hymer (1972). For discussions of European trends, see Chandler and Daems (1974), Daems and van der Wee (1974), and Dyas and Thanheiser (1976).
2. For example, Dalgety, British South Africa Co., British Central Africa Co., Union Bank of Australia, Standard Bank of South Africa, Peninsular & Oriental.
3. Table 3.1 therefore excludes the British subsidiaries and associates of these parents, even when they appeared in the top 200.
4. British Westinghouse had between one-fifth and one-quarter of its shares held by US Westinghouse; Linotype & Machinery was owned by US Mergenthaler Linotype.
5. Although British Westinghouse exercised a major influence over the affairs of Mersey Railway, as it owned debentures and was contractor for conversion to electric power, the two companies were not interlocked.
6. The uninterlocked foreign parent was Van den Bergh from the Netherlands, later a part of Unilever. The financial sector of 1904 included three companies subject to foreign ownership, all of which were merchant banks and two of which had been set up by migrants from Europe to America. Lazard originated as the London branch of the business of the Lazard brothers, migrants from Alsace who set up banks in New York, Paris, and London. Brown Shipley, of London and Liverpool, had its origins in the trading and banking business set up at the beginning of the nineteenth century when (Sir) William Brown, of a Scots-Irish family, migrated to Baltimore. Morgan Grenfell, by contrast, originated in the London business of an American financier, Junius Morgan, and preceded the expansion of its eventual parent, J. P. Morgan & Co.
7. The activities of the Philipps family are discussed below in relation to the Kylsant shipping group.
8. Edmundson's Electricity and Ford were in the large component. British United Shoe Machinery was part of an isolated pair (it was interlocked with Linen Thread). F. W. Woolworth and Anglo-American Oil were uninterlocked.

9. See Jones and Marriott (1970). The stake in GEC was being reduced at this time. AEI was a merger which included British Westinghouse from the 1904 network.
10. The Oppenheimer mining group, based in South Africa, involved British and dominion ownership as well as participations by foreign interests such as the French Rothschilds. See Emden (1935), Gregory (1962), Copeman (1971), and Lanning et al. (1979).
11. IBM had two interlocks with National Westminster Bank, and STC had two interlocks with Prudential Assurance. The latter has no connection whatsoever with the similarly named Prudential Insurance of the USA.
12. BPB had a liaison scheme with US Gypsum, and BICC with General Cables. Neither of these, of course, resulted in an interlock within the British network. The two joint ventures were Rank Xerox and British Aluminium. On international interlocks, see Fennema (1982) and Fennema and Schijf (1984).
13. The Post Office was at that time concerned solely with the carriage of mail and inland telegraphs. Telephones remained a private enterprise until 1911.
14. The Metropolitan Water Board was formed by the amalgamation of existing private enterprises. The 1904 data set included some private water undertakings but not the Board itself, as it was still in process of formation.
15. These 'public corporations' had no share capital and, therefore, no voting members. Their existence and right to raise capital are defined by Act of Parliament and their boards are appointed by government or by specified persons. The BBC was originally a private company owned by a consortium of electrical manufacturers.
16. The public stake in Cable & Wireless was taken after the period to which selection of the 1938 data set relates.
17. Of a stratified random sample of 10 companies from the top 200, 4 were connected into 2 pairs at distance two and the other 6 had no connections to one another at this distance. If a railway had not been included in the sample only 2 of the 10 would have had distance two connections.
18. Among the enterprises with indirect state participations the isolates were Rolls-Royce, ICL, British Sugar, and Finance for Industry. The National Enterprise Board was interlocked with two other public corporations, but had no interlocks with its own subsidiaries. However, an error in the *Directory of Directors* may have led to the failure to identify an interlock between the NEB and British Leyland, as John Gardiner joined the BL board during the year 1976–7.
19. In graph theory the relations between sectors can be measured by the bi-partite density, the density of lines between one sector and all others.

20. For sector studies in other countries, see Zijlstra (1979) on the Dutch nuclear sector, and Gogel and Koenig (1981) on American primary metals.
21. Sources on the heavy industrial sectors include the following: *Shipbuilding:* Pollard and Robertson (1979), Dougan (1968), Parkinson (1960), Reid (1964), and Hogwood (1979). *Coal:* Fitzgerald (1927), Neuman (1934), Heinemann (1944), and Carney et al. (1977). *Steel:* Owen (1946), Minchinton (1957), Burn (1961), Keeling and Wright (1964), Vaizey (1974), and McEachern (1980). Sources on utilities are as follows: *Electricity:* Garcke (1907), PEP (1936), Byatt (1979), and Hannah (1979). *Gas:* South Metropolitan Gas (1924), PEP (1939), Chandler and Lacey (1949), Everard (1949), and Jenkins (1959). *Telephones and telegraphs:* Murray (1927), Haslewood (1953), Scott (1958), Sturmey (1958), and Kieve (1973).
22. On Vickers and Beardmore, see Hume and Moss (1979). The McLaren group in the large component is discussed in Firth Brown (n.d.), Hudson (n.d.), Cammell Laird (1959), Grant (1960), Deeson (1972), and Cottrell (1980).
23. The pairs were Metropolitan Electric/Direct US Cable, Commercial Gas/Primitiva Gas and Electric, Gas Light and Coke/Imperial Continental Gas, and the Newcastle and Gateshead gas and water companies.
24. On the Pender combine, see Eastern Associated (1922), Baglehole (1968), Barty-King (1979), Lawford and Nicholson (1950), Haigh (1968), and Baker (1970). The four Pender companies of 1904 were interlocked with Anglo-American Telegraph, which was not strictly part of the Associated Group itself.
25. See John (1950), Addis (1957), and Elletson (1966).
26. Stewards & Lloyds had a liaison scheme with United Steel from 1932 to 1936 and then entered into liaison with Tube Investments. See Andrews and Brunner (1951), Stewards & Lloyds (1953).
27. The three remaining components were the joint venture of Dorman Long and Pearson, a personal union between Bolsover Collieries and Consett Iron, and a multiple interlock between Colvilles and Harland & Wolff. The latter represented a survival of the Kylsant group, which is discussed below.
28. Maximal interlocking exists where all possible lines are actually present.
29. See Balfour Beatty (1959).
30. Edmundsons was controlled by Utilities Power & Light of the USA, though American involvement was kept secret through the use of Lazards as their British nominee. Edmundsons was involved with over 70 electricity supply companies and participated in the control of English Electric.

31. The two London companies were both uninterlocked with any others from the top 250. London Associated Electricity was formed to amalgamate some West End power companies and was controlled by the Gatti family of restaurateurs and theatre proprietors. County of London Electricity was a much larger and complex undertaking and formed part of a combine whose other members were not included in the data set. Formed by stockbrokers Foster & Braithwaite, and headed by one of their partners, the four companies in the combine were backed by investment trusts associated with BET (and possibly by BET itself). The combine was subject to central direction through a joint committee of the four companies and was the largest of the electrical grids operating under the CEB.

32. A large part of the steel industry was nationalised in 1950, but was denationalised during the 1950s. In 1967 the biggest steel firms were again nationalised to form British Steel. Throughout the postwar period the industry was considerably restructured.

33. Electricity Council, British Gas, Post Office, and South of Scotland Electricity Board. Cable & Wireless, which had been nationalised, was not in the top 200.

34. Market shares in electric cables and telephone equipment, industries closely associated with the nationalised utilities, can be found in Hart et al. (1973, pp. 106, 108); and Cowling et al. (1980, p. 206).

35. On brewing, see Vaizey (1960), Protz (1978), Dunn (1979), and Hawkins and Pass (1979).

36. Viscount Duncannon (later the 8th Earl of Bessborough) of Gordon Hotels was also chairman of Apollinaris and of the Bovril meat extract firm. W. E. Lawson-Johnston, owner of Bovril, joined Lord Duncannon on all of these boards.

37. Ind Coope and Samuel Allsopp merged in 1934 to form Ind Coope & Allsopp, both enterprises having been extensively reorganised after their initial flotation.

38. Allied Breweries emerged as the first truly national group in 1961, when Ind Coope & Allsopp merged with a number of regional brewers. E. P. Taylor, a Canadian whose interests included Carling Lager and Massey Fergusson, amalgamated a number of British brewers during the early 1960s and reversed this group into Charrington in 1962. The previous year Bass had merged with Birmingham brewers Mitchells & Butler, and in 1976 Bass and Charrington merged. Southern brewers Courage and Barclay Perkins merged in 1956 and were acquired by Imperial Tobacco (now Imperial Group) as part of its move out of tobacco (Alford, 1973; Pudney, 1971). Watney Combe Reid merged with Mann Crossman & Paulin in 1958, and the combined group was acquired by Grand Metropolitan Hotels in 1972, the latter having acquired

Truman in the previous year. The three other member of the 'big seven' were Whitbread, Guinness, and Scottish & Newcastle. See Whitbread (1964), Keir (1951), and Donnachie (1979). Distilling was dominated by Distillers (Knightley et al., 1979).

39. Reckitt (1952), Gardiner (n.d.), *Time and Tide* (1969), Vernon (1958), Keevil (1972), and Bibby and Bibby (1978) discuss various food companies. On Ranks, see Burnett (1945), Dence (1948), Wood (1952), and Anon. (1955).

40. See Dyos and Aldcroft (1969). Shipping records are surveyed in Mathias and Pearsall (1971).

41. The main dock companies were floated by mercantile interests in the early nineteenth century. Financial difficulties led to mergers which eventuated in the operation by London and India Docks of 4 of the 7 London docks as well as those at Tilbury (Pudney, 1975). Merchants on shipping boards were Liverpool familes such as Gladstone, Rathbone, Forwood, Watson, Beausire, and Rankin.

42. Ellerman Lines/Frederick Leyland, P & O/Union-Castle. On Ellerman, see Taylor (1976); on P & O, see Cable (1937) and Divine (1960); and on Union-Castle, see Murray (1953). Union-Castle eventually merged with Clan Line to form British and Commonwealth Shipping (Muir and Davies, 1978).

43. Liaison schemes involved Birmingham Canal Navigation, which was effectively controlled by the London and North Western Railway, and the Sheffield and South Yorkshire Navigation, which was almost half-owned by the Great Central. These shareholdings were combined with multiple interlocks. Grand Junction Canal and the Leeds and Liverpool both had cooperative agreements. The Leeds and Liverpool was interlocked with the Aire & Calder Navigation.

44. Manchester City Corporation gave financial support and appointed half the directors. Preference shares were floated by Rothschild and Baring.

45. These joint ventures were Birkenhead Railway and Forth Bridge Railway.

46. On the Underground combine and the Metropolitan Railway, see Barker and Robbins (1963 and 1974), Douglas (1963), Lee (1966 and 1972), White (1963), and Jackson and Croome (1962). On BET, see Fulford (1946).

47. The fact that Metropolitan District was controlled by and interlocked with UERL means that the London, Tilbury and Southend Railway was also a part of the Midland/Underground community of interest.

48. All railways had been taken under government control during the First World War and were operated as a single Railway Executive Committee responsible to the Board of Trade. Although returned

to private control in 1921, the financial difficulties of the railways were responsible for the eventual formation of the four regional groups. Studies of particular groups include Ellis (1970) and Dendy Marshall (1963).

49. Owen Philipps (later Lord Kylsant) first went into shipping with his brother John (later Lord St Davids) in 1889. He became dominant in Pacific Steam Navigation in 1902 and in Royal Mail in 1903. Over the next two decades Kylsant acquired Elder Dempster, Union-Castle, and Coast Lines, and forged links with Lord Pirrie's heavy industrial combine of John Brown, Harland & Wolff, and Colvilles. The whole combine came under the control of Kylsant following Pirrie's death in 1924 and was a major vertically integrated force in shipping, ship building, and steel. In the late 1920s Kylsant contracted to buy Oceanic Steam Navigation (the White Star Line) from J. P. Morgan's American-based International Mercantile Marine, but troubles in the Kylsant combine prevented this deal from being completed. The structure of the combine – a complex pattern of cross-shareholdings – led to a chain reaction in which confidence in the group's shares declined rapidly to the point of collapse in 1931. The Bank of England became the centre of a rescue programme: the cross-holdings were scaled down, White Star was sold to Cunard, companies such as Union-Castle were floated off, the links with the Harland & Wolff group were broken, and a new Royal Mail company was set up to consolidate much of the rest of the business. A new Elder Dempster company was set up, and this later became part of Ocean Transport & Trading. A key figure in the reconstructed group was Lord Essenden, chairman of Furness Withy, which took a large holding in Royal Mail Lines. Royal Mail subsequently became a wholly owned subsidiary of Furness Withy. On the history of the Kylsant combine, see Green and Moss (1982), Davies (1973 and 1981), and Brooks (1933). Lord St Davids is discussed in Cottrell (1974). Studies of other shipping companies include Hyde (1956 and 1973), Henderson (1951), and Marriner and Hyde (1967).

50. On interwar airlines, see Aldcroft (1974), Birkhead (1958 and 1960), and Davies (1964). For the postwar period, see Jones (1976–7), Eglin and Ritchie (1980), Hunting (1968), and Jenkins (1959).

51. The three lines connected British Rail to British Airways and to National Freight, and the latter to Ocean Transport & Trading.

52. Sources for this discussion include PEP (1938 and 1958), Berry (1947), Ross et al. (1949), Murdock and Golding (1973 and 1978), Klingender and Legg (1937), Betts (1973), and Armes (1978).

53. Lord Camrose (William Berry) took the *Daily Telegraph*, the *Financial Times*, and Amalgamated Press (bought from

Harmsworth), and Lord Kemsley (Gomer Berry) took the *Sunday Times, Daily Graphic, Daily Record,* and *Daily Sketch.* By 1976 only the *Telegraph* remained in Berry hands.

54. Illustrated Newspapers was controlled by Sir John Ellerman. Outside the top 200 the Pearson and Rowntree families controlled Westminster Press, and United Newspapers was controlled by Inveresk Paper and the St Davids' investment trusts.

55. Gaumont began as the London agency for the French Gaumont company, but in the 1920s came under the control of the Ostrer brothers. The Ostrers were wool merchants from Bradford (the large woollen textile firm of Illingworth Morris remained under family control until the 1970s) who had used their immense wealth to branch out into investment banking for theatres and radio. In 1929 Twentieth Century Fox of the USA took a large stake in Gaumont, and the Ostrers began reducing their holdings – non-voting shares and an option on voting shares were granted to the rival ABC group. The latter dated from the middle 1920s and was formed in Scotland with Scottish backing. The predominant ownership interest, with 34 per cent, was John Maxwell and his associates, with Scottish investment trusts having a further 15 per cent and being represented on the board by R. G. Simpson of Chiene & Tait. By 1938 the group had acquired control of Union Cinemas.

56. In the early 1930s Arthur Rank (later Lord Rank) was associated with the Portals and Wiggins Teape paper interests, Prudential Assurance, and the merchant bankers S. Japhet in the formation of General Cinema Finance, which distributed Universal films from the USA and Rank's own films. This became the base for Rank's build-up to dominance in British films: Rank, Philip Hill, and Eagle Star bought the Odeon group in 1939, and in 1941 they acquired the Ostrer interests in the Gaumont group. By the early 1940s the Odeon company was the central holding company for the various Rank interests – the group had over 600 cinemas in 1944. See Burnett (1945) and Wood (1952), and the sources in note 39.

57. Following the death of John Maxwell in 1941, Warner Brothers of the USA took a 25 per cent holding in ABC and built up this holding to over a third of the capital. The Maxwell family continued to hold 20 per cent, and the enterprise was chaired by Sir Philip Warter (son-in-law of Maxwell).

58. Some of the issues involved in this claim are debated in Baldwin (1977) and Clement (1977), though that dispute concerns definitions rather than the empirical basis of the claim.

59. The North British & Mercantile Insurance was the result of a merger between an English and a Scottish company and had a peculiar federal structure comprising Edinburgh and London

boards with a common chairman. The 15 non-Scottish lines of NBM were all carried by its London board. In the general analysis in the rest of this book all lines were included.

60. Under company law a British company may have its registered office in Scotland or in England. Those with an office in Scotland must make their annual returns to the Companies Registration Office in Edinburgh.

61. Colville originally came under the aegis of Lord Kylsant's Royal Mail group, but the collapse of the latter weakened its links to the combine. It remained allied with Harland & Wolff.

62. The secondary lines include one of multiplicity two, both of its constituent interlocks being secondary.

63. Although the density for the north-west region in 1904 was slightly higher than that for Scotland, this reflects the considerably larger number of Scottish-registered companies. See table 3.5.

64. British Insulated Helsby Cables and United Alkali.

65. The other financial company in the component was District Bank.

66. This line connected Royal Insurance with Ocean Transport & Trading.

CHAPTER FOUR

Family, Kinship, and Corporations

The disappearance of family enterprises through takeover and amalgamation and through the sheer increase in the scale of business activity has stimulated considerable debate among lawyers, economists, and sociologists over the implications this has for capitalist relations of production. Though raised by Marx and the Austro-Marxists, this question received its most forceful and influential statement in the work of Berle and Means (1932). While the whole of the ensuing debate cannot be summarised here (see Scott, 1979), certain important issues must be reviewed. Berle and Means argue that the joint stock company allows entrepreneurial control to be weakened as the founders of an enterprise issue shares to the public and so dilute their own shareholding. When the shares are dispersed to the point at which no single shareholder has a large enough block of shares to ensure command of company meetings, the board of directors becomes dissociated from any control exerted by the body of shareholders. In consequence, internal executives gain enhanced opportunities for participation in the control of the business, and the enterprise can be described as subject to 'management control'. Other writers (R. A. Gordon, 1936, 1938, and 1945; Larner, 1970) have extended the empirical basis of this analysis to claim that by the 1960s the transition from family to managerial enterprise was all but complete, and the managerial revolution was over.

The main implications of such a trend have been traced in relation to economic performance and administrative structure. Proponents of the managerial revolution thesis have variously argued that the managerial enterprise is better able to pursue pure profitability than was the family enterprise, which was concerned with the perpetuation of the family dynasty; or that it is less likely to pursue maximum profits because of the weakened constraints of the capital market. Studies aimed at establishing a link between ownership and performance, however, have been contradictory and inconclusive.[1] Indeed, it can be argued that an improved understanding of the mechanisms through which control is exercised is necessary before any attempt can be made to demonstrate the link between these mechanisms and performance measures. It is in this connection that studies of administrative structure are relevant. Drawing on the argument of Berle and Means, Chandler (1962) claims that changes in patterns of ownership are the basis of changes in corporate strategy which, in turn, result in changes in the internal administration of the enterprise.[2] The emergence of a multidivisional organisation limits any possibilities for managerial discretion which may have been created by the dispersal of shareholdings because it establishes internal control processes over managers: top executives concentrate their attention on formulating a profit strategy, while lower-level managers are constrained to conform if they wish to ensure promotion in the 'career' hierarchy (Williamson, 1970, p. 9).[3]

The predominant viewpoint among the more sophisticated proponents of the managerial revolution, therefore, is that any shift from family ownership to management control is unlikely to have weakened the constraints of profitability. These constraints are built into the hierarchies which have been established in the multidivisional organisation. But the issue of the managerial revolution cannot be left there. Radical critics of the thesis have argued that the empirical basis of its central tenet – that family ownership has given way to management control – is insecure. Specifically, it has been claimed that families and individual shareholders can continue to influence corporate strategy despite a fall in their percentage shareholdings, and that there has, in any case, been a move back towards concentrated shareholdings. This reconcentration is a consequence of the rise of the financial intermediaries – banks, insurance companies, pension funds, etc. – as major shareholders since the 1930s (Zeitlin, 1974; Zeitlin and Norich, 1979; Scott, 1979). The broader implications of this will be discussed in the following chapter, but the important point for the present discussion is that executive managers increasingly face not an anonymous mass of powerless individual shareholders, but an aggressive group of large financial interests. Although the dominant shareholders in an enterprise may not comprise a cohesive controlling group, neither do they comprise a purely passive body of loyal supporters of managerial leadership.

The composition of the board reflects the constellation of financial interests in which the enterprise is embedded, and the internal executives are unable to release themselves from the constraints of proprietary control. If modern corporate management is committed to the criterion of profitability, this is because it is constrained not only by product market imperatives and internal control systems but also by the dominant proprietary interests.

This and the following chapter will review some of the major issues raised in this debate in so far as they can be studied in and through interlocking directorships and other personal relations. On the basis of an examination of share ownership in Britain, it will be possible to investigate the interlocking of family and other enterprises and the ways in which interlocks can be complemented and extended by bonds of kinship. An examination of the interdependence of these forms of personal relation on a class-wide basis will provide the foundations on which the characteristics of the 'inner circle' (Useem, 1984) will be analysed in chapter 5.

OWNERSHIP, CONTROL, AND INTERLOCKING

Central to the thesis of the managerial revolution is the idea that share dispersal was so great in most enterprises that no single shareholding interest was able to dominate the board and determine corporate strategy. If such a trend has occurred, then members of the board will hold an insignificant or small proportion of the shares. Table 4.1 presents comparative data for the USA (1975) and Britain (1976) on directors' holdings. It can clearly be seen that the proportion of enterprises in which the board held less than 1 per cent of the shares was similar in both countries at about two-thirds. More than four-fifths of the enterprises had boards holding less than 5 per cent. The major divergence between the two countries lies in the number of wholly owned subsidiaries. Herman (1981) shows that only one of the largest American enterprises was foreign owned. By contrast, a quarter of the largest British enterprises were wholly owned – most being the North American and European subsidiaries discussed in chapter 3. There are also slight differences at the other end of the scale. Ten per cent of the American enterprises

Table 4.1   Proportion of Voting Shares Held by Directors in the
Top 200 Non-Financials: USA (1975) and UK (1976).

% held by directors	USA (1975)		UK (1976)	
	No. of companies	%	No. of companies	%
Wholly owned[a]	} 132	66.0	48	24.0
Less than 1%			88	44.0
1–4.9	40	20.0	26	13.0
5–9.9	8	4.0	5	2.5
10–19.9	3	1.5	10	5.0
20–49.9	} 17	8.5	7	3.5
More than 50%			16	8.0

Sources: Data for USA from Herman (1981), table 3.9, p. 87; data for UK from
Company Analysis Project.
Note: [a] 'Wholly owned' includes bilateral and multilateral joint ventures in
which the whole of the share capital is held by other enterprises.

had boards holding more than 10 per cent of the shares,
compared with 16.5 per cent of British enterprises.

There was little sign of any relationship between directors'
holdings and the size of the enterprise in the British data set.
Disregarding those which were wholly owned, the proportion of
enterprises in which the board held less than 1 per cent was
similar in the top 50 and in those ranked 151–200, and the
distribution in other categories was also similar. There was,
however, a clear association between directors' holdings and
interlocking. Four-fifths of those enterprises in which directors
held less than 5 per cent, again disregarding the wholly owned,
were interlocked, while the proportion in other categories was
somewhat lower.[4] This relationship was particularly marked if
directors' holdings, size, and interlocking are taken together. Just
1 of the top 50 enterprises with a board-holding of less than 1 per
cent (Cavenham) was uninterlocked, while the number in the
other 'slices' of the size hierarchy varied from 4 to 5. Similarly
only 1 of the top 100 with a board-holding of between 1 and 5 per
cent (Grand Metropolitan) was uninterlocked, compared with
4 in the 101–200 slice. Small numbers make it difficult to draw
firm conclusions, but it is perhaps significant that the negative
association between size and interlocking was not found among
those enterprises in which directors held a majority of the shares.

It may be concluded that the majority of non-financials did, indeed, have small board shareholdings and that they were rather more likely to interlock than were other enterprises. Although this appears to support the managerial thesis, the high propensity to interlock must be regarded as a pointer to possible inadequacies in the thesis. It is not sufficient to analyse simply the proportion of shares personally held by directors. It is necessary to establish that no other large blocks of shares exist. As was argued in the introduction to this chapter, there has been a substantial shift towards the reconcentration of shareholdings in large enterprises in the hands of financial intermediaries. Enterprises characterised by this form of ownership (see table 2.10) should be classified not as management-controlled but as controlled through a constellation of interests. Enterprises controlled in this way may be expected, for the various reasons discussed in the next chapter, to interlock more extensively than either family or managerial enterprises. It is important, therefore, to discuss the actual ownership patterns found in large British enterprises.

In their original investigations Berle and Means documented a transition from personal ownership of productive assets by the individual entrepreneur to the forms of 'majority ownership' and 'minority control' which they saw as preceding the stage of management control. Individual- and family-owned undertakings which were organised as joint stock companies could remain under the control of the original owners. 'Majority ownership' is that form of strategic control in which a shareholder with more than 50 per cent of the issued shares has virtually complete powers of ownership, as it is possible to out-vote any opponents. On the other hand, 'minority control' occurs where a shareholder has less than 50 per cent of the shares but is faced by a mass of other shareholders with even smaller holdings. Such a shareholder can normally expect to win a vote, but the control is far less secure than that held by the majority owner. Berle and Means suggest that minority control could be exercised on the basis of as little as 20 per cent of the shares, and recent research has suggested that 10 per cent might be an appropriate figure for the postwar period.[5]

Berle and Means typically discuss what may be termed 'exclusive control', where a single shareholder or a small and unified group (for example, a family) hold a controlling block of shares. It is important to extend this by introducing the concept of 'shared control', where control is exercised by two or more separate but cooperating shareholders. Bilateral and multilateral joint ventures, for example, demonstrate shared control.[6] This points to a second important distinction, between corporate and personal control. Although many cases of majority and minority control involve personal controllers such as individuals and families, it is possible for control to be exercised by a corporate agent such as another enterprise, a charity, or a state agency. It is clear that where control is exercised by another enterprise, it is important to push the analysis a step further by examining the control situation of the controller itself. To handle this, Berle and Means distinguished between 'immediate' and 'ultimate' control. An enterprise may be immediately controlled by another enterprise, but ultimately controlled by whoever controls the parent company. Table 1.2 summarises some of these distinctions by showing the various forms of immediate control by other enterprises. Any enterprise which has a majority or minority block of shares held by one or a small group of enterprises can be classified into one of the four categories.

The largest category of enterprises controlled by other enterprises was foreign subsidiaries. It was not generally possible to trace their patterns of ultimate control, as information on the ownership of the foreign parents was not always available. But from the standpoint of the British network the foreign subsidiaries must be regarded as standing in a distinct situation. Many of the subsidiary boards consisted of internal executive managers, but it is unrealistic (*pace* Barratt Brown, 1968) to regard them as cases of management control. Foreign subsidiaries are enmeshed in the global strategies pursued by their overseas parents. The ultimate controllers of the parent may be the parent's internal managers, but they may equally be financial intermediaries or personal shareholders.

Figure 4.1 attempts to summarise the various categories of ultimate control.[7] Personal majority ownership, whether shared or exclusive, may be possessed by the founders of the enterprises or by their heirs, and the personal owners may be families or individual tycoons. When the controlling holding falls below 50 per cent the personal shareholders may nevertheless retain minority control, but their holding may be reduced to the point where there is no single controlling interest. Depending on the exact distribution of shares this may result in either management control or control through a constellation of interests. An enterprise which is in any of these control situations may be subject to takeover by another enterprise, in which case its immediate

Figure 4.1   Ultimate Control: Main Historical Trends

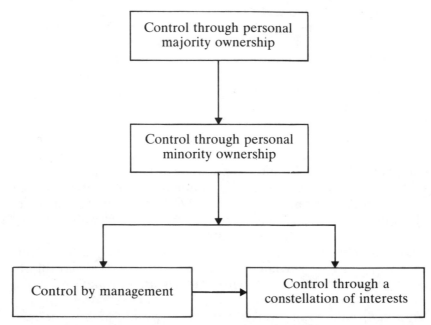

control can be conceptualised by the categories of table 1.2. The share ownership of such a company may then be dispersed as the acquiring enterprise sells off part of its holding, and this may eventuate in a minority holding becoming so diluted that the categories of management and constellation of interests are once again appropriate. Although movement from any one category to any other is logically possible, the main historical trend from the 1880s to the 1980s in Britain has been from personal majority ownership to control through a constellation of interests and control by foreign enterprises. But there has been no unilinear evolutionary trend. The struggle for control is a dynamic process in which shifts in the balance of power produce regular and frequent movement backwards and forwards between the categories. New entrepreneurs have bought majority or minority shareholdings in enterprises formerly controlled by constellations of interests, and both entrepreneurs and constellations have been displaced by other enterprises and by state ownership.[8]

No classification can meet all eventualities, and various intermediate situations are possible. The most frequently occurring, and the most problematic, cases are those on the borderline of minority control and the two dispersed forms of control. It has already been suggested that any percentage cut-off for minority control tends to be arbitrary unless account is taken of the overall distribution of shares in the enterprise. The most important examples of this are those which can be termed 'limited minority control'. These are enterprises in which the largest shareholder has more than 10 per cent of the shares but can be out-voted by a coalition of other large holders.

Where personal ownership has given way to other forms of control, 'entrepreneurial capitalists' have been replaced by 'internal capitalists' and 'finance capitalists'. As the financial intermediaries acquire controlling positions, so a high proportion of board positions come to be held by people with small personal shareholdings in any one company but a large number of director-ships. These finance capitalists, or 'co-ordinating controllers' (Barratt Brown, 1968), play a central role in the business system and largely set the terms within which the executives, the internal capitalists, may act. It is the interplay of internal, entre-preneurial, and finance capitalists which structures the modern business system. Thus Herman (1981) has suggested that even in the absence of personal 'proprietary' control, outsiders on the board may be able to limit managerial options. Similarly, Carchedi (1983, pp. 187–8) argues that executives are 'dependent capitalists' because they are ultimately responsible to the domi-nant stockholders. The internal capitalists, nevertheless, are distinct from the managerial workers of the service class, which makes up the core of the middle layers of the stratification system (see also Gordon, 1945, chapters 4, 5).

Examples of management-controlled enterprises – those in which there is a high level of share dispersal and internal capital-ists have enhanced opportunities for action – are difficult to find. None of the top 200 of 1976 fell into this category; in all cases where there was no dominant interest, the control was through a constellation of interests or, in a very few cases, limited minority control. Those enterprises which might be expected to have had a wide spread of share ownership in the earlier periods are the big four railways of 1938, though the degree of dispersal was not so great as might be anticipated and their boards were among those least dominated by executives (Parkinson, 1944). It can plausibly be argued that management control was a short-lived feature of the transition from majority control to control through a constellation of interests, and that it was even more tenuous and short-lived in Britain than in the USA.[9] This can be illustrated by an examination of two of the more likely cases of management control, Dunlop and ICI.[10]

Dunlop was for a long time controlled by the DuCros family of financiers, but financial problems in the 1920s led to their withdrawal from the business and its reorganisation by Sir Eric Geddes and the financier F. A. Szarvasy.[11] The largest single shareholder was Nobel Industries, with 4.3 per cent, though its holding was somewhat reduced when Nobel was amalgamated with ICI in 1926. By 1936 the top 20 shareholders held just 5.1 per cent, the largest being a financial intermediary, and the directors collectively held only 0.09 per cent. The 1938 board included Szarvasy, four men with links to Geddes and his interests (Geddes had died in 1937), a director of one of Dunlop's bankers, and just two career executives. By 1951 the proportion of shares held by the top 20 had risen to 9.6 per cent, the largest holder being Prudential Assurance with 2.3 per cent, and the proportion of shares held by directors had fallen to 0.03 per cent. The board comprised 5 men associated with Geddes's interests (including his own son and another father/son pair), 2 merchant bankers, and 3 executives. At no time up to the 1950s did internal capitalists make up a majority of the board, despite a wide dispersal of shares. This had hardly altered by 1976: Geddes's son was then chairman, outside interests were represented on the board, and 5 of the 12 directors were career executives. Although the board's holding had fallen to 0.015 per cent, the proportion held by the top 20 had doubled to 20.14 per cent. At the very time that internal capitalists had enhanced their board position, ownership was becoming more concentrated. Dunlop in 1976 was controlled through a constellation of interests.

ICI was formed in 1926 as an amalgamation of four large chemical concerns, its size meaning that the holdings of the founding families of the original enterprises were extremely small.[12] By 1936 the largest shareholder in ICI was the Belgian Solvay firm, which had long held a stake in one of the constituent companies. The top 20 shareholders held 21.0 per cent, including Solvay's 5.1 per cent, and the board held 0.2 per cent. For a long while the dominant board member had been Lord McGowan, who was indeed a career executive from one of the constituent companies. McGowan had, however, an important economic and political base outside ICI and brought men such as Lord Weir and

Lord Ashfield onto the board, the first coming from a family-owned Scottish industrial and the second being a representative of American financial interests in the London Transport combine. McGowan, Weir, and Ashfield, had all been involved in the Lloyd George experiment of associating businessmen more closely with government, and were part of an extensive group of businessmen involved in numerous British enterprises – Geddes of Dunlop was a member of this group, and Lord Weir's son was a Dunlop director in the 1950s. McGowan was able to use the support of Weir and Ashfield to buttress his own position in a boardroom struggle in 1937, when McGowan's power was opposed by the Mond and Solvay interests. By 1951 the Solvay holding had been sold, the share of the top 20 had fallen to 9.3 per cent, and the share of the directors had fallen to 0.1 per cent. McGowan was succeeded in the 1950s by a series of career executives, but the board continued to be numerically dominated by directors of other large industrials, members of the original controlling families, and by representatives of banks and insurance companies. At the same time, shareholdings by financials were increasing to the point at which the top 20 of 1976 held 13.6 per cent: the enterprise was controlled through a constellation of interests.

The two strongest contenders for the designation 'management-controlled', therefore, show only limited evidence for its existence. The extent of the drive towards control through a constellation of interests can be seen in table 4.2. By 1976, 42 per

Table 4.2   Control Type and Interlocking in the
Top 200 Non-Financials, 1976

	No. of companies		
Control type	*Interlocked*	*Uninterlocked*	*Totals*
Public corporations	11	2	13
Exclusive majority	23	34	57
Shared majority	5	3	8
Exclusive minority	19	5	24
Shared minority	6	1	7
Limited minority	5	2	7
Constellation of interests	73	11	84
Totals	142	58	200

cent of the top 200 non-financials could be classified in this way, making this the single largest category. It can be seen that these enterprises were also the most likely to interlock with other large industrials or with the top 50 financials. Enterprises subject to exclusive majority control showed the lowest tendency to inter-lock: the presence of a single overweaning ownership influence, whether corporate or personal, tended to be associated with isolation from the network. It is perhaps significant that the propensity to interlock of enterprises in this category increased as the size of the controlling block fell. Under half of the enterprises in which a single holder had more than 50 per cent but less than 100 per cent were interlocked. This relationship was also found in family-controlled enterprises. As shown in table 4.3, most of the enterprises subject to family majority ownership were

Table 4.3   Family Control and Interlocking in the
Top 200 Non-Financials, 1976

Extent of family influence	Interlocked	Uninterlocked	Totals
Majority ownership	5	12	17
Minority control	16	6	22
Participation and representation	17	7	24
Participation only	7	1	8
Totals	45	26	71

Note: The data relate to those of the top 200 enterprises which were subject to family control or influence.

uninterlocked while most enterprises in the other categories were interlocked. The propensity to interlock increased from 3 in 10 in cases of majority ownership to almost 7 in 10 where family minority control existed. As family influence wanes and share-holdings by financial intermediaries increase, so the propensity to interlock increases. Enterprises where families were participants in the controlling constellation and were represented on the board were rather less likely to interlock than were those where family participants were not represented on the board.

It has been argued that enterprises in which family control or influence is present have a low propensity to interlock with other enterprises and that the growth of control through a constellation of interests, which has encouraged an expansion in the role of the internal capitalists, has produced enterprises with a high propensity to interlock. But interlocking directorships are not the only type of personal relation which can exist between enterprises. The very fact of writing about 'family' enterprise raises the issue of kinship relations and their implications for corporate behaviour. As Zeitlin has argued:

> Without research into the web of kinship relations binding apparently unrelated individuals into a cohesive owning unit for purposes of control, analysis of the locus of control of the large corporation is hobbled at the outset. (Zeitlin, 1974, p. 1108)

In the following section the 'web of kinship' will be discussed in so far as it relates to the control of particular enterprises. The final section will extend this to the web of connections between enterprises.

ENTREPRENEURIAL CAPITALISTS: FOUNDERS AND HEIRS

The family firm, the cornerstone of classical economics, was the basis of the Victorian economy, and many of the features of contemporary family enterprise have their origins in the nineteenth century. Central to the concept of family enterprise has been the virtual equation of the enterprise, the kinship group, and the family name. Crozier has described this complex as the 'patrinominal kinship nucleus' (1965, p. 15). The enterprise consists of a plant, office, or group of establishments whose leading participants are recruited from kin whose members bear the same patronym by virtue of their descent through male lines from a common ancestor, and itself takes the family name. The family enterprise has rarely involved the kind of strict primogeniture which existed in the large landed estates, and has, therefore, been able to recruit its leadership from a larger pool of kin. Up to the First World War, capital mobilisation in many of the largest enterprises depended upon the ability of this web of kinship to provide an alternative to the formal capital market (Kennedy, 1976). Although primogeniture was not followed, inheritance through the male line was customary. The male line was the bearer of the 'name', and unless a family was unable to produce male children it was possible to perpetuate the patrinominal kin enterprise. As in so many areas of life, women were forced into a subordinate position:

while the maternal kin played an important role in the life of any individual . . . the important structural principle was patrinominal and it was with the patrinominal family that the individual identified himself . . . The impression is that women even after marriage were still regarded for many purposes as members of their patrinominal families, but their issue were not. (Crozier, 1965, p. 40)

These processes can be grasped through Bourdieu's (1921) notion of 'marriage practices', which can usefully be broadened into the concept of 'kinship strategies'. This concept indicates that kinship practices are intentional social actions and, as such, have unintended consequences. Although inheritance and marriage are concerned, explicitly and implicitly, with the maintenance and perpetuation of definite family units and their property, they are also implicated in class structuration. Inheritance is the principal means through which a kinship group can perpetuate its position over time. But succession to positions of privilege is determined also by a person's connections with the wider network of kin. Uncles, cousins, and brothers-in-law are important contacts which can be mobilised to enhance a person's own opportunities (Tepperman, 1972). Where a family pursues a strategy aimed at enhancing its position in relation to other families and at the transmission of its name and property, and perhaps a title, the result is the formation of a dynasty. Marriage arrangements are part of a broader network of transactions in which each family aims to cement alliances and maximise its advantages (Kann, 1973; Fichtner, 1976). Tepperman has argued that upper-class dynasties are maintained through cousin marriage and through cooperative business enterprises (Tepperman, 1981).

Dynasty formation, however, is constrained by demographic factors. Although there is a 50 per cent probability of a male heir, there is no guarantee that this will result in the birth of a male heir in any particular family. The presence of a suitable male heir depends also on a variety of other circumstances. The heir may die in childhood, he may die in adulthood but during his own father's lifetime, he may prove to have a mental incapacity, or he may have an unfortunate propensity for fast women and slow horses. Even more unfortunate from the standpoint of dynasty formation, the family may be inflicted with a string of daughters but no sons. In such cases the continuity of the family property – and the family name – is seriously threatened. In many such cases inheritance by sons-in-law has been associated with a change in their name to the patronymic of their wives. Of course, the recruitment of business leaders and partners from a wider patrinominal pool helps to offset the failure of any particular male line, but demography often results in the demise of a dynasty.

Because of the degree of intermarriage among a relatively small number of persons, identification of the boundaries of a particular 'family' may be only arbitrary. Even those families which place great emphasis on the name and continuity of the family and its patrimony will overlap with neighbouring families, so making it difficult to determine whether particular persons are members of this or that family. Nominally separate nuclear families may be laterally joined to one another in larger kin groupings by virtue of their standing to one another as uncles, aunts, and cousins, or by their common interest in particular units of capital. Thus, Zeitlin et al. (1975) introduce the concept of the 'kinecon group' to refer to those groups which go beyond the limits of a particular nuclear unit. Within the wider kinecon group, the family elders may play a dominant role: a group of collateral senior members may make the important decisions relating to the group as a whole. The kinecon group is 'the set of interrelated kin who control the corporation through their combined ownership interests and strategic representation in management' (Zeitlin et al., 1975, p. 1110; Berkowitz, 1976, pp. 183–4, 200).

Striking examples of such kinecon groups are provided by the Cadbury and Guinness families. The Cadbury chocolate business was controlled by a large number of family members together with members of the Fry and Pascall families, whose firms had been taken over. Although some female members of the family were involved in running the business, control remained firmly in male hands and the kinecon group held majority ownership, partly through private and investment trusts, and filled all the main executive positions until a merger with Schweppes in 1969. After the merger, the family were left in a position of minority control with a lessened participation in the executive, and by 1976 the family holding had shrunk to 6.02 per cent. At this stage only one member of the family was on the board, and the block of shares was held in a large number of separate family accounts. In Cadbury Schweppes, therefore, control had progressed from majority to minority to family participation in the dominant constellation, with the organisation of the family as a kinecon group being crucial for continued family influence.

Arthur Guinness is an enterprise of which a large kinship group was able to maintain control throughout the period of this study. Lord Iveagh was a third-generation member of the brewing family and bought out his brother prior to forming the business into a public company in 1886. Through intermarriage over several generations with families such as Channon, Lennox-Boyd, and Hamilton-Temple-Blackwood, as well as with other branches of the Guinness family,[13] Lord Iveagh's descendants built up an extensive kinecon group which in 1976 held 18.98 per cent of the brewery company and made up about half its board. A similar pattern of intermarriage was found in the kinecon group which participated in the controlling constellation of Marks & Spencer. From early in its history the Marks and Sieff families were closely intermarried, and their members also married into the Sacher, Blond, Lerner, Susman, and Goodman famlies. Majority ownership was maintained until 1964 through the issue of non-voting shares, but by 1976 the kinecon group had just 1.6 per cent – though they filled almost half the board positions (Rees, 1973). Clearly, the survival of family influence depends upon many factors, but the ability to retain a significant block of shares through appropriate marriage strategies is a key element in that survival.

Intermarriage, however, generates two important problems for family dynasties. To the extent that the intermarried families each pursue a dynastic strategy various forms of shared control may emerge, and to the extent that the kinecon group becomes larger the shareholding may become fragmented. Both problems make family influence less secure, and they become particularly marked where families share control of an enterprise but pursue their separate interests. This was the situation in many of the turn-of-the-century amalgamations which produced enterprises such as Imperial Tobacco, where the Wills family eventually subordinated other families to itself. Where families are evenly balanced, as in Tate & Lyle, an effective condominium may persist for long periods. Such situations raise important research problems, as it is necessary to assess the potentials for conflict and cooperation between families in each particular case. This is especially difficult where the second problem – fragmentation of the controlling block – takes place. In such circumstances, family control and influence depend upon the ability of the family to coordinate its activities (Tepperman, 1972, p. 113). Where the family enterprise is organised through the use of trusts and settlements a large kinecon group can be supported through money payments rather than the direct distribution of shares, thus enabling concentrated control to coexist with dispersed benefits (Crozier, 1965, p. 16). This may be enhanced when the board includes trustees, such as lawyers, who are not themselves members of the family. Because of the seriousness with which the trustees view their fiduciary role, they are more actively involved in corporate affairs than are their fellow outside directors and so become advocates of family interests (Mace, 1971, pp. 61–2).

Maintenance of the influence of a large kinecon group may depend upon a variety of organisational devices, such as trusts, foundations, settlements, and private investment companies, which regulate the family property. Family members and their trustees jointly coordinate family holdings, decide on voting policy and board membership, and determine the incomes and allowances of those who benefit from the property. In its most developed form, this may involve a 'family office' in which a central administrative staff takes on the additional tasks of managing family tax matters and investment portfolios, and providing banking facilities to family members. Where the family office is an integral part of an investment company, it may also undertake management on a commercial basis for non-family members. American research has discovered that some family offices have handled the collection and distribution of political donations and the payment of club subscriptions and shopping bills (Dunn, 1980, pp. 19, 43; Lundberg, 1968, pp. 225–36).

J. Lyons is an enterprise which shows an informal, but effective, organisational device for coordinating the affairs of a kinecon group. The intermarried Salmon, Gluckstein, and Joseph families set up in catering in the late nineteenth century and maintained tight control over the business through issuing non-voting shares. The voting shares were divided equally among the family directors, wealth was distributed equally, and the oldest member of the family automatically became chairman. Operational management was largely undertaken by the Salmons, with the Glucksteins running their law partnership and handling family investments (Aris, 1970). Although non-family directors were given greater powers in the 1960s, the non-voting shares were not enfranchised until late in 1976. In S. Pearson a small and compact kinecon group, consisting of Pearson, Gibson,

Hare, and Burrell, had the bulk of their shares held in two family trusts which enabled the family to coordinate a 25.5 per cent minority block.[14] Both Unilever and Rowntree Mackintosh show a further development of the idea of a family trust. Rowntree Mackintosh in 1976 was minority-controlled by two Rowntree trusts which were operated as a single unit and which were used to extend family investment interests and to finance social research such as the poverty studies carried out by family members themselves.[15] The family, however, were not represented on the board although the Mackintosh family, which held less than 2 per cent, was. Unilever showed a particularly complex pattern. It was organised as an integrated Anglo-Dutch operation with centralised strategic control, but the central board was jointly appointed by two separate parent companies. For a long time the British parent had a legal device for maintaining voting control within the group itself through a system of cross-holdings and special voting rights. By the 1950s all the shares had been enfranchised and this device was ended, leaving control in the hands of the Lever family's Leverhulme Trust. By 1976 the trust was minority controller with 16.56 per cent, the trustees being Lord Leverhulme together with past and present Unilever chairmen, and the principal beneficiaries being the Lever family.[16] Undoubtedly the closest approximation to the family office was the device through which the Vestey family controlled Union International and managed numerous other investments. A private investment company held all the shares and acted as bankers to the family, and was itself controlled through four family-owned 'management shares'. The bulk of the capital of the investment company was held by one of the family's overseas trusts, which had been built up from income generated by the operating companies and which financed the activities of the investment company (Knightley, 1981, pp. 39–41).

Family control has had a great impact on the development of forms of administration in British enterprises. Family enterprise has mainly come under pressure if and when diversification occurs, and a failure to diversify has often been associated with the desire to maintain family control. Because the family leadership has a vested interest in maintaining the existing administrative structure, the system of management will not come under direct pressure to change until there is some kind of crisis of family control, such as their withdrawal from the executive or the rise of a younger generation (Channon, 1973, pp. 75–6; Child and Kieser, 1981, p. 52). Such change may be externally induced when a faltering family enterprise becomes the object of a takeover bid, the crisis enhancing the power of executives or outsiders who were previously unable to alter board policy.[17]

Family enterprise, taking this term to include founders, heirs, and 'tycoons' as well as the classical family enterprise (Barratt Brown, 1968; Savage, 1979; Nyman and Silbertston, 1978; Francis, 1980), remained an important aspect of the British business system, and the entrepreneurial capitalists which they produced were key agents in business leadership. In many ways the scope for family influence has increased as the drift towards concentrated shareholdings by financial intermediaries has opened up greater possibilities of stock diversifiction by wealthy families. It is no longer necessary to choose between complete withdrawal and the maintenance of full control, perhaps with a minority holding. Families have increasingly been able to become participants in the controlling constellations and so to spread the bulk of their wealth in a diversified portfolio. At the same time, such families have been forced to share their influence with other participants and so become more closely tied into the network of intercorporate relations.

KINSHIP NETWORKS AND CORPORATE LINKS

Kinship relations connect individual families and kinecon groups into a wider kinship network, and this 'partial network' has implications for the partial network of intercorporate relations. Kinship relations are not biological, they are social relationships constructed in terms of specific social meanings. The links of kinship 'exist in the understandings that the actors have of the implications of the relationships among them for their behaviour' (Mitchell, 1973, p. 28; Berkowitz, 1982, chapter 2). In constructing kinship networks, agents orientate themselves in terms of 'rules' which specify the meaning of kinship terms and how they are to be used to define social relations (Truex, 1981; Farber, 1981). The application of these rules, the kinship semantics, defines others as kin or non-kin and specifies their relations of 'descent', 'generation', 'lineality', 'residence', and so on. In this way, agents are defined as occupying one or more kinship roles:

mother, daughter, sister-in-law, cousin, etc. The rules governing
kinship will also specify the circumstances under which different
kinds of instrumental and symbolic transaction can be expected to
take place. That is to say, they will define the obligations which
particular categories of kin have towards one another to provide
advice, services, emotional support, financial provision, preferential business dealings, and so on (Mitchell, 1969, p. 40;
Ben-Porath, 1980; Verdon, 1981; Mitchell, 1973, pp. 27–8). In a
capitalist society, kinship relations are highly institutionalised,
being both intense and durable. They are intense because of the
affective quality which defines the relationship, though it must be
emphasised that this does not refer to the actual feelings of agents
but to the normative content of the relationship and hence to the
kind of obligations that can be called upon. Kinship relations are
durable because they are typically regarded as life-long relations
which may only be broken under special circumstances. Even
when a man and woman are divorced, kinship relations will still
exist between them and any children they may have had – and
therefore there will still be kinship relations with the grand-
parents, aunts, and cousins of those children. This reflects the fact
that, so far as any individual is concerned, kinship relations are
not a matter of choice:

> From a genealogical point of view then a framework of kinship is
> largely constructed for a person without his volition. This implies
> that a capacity for actions and decisions which may radically affect
> a person's life is placed in the hands of people of pre-selected
> status, irrespective of their fitness for such a role. (Firth et al.,
> 1970, p. 11)

Kinship relations are entwined with relations of 'friendship', and
'friends' are often co-opted into quasi-kinship roles. An example
of this would be the working-class practice of referring to female
friends of a mother as 'auntie', regardless of the absence of 'real'
kinship (Barnes, 1972, p. 20; Mills, 1956, p. 32). The circle of a
person's friends is frequently extended through their kinship
relations and is often the basis of the marriage choices made by its
members and their kin. The partial networks of kinship and
friendship overlap and intersect to produce a network of informal
personal relations which comprises the 'social assets' that people
are able to mobilise to achieve such goals as occupational
placement. Such personal relations thereby become principles of
recruitment and cooperation (Firth et al., 1970, p. 6).

Studies of kinship and business have rarely shown any interest in the structural features of the kinship system considered as a network of relations. Lupton and Wilson (1959) constructed geneaological diagrams in a path-breaking paper, but they failed to consider the systemic implications of kinship. Whitley (1974) advanced this approach by examining the connections between enterprises which were created through kinship links, but he also did not examine the structure of the kinship relations themselves. A major difficulty in pursuing this approach is deciding when two people are, or are not, related. Whitley's solution was to define relatedness in terms of the degrees of cousinhood: two people are related if they are second cousins or closer, whether they be cousins by blood, marriage, spouse, or step-parents. The problem in developing this into a network analysis is that it involves an arbitrary cut-off point for relatedness. To overcome this, Zeitlin and Ratcliff (1975, pp. 25–6) have proposed the use of the network concepts of path and distance. A path of distance one in a kinship network is defined as a relationship within a nuclear family. On this basis it is possible to define the kinship relation between any two individuals as a path with a given distance. Although Zeitlin and Ratcliff concentrate on egocentric first- and second-order stars, their aproach is generalisable to the network as a whole. If a distance matrix for a given set of persons is constructed, then the associated graph can be derived and then analysed for density, centralisation, cliques, and so on. Dynasties, for example, can be regarded as cliques in the network of lines of male descent.

Although a full application of this approach would require a massive amount of kinship data on all directors of the top 250 enterprises, its power can be illustrated by examining the network of lines between enterprises which results from kinship relations. The presence of kinsmen on two distinct enterprises creates a kin interlock, or 'kinterlock', between them. In the 1904 network such kinterlocks were numerous, especially in the City of London core, and by 1938 they had been extended to encompass many parts of the network. The largest enterprise of 1938, the London, Midland & Scottish Railway, had 18 directors and an adjacency in the interlock network of 33. The kinterlocks generated by its directors were difficult to trace, even on a restrictive cut-off for relatedness of distance four. When distance was increased to a more realistic 6 or 7 (to cover, for example, cousinhood through a common great-grandfather) the number of kinterlocks became equal to the number of interlocks, creating a massive web of personal relations at the heart of the intercorporate network. By contrast, the largest enterprise of 1976, BP, had no traceable kinterlocks at close degrees of cousinhood. Kinterlocks still existed in 1976 (see Scott and Hughes, 1980, figure 4.7), but they had become less extensive than they had been in earlier years. At the turn of the century the members of the City of London core were linked through both interlocks and kinterlocks, and the bonds of kinship continued to reinforce the pattern of interlocks as the level of interlocking increased in the interwar years to produce the outlines of a more extensive intercorporate network. The decline in density and multiplicity as the national network was consolidated was associated with a decline in kinterlocking, though this was not a necessary consequence of the fall in interlocking. Kinterlocks may be used deliberately to forge bilateral or multilateral relations between enterprises, but they are also unintended consequences of intermarriage among the leading business families. For this reason, the decline in kinterlocking in the postwar period must be seen as a consequence of changes in the kinship network itself.

A major structural change in the upper-class kinship network has been the gradual incorporation of formerly distinct 'cousinhoods' into a more even-textured network. A tendency towards cousin-marriage can be explained in terms of the logic of marriage strategies. Marriage partners tend to be chosen from a person's close social contacts, a group which is likely to include a large number of kinsmen, and when senior family members attempt to retain the family patrimony within existing degrees of kinship there will be a tendency for marriage partners to be chosen from one's 'cousins' (Rytina, 1982). In such circumstances the kinship network will contain a large number of multiple lines. Where ethnic or religious groups prescribe endogamy this tendency is taken to its extreme, and dense 'cousinhoods' emerge. A cousinhood is a cluster of closely related families which are allied through a series of partnerships, joint participations, and shareholdings. Marriage and business reinforce one another in such a way that large amounts of capital can be mobilised from within the cousinhood (Berkowitz, 1976, pp. 142, 176). Secondary sources suggest the existence of two extensive cousinhoods in Britain, both of which are evidenced in data collected for the Company Analysis Project: the Anglo-Jewish cousinhood and the Quaker cousinhood.

Since the seventeenth century Jewish merchants, bankers, and others have immigrated from Spain, Portugal, Holland, and, later, from Germany and Poland. By the mid-nineteenth century they formed a tightly knit community of bankers, stockbrokers, bullion merchants, lawyers, and politicians, and although some (such as Hambro and Lazard: see Bramson and Wain, 1979) adopted Christianity after their arrival the majority remained Jewish (Bermant, 1971 and 1977; Aris, 1970). There was a tendency for their business interests to be maintained within the group because of their own endogamy and because of prejudice against Jews on the part of established business interests. Their extensive international connections through their cousins in other European capitals were of particular importance. Acceptance by the established order was spearheaded by the Rothschilds in the second half of the century – a Rothschild entered the House of Commons in 1858 and the Lords in 1885. The core families of the cousinhood (see table 4.4) were linked through a dense network of kinship ties and business alliances, though the Rothschilds remained partially separate as Mayer Rothschild's will had stipulated that his descendants should not marry outside the family. Table 4.4 shows that members of these families were directors of 6 of the top 250 enterprises in 1904, of which 4 were

Table 4.4   The Jewish and Quaker Cousinhoods, 1904–76

	Top 250 directorships held by core families		
	1904	*1938*	*1976*
Jewish families[a]	6	7	10
Quaker families[b]	23	19	6

Notes: [a] Families in the Jewish core are Cohen, Samuel, Montagu, Sebag-Montefiore, Stern, Rothschild, Goldsmid, Sassoon, Franklin, Keyser, and Jessel.
[b] Families in the Quaker core are Barclay, Bevan, Gurney, Fry, Tritton, Lloyd, Hanbury, Buxton, Pease, Backhouse, Hoare, Tuke, Rowntree, Seebohm, and Fox.

financials.[18] Three of these enterprises – Shell, Rothschild, and Alliance Assurance – were interlocked with one another, but many of the Jewish banks and merchant houses fell outside the top 250. By 1938 the number of companies on which the cousinhood was represented had risen only to seven.[19] The Jewish cousinhood remained somewhat marginal to the main network, although they created numerous kinterlocks among the second-rank City enterprises. The cousinhood was represented on 10 of the top 250 enterprises in 1976,[20] and the number of Jewish enterprises outside the sphere of the cousinhood had increased following a new wave of immigration. Members of the cousinhood had extended their influence within the top 250, but the enterprises were more likely to have outside shareholders – indeed, Shell was an example of an enterprise which had passed from full Samuel family ownership to control through a constellation of interests (Henriques, 1960). The cousinhood formed a large, and still endogamous, cluster within the wider kinship network.

From the eighteenth century Quakers had become involved in banking and industry because of their exclusion from other avenues, and for the same reason they developed a high degree of mutual support (Grubb, 1930; Emden, 1939; Raistrick, 1950; Isichei, 1971; Windsor, 1980). Business activity was reinforced by religious prescriptions and proscriptions: Robert Barclay, the Quaker 'apologist', was the basis for Max Weber's construction of the ideal type of the Protestant ethic, and his son David became a banker and merchant (Barclay, 1924–34; Mathews and Tuke, 1926; Tuke and Gillman, 1972). The evangelical nature of the religion meant travelling in the ministry and so a nation-wide friendship system emerged around the practice of 'intervisitation'. The network of friendship was the basis of marriage choice, and both friendship and kinship became the bases of business partnerships. David Barclay brought in his cousin and nephew, a Bevan and a Tritton, to the banking business and expanded into brewing, and later business partnerships involved other Quaker families (Sessions and Sessions, n.d.; see also Lloyd, 1975; Sayers, 1957). The Quaker cousinhood emerged as a series of overlapping family compacts (Berkowitz, 1982, pp. 116–19; Berkowitz, 1976).

It can be seen from table 4.4 that the number of top boards on which the Quaker cousinhood was represented fell from 23 to 6, most of this decline occurring in the postwar period. The dilution of the cousinhood began in the late nineteenth century, when most of the Barclays, Gurneys, Hoares, and Lloyds left the Society of Friends to become Anglicans, and the Society itself lifted its proscription on marriage to non-Quakers. Nevertheless, it is startling to find that the cousinhood was represented on 23 boards in 1904, with 8 of these enterprises having 2 or more

Quaker directors. Multiple representation of this kind had declined by 1938, though Barclays Bank had 10 Quaker directors and Lloyds Bank had 4, and the total number of boards on which they sat had fallen slightly. A major decline in Quaker influence occurred during the postwar period, the cousinhood being represented on just six boards in 1976 – though Barclays Bank still had six directors recruited from this group. Barclays Bank, Lloyds Bank, and Commercial Union Assurance showed Quaker representation throughout the period studied. The Quakers, therefore, were more strongly represented in the largest enterprises than were members of the Jewish cousinhood, but their influence has waned in the second half of the century.[21]

The Jewish cousinhood remained a distinct structural feature of the kinship network in 1976, but the Quaker cousinhood had largely merged into the wider network. This network extends horizontally to encompass many business families and has its core members drawn from a number of prominent families: Brand, Lubbock, Tiarks, Grenfell, Glyn, Hill-Wood, Hambro, Gibbs, Göschen, Hubbard, Gladstone, and the Smiths (the double-barrelled families of Abel Smith, Colin Smith, and Hugh Smith; Lords Bicester and Carrington).[22] The most prominent members change from period to period, and both families and individuals move to and fro between business and politics. Virtually all the major City enterprises can be connected through kinterlocks at very low kinship distance. The symbolic transactions in which kinsmen engage become the informal conditions of instrumental transactions; the 'trust' which was central to City business practices was firmly rooted in an extended kinship network. Kinship and friendship operate as channels of communication between people and enterprises and so allow other transactions to proceed more smoothly (Lupton and Wilson, 1959).

This network of personal relations is articulated with a network of economic transactions between members of the upper class. As Zeitlin and Ratcliff argue:

> Extensive intermarriage among propertied families is not only a consequence of close mutual interaction but also serves to create reciprocal obligations and loyalties and to buttress the economic foundations of class unity. (Zeitlin and Ratcliff, 1975, p. 23; see also Blumberg and Paul, 1975)

It is through kinship and its associated informal social interactions that mere 'economic' classes become translated into 'social' classes:

> The complex pattern of extensive intermarriage among propertied families both results from, and, in turn, reinforces and extends, a web of social interaction and of mutual obligations and loyalties. Already sharing common interests, based on their common location in the productive process and propertied system, they are, thereby, unified into a social, rather than merely 'economic' class. (Zeitlin and Ratcliff, 1975, p. 33)

The structure of this class can be understood in terms of Sweezy's model of a central core surrounded by 'fringes which are in varying degrees attached to the core' (1951, p. 124). The central core of the network was the cluster of old-established families which had a particularly dense nexus of kinship lines and which created numerous kinterlocks between enterprises. It will be shown in the following chapter that these same families were part of a dominant status group, the 'establishment', which linked business with politics.

NOTES

1. Recent reviews of British evidence can be found in Holl, 1975 and 1977.
2. Drawing on Braverman (1974), both Burawoy (1979) and Edwards (1979) have developed Marxist analyses of control over the labour process which complement Chandler's discussion of managerial restructuring. See Gospel and Littler (1983).
3. One of the few empirical studies of the relationship between ownership and administration is that of Pugh and Hickson (1976), who found no relationship between 'ownership' and centralised authority. Their analysis, however, employed an idiosyncratic definition of ownership.
4. This point must be treated with caution in view of the small number of enterprises in these other categories.
5. Strictly, the percentage will be variable over time and depends upon the specific pattern of shareholdings in the company. Rather than specifying an arbitrary percentage cut-off, it is preferable to define minority control as the situation where the largest shareholder is able to out-vote the next largest holders. Florence (1961) suggests that this be based on an analysis of the 20 largest holders. These

points will be discussed in a later publication. Analysis of share registers shows that a practical working definition of minority control in British companies in 1976 is that a single shreholder has between 10 and 50 per cent of the shares.

6. When this involves more than two controllers it becomes less stable, the board reflecting shifting balances among the holders. It is also more difficult to demonstrate the existence of the necessary cooperation, and each example has to be judged on its own merit.

7. Compare diagram 1 in Francis (1980, p. 7), which fails to give sufficient attention to financial intermediaries.

8. From the standpoint of the argument in this chapter, control by the state and state agencies can be assimilated to the category of control by another enterprise.

9. Barratt Brown (1968) gives various examples of 'management control', but he defines this in terms of the proportion of insiders on the board and takes no account of the share dispersal. Similarly, Francis (1980) takes the background of the chairman as the indicator of control type – though he finds very few 'managerial' enterprises. Useful as they are for many purposes, neither study approaches the heart of the question of management control.

10. Unilever is the one case cited by Francis (1980). For reasons given below, this case is rejected here.

11. In addition to Company Analysis Project data and Florence (1961), sources on Dunlop are Anon. (1908), J. B. Dunlop (1924), Dunlop (1938), Du Cros (1938), and Jennings (1961).

12. Sources on ICI are Reader (1970), Koss (1970), and Crathorne (1973).

13. The other branch of the family had never been involved in the brewery and were Dublin lawyers who set up the merchant bank Guinness Mahon in 1836. The bank was closely involved in airlines in the 1930s and was forced into a merger to form Guinness Peat in 1972. By this time the Guinness family were no longer represented on the board, but were reputed to retain a small shareholding.

14. On the history of the Pearson group and its interwar involvement in electricity, airlines, coalmining, oil, newspapers, and banking, as well as the original contracting business, see Spender (1930), Middlemas (1963), and Young (1966).

15. On Rowntree, see Vernon (1958).

16. On Unilever, see Wilson (1954 and 1968), Reader (1960 and 1980), Fox (1931), and Mathias (1967).

17. Channon's argument is based on that of Chandler (1962), and the general thesis has been examined in other European countries by Dyas and Thanheiser (1976), Daems and van der Wee (1974), and Chandler and Daems (1974).

18. The board of National Telephone included a George Franklin, but this was not included in the total as his kinship was not known.
19. Two Franklins and a Goldsmith of unknown kinship were not included. Families such as Salmon and Gluckstein and the Marks kinecon group were not part of the cousinhood. Lewis's Investment Trust was headed by Sir Rex Cohen, who Bermant (1971) claims was part of the cousinhood, but this could not be confirmed.
20. Sir James Goldsmith's precise kinship could not be determined and he was not included in the total, though he is reputed to come from an 'impoverished' branch of the cousinhood (Ingrams, 1979). The Cavenham board did, however, include two Franklins.
21. Quaker families outside the cousinhood include Cadbury and Reckitt, and numerous others.
22. See Leighton-Boyce (1958).

CHAPTER FIVE

Finance Capital and the Finance Capitalists

It has been suggested that the personal relations of kinship and friendship foster the cohesion of the leading members of a propertied upper class. The communication between these members is the basis of the trust and informality which sustains the network of instrumental transactions between individuals and among enterprises. Interlocking directorships must be seen as a key expression of such instrumental transactions. They not only constitute personal relations between enterprises, but between the persons themselves, and they reinforce the solidarity of business leaders. People may be connected, therefore, through kinship, through friendship, and through the fact that they meet one another on company boards. The network of 'meetings' which links directors together is an important aspect of their social cohesion, and variations in cohesion may be expected to be associated with variations in the structure of that network. In the USA the group of 'multiple directors' among which this unity is fostered has been described as an 'inner circle' (Useem, 1984) or a group of 'finance capitalists' (Soref, 1980), the common view being that they form the dominant segment within the upper class (Zeitlin, 1980, p. 13).[1] The aim of this chapter is to summarise the debate about finance capitalists in the USA and to examine whether British multiple directors can be regarded in the same light.

THE DEBATE OVER THE MONEY TRUST

Concern over the existence of a 'money trust' of big financiers grew alongside the monopolisation of the American economy. The period from 1870 to 1900 saw a growth in the scale of business, and the massive capital requirements of the large national enterprises gave investment banks and other providers of credit a key role in their affairs. In many industries company boards were dominated by the bankers or their representatives, and large numbers of enterprises came under bank control. Sometimes this development resulted from business failures. In railways, for example, bankruptcies and threatened bankruptcies in the 1880s and 1890s forced bankers to move in to protect their interests through consolidation and reorganisation (Kotz, 1978, pp. 26–30; Herman, 1981, pp. 118–19). In other cases bank control resulted from the raising of corporate finance. During the 1890s a number of large industrial concerns went public, and the already powerful investment bankers were well-placed to take advantage of the search for capital. This power was used to promote large amalgamations such as General Electric and US Steel. While some industrialists, such as Rockefeller and his Standard Oil Trust, could achieve a partial independence from the banks, the major banking and industrial groups had come to a *modus vivendi* by the early years of the century (Kotz, 1978, pp. 34–9). By the 1890s J. P. Morgan was pre-eminent in a group of bankers which used ownership, credit, and board represen-tation to control the many large companies they had created. There was a rapid growth in public concern about the 'captains of industry', 'masters of capital', or – more criticaly – 'robber barons' who used holding companies and trusts to consolidate their power. This small group of multiple directors had by 1910 come to be known as the 'money trust', and in 1912 the Pujo Committee was set up by Congress to investigate the concentra-tion of economic power in their hands. The result of their deliberations was the passage of the Clayton Act (1914), which imposed restrictions on interlocking directorships and on other means of concentrating economic power. By 1919, however, public concern about the money trust had begun to wane. The public image of big business had been transformed (Bunting, 1976a).

The decline and fall of the money trust have been documented in a recent series of interrelated studies by Bunting and Mizruchi, which have examined changes in the American intercorporate network. The 166 largest American enterprises of 1904 had a very high average of 18.4 interlocks each. Sixteen enterprises had more than 50 interlocks each, and only 12 were isolated. The network had a density of 0.72 (Mizruchi, 1982, pp. 99, 105).

The big investment and clearing banks were at the centre of the network of weighted primary interlocks: J. P. Morgan, National City Bank, First National Bank, and Kuhn Loeb often had executives sitting as outsiders on the boards of industrials such as US Steel and International Harvester (Mizruchi, 1982, p. 100). The multiple directors held 38.5 per cent of all directorships; and those with the most directorships tended to have their primary business interests outside the network of large firms, thus generating secondary interlocks. It was found that 40 per cent of all interlocks were *between* financials and non-financials (Mizruchi, 1982, pp. 100, 107, 121). The general level of interlocking remained constant until 1912 but then fell substantially. Much of this fall occurred between 1912 and 1919, and this decline was far sharper in railways and banks than in manufacturing (Mizruchi, 1982, pp. 101–4).

Bunting operationally defined the money trust as including all those directors who held 6 or more positions in the top 167 companies. The economic foundation of the trust was defined as those companies with 30 or more interlocks (i.e., with adjacency of 30 or more). These definitions are, of course, contestable as the money trust was defined simply in terms of arbitrary numbers of directorships and interlocks. Bearing this qualification in mind, certain conclusions can be drawn. The trust included 16 people in 1899, 20 people in 1905, 27 people in 1912, and 14 people in 1919; and it included 16 companies in 1899, 31 companies in 1905, 36 companies in 1912, and 13 companies in 1919 (Bunting, 1976a, p. 10). The decline between 1912 and 1919 was explained in terms of the passage of the Clayton Act and the associated growth in public concern.[2] In the earlier period, much of the high centrality of banks was due to the interlocking between banks which the Clayton Act outlawed (Mizruchi, 1982, p. 124).

The period from 1919 to 1935 saw a decline in interlocking and of the investment banker. Foreign capital, formerly controlled by the investment banks, declined in importance and so the bankers no longer had the power which this control had given them. Similarly, the growth of new industries led to the rise of new entrepreneurial capitalists, such as Ford, outside the existing bank-centred system (Kotz, 1978, pp. 41–3). The growth of public investment in stocks and shares as company shareholdings were dispersed led other financial intermediaries to challenge the investment banks. While the latter remained 'wholesale' underwriting banks, the commercial deposit banks moved into this new area of 'retail' custom and emerged as rival centres of economic power. The mushrooming of utility holding companies and investment trusts reinforced this challenge as the old investment banks cashed in on the speculative mania (Kotz, 1978, pp. 43–9). The Depression and the New Deal banking legislation, which forced a separation of investment and commercial banking operations, further weakened the financial intermediaries. There was, therefore, a general decline in the predominance of the banking system and the emergence of greater rivalries among the banks.

Mizruchi shows that this period involved a decline in the level of interlocking by investment banks. Although the level of their interlocking had always been lower than, say, insurance and railway companies, the investment banks still experienced a significant decline over the period 1919–35 (Mizruchi, 1982, p. 104). By 1935 the network density had fallen to 0.4, a level at which it stabilised. The multiple directors held just 27.8 per cent of directorships, and 50.8 per cent of interlocks were between financial and non-financial enterprises (Mizruchi, 1982, p. 121). Much of the decline in interlocking, argues Mizruchi, was a result of the declining importance of personal, entrepreneurial capitalists in the network. As the system of intercorporate relations was institutionalised, so it could be maintained without the personal domination exercised by men with extremely large numbers of directorships. People such as Morgan and Stillman had created a system in which individually powerful men such as themselves were no longer necessary (Mizruchi, 1982, p. 187).

In the period after 1935 the level of interlocking rose but did not again reach its 1904–12 peak. The proportion of interlocks between financials and non-financials continued to rise slightly to a high point of 55.6 per cent in 1969 (Mizruchi, 1982, p. 121). This period was, however, marked by a fall in the number of bank interlocks carried by bank executives. The links between financials and non-financials were by then just as likely to be carried by those with their primary interests in an industrial company as by bank executives. This signifies an enhanced influence of industrial interests on bank boards and is an indicator of the ever fuller merger of banks and industry to form 'finance capital' (Mizruchi, 1982, pp. 127, 129).

By 1974 there were just 3 companies with 30 or more interlocks and there were no directors with 6 or more directorships (Bunting, 1976a–c, p. 29; see also Bunting and Barbour,

1971). The total number of companies which were interlocked remained comparable over this period (140 in 1912, and 145 in 1974), but they were interlocked at a much lower intensity. One important trend was that indirect connections at distance two between competitors – especially those mediated by a bank – were of increasing importance relative to direct interlocks. This was especially true of the period 1964–74 (Bunting, 1976b, p. 33).[3]

During its heyday, in the period 1890–1912, the money trust was based on the predominate power of the entrepreneurial capitalists who headed the major investment banks. The fusion of the groups of enterprises associated with each of these banks created a large component in the intercorporate network. Morgan dominated the other investment banking syndicates and established a 'Pax Morgana': through the growth of trust companies the process of industrial consolidation ('morganisation') took place within an economy in which a degree of cooperation had been established among the various competing banking interests (Berkowitz, 1976, p. 301ff.). The decline of the investment banker led to a break-up of the money trust, and by 1976 an extensive and loosely connected national network had emerged. There still existed a small group of multiple directors, but this inner circle of finance capitalists no longer constituted an all-powerful money trust.[4]

In the work of Mills (1956) and Sweezy (1951), the rise and decline of the money trust have been seen as part of a wider transformation in the upper class. The upper class of the mid-nineteenth century comprised a number of distinct local upper classes, which only became forged into a cohesive, intermarrying national class after the 1870s, as their enterprises were amalgamated into large national enterprises. Berkowitz claims that between 1890 and 1900 regionalised kinecon groups became linked into a national kinship network of propertied families (1976, p. 201). Thus, the money trust was both an outcome of and a contribution to the emergence of a national upper class (see also Baltzell, 1958, p. 8ff., 25ff.). Lundberg (1937) argues that it was still possible to recognise an 'inner circle' of wealthy kinecon groups based on the great wealth generated in the large enterprises of the expanding national economy.[5] These kinecon groups had their focus in the 'New York Rich' (Berkowitz, 1976), and New York 'Society' became the dominant segment in the upper class.

The period since the 1920s – the period of decline for the New York bankers – has been described as involving the further consolidation of a national upper class through a process of 'managerial reorganisation'. Propertied families and managers of corporate property became welded together into a group of 'corporate rich' (Mills, 1956, p. 116) with interests in the profitability of the corporate system as a whole. The wealth of the rich came to take the form of a diversified portfolio rather than large holdings in particular companies, and this was reinforced by the growth of intercorporate connections such as interlocks (Mills, 1956, p. 123):

> The growth and interconnections of corporations . . . have meant the rise of a more sophisticated executive elite which now possesses a certain autonomy from any specific property interest. Its power is the power of property, but that property is not always or even usually of one coherent and narrow type It is, in operating fact, class-wide property. (Mills, 1956, p. 122; see also Zeitlin, 1974; a related view is Lundberg, 1968)

Koenig and his collaborators (Koenig et al., 1979; Koenig and Gogel, 1981) follow Mills's analysis and argue that interlocks are very significant as channels of communication, of symbolic transactions, between people. The interlock network permits the emergence of common values and a sense of identity and cohesion. They reinforce other informal relations between people and permit the development of a common political outlook, which is itself expressed in the government of charities and universities, and in national politics (Useem, 1981a; Useem and McCormack, 1981; Domhoff, 1978). The upper class which resulted from the economic transformations of the period since 1870 itself underwent a series of transformations. Although the money trust declined after 1912, the network of the 1970s still contained an 'inner circle' of multiple directors (Useem, 1984). Instead of entrepreneurial capitalists, however, the inner circle comprised mainly finance capitalists (Norich, 1980) who owed their position to the emergence of an extensive network of intercorporate shareholdings.

THE INNER CIRCLE AS FINANCE CAPITALISTS

The gradual development of a national intercorporate network and the creation of closer links between financials and non-financials were common to both Britain and the USA, but grew from different starting points and at different rates. The development of an extensive national network occurred later in Britain than in the USA, and it is possible to assess whether the British economy was, at any stage, dominated by a money trust of the type found in the USA. The material presented so far suggests that evidence for the existence of a money trust is more likely to be found in the data for 1938 than in that for 1904. The expansion of the City of London core created an inner circle of major businessmen with interests in a wide range of enterprises. Direct comparisons between the findings of the Company Analysis Project and those of Mizruchi are difficult because a different number of companies were analysed, the British data relating to a larger network. But certain comparisons can be made between the 1938 British network and the 1904 American data.

The British network of 1938 comprised enterprises with an average of 4.6 interlocks (compared with an average of 18.4 in the USA); 1 enterprise had 30 or more interlocks (35 in the USA), there were 9 people with 6 or more directorships (20 in the USA), and the multiple directors held 31.3 per cent of all directorships (38.5 in the USA). By contrast, the British network of 1904 comprised enterprises with an average of 3.2 interlocks; no enterprises had 30 or more interlocks; 1 person had 6 or more directorships, and the multiple directors held 26.8 per cent of all directorships. Clearly the inner circle of 1938 was far more extensive and influential than that of 1904, but it can hardly be characterised as a money trust of the kind that existed under the Pax Morgana. Although the British multiple directors held a similar proportion of directorships as their American counterparts, this did not represent the activities of a small number of people with a large number of directorships each. The British multiple directors comprised an inner circle but not a money trust. It is, nevertheless, the case that the inner circle of 1938 was the outcome of a long process of concentration in the economy and that many of those with the largest number of directorships were directors of the big clearing banks. A parallel also exists between Britian and the USA in the relative decline of the group.

The large British enterprises of 1976 had an average of 4.3 interlocks; 2 people held 6 or more directorships and no enterprises had 30 or more interlocks. This decline between 1938 and 1976 runs parallel with the decline in the American money trust between 1912 and 1935. In both Britain and the USA an intensively interlocked network emerged and subsequently moved towards a similar, and lower, level of interlocking by the 1970s.

The British intercorporate network, therefore, never contained an overweening money trust, though the power and influence of its inner circle increased substantially between 1904 and 1938. By 1976, as has been emphasised at a number of points in this book, the British network was an inclusive and cohesive national network and was built from lines of a lesser intensity than previously.

Some insight into the nature of the British inner circle of 1976 can be gained from an analysis of the business background and interests of its members. The main institutional base of a director can be termed his or her 'primary interest', and a director's primary interest was initially operationalised as the holding of a full-time executive position in one of the top 250 enterprises. It was found that the 1976 network contained 84 people with a primary interest in one of the top 50 financials and 95 with a primary interest in one of the top 200 non-financials. The 84 directors with a financial base generated 133 primary interlocks – those running from the base company to others, as defined in table 1.4 – and 'induced' a further 74. The 95 directors with primary non-financial interests generated a further 146 primary and 70 induced interlocks. Thus, directors with a primary interest in the top 250 were responsible for almost three-quarters of all interlocks in the network. Table 5.1, which shows the relationship between the number of directorships held and the type of interlock generated, demonstrates that those with a primary interest within the top 250 generated more interlocks than those without such an interest, regardless of the number of director-ships they held.[6] What is perhaps most significant is that the 50 financials produced 84 of the directors with primary interests in the top 250, while the much larger group of 200 non-financials produced only 95 such directors. The executives of financial enterprises accounted for almost half of all the primary interlocks and so contributed disproportionately to the overall structure of primary interlocks which is discussed in the following chapter.

Table 5.1   Interlocks and Number of Directorships, 1976

No. of directorships held	% of interlocks generated		
	Primary	Induced	Secondary
2	19.0	—	14.0
3	14.9	7.4	8.1
4	7.1	7.1	2.5
5	5.4	8.1	1.7
6	0.8	1.7	2.5
Totals	47.2	24.4	28.4

Note: The total number of interlocks was 591. By definition, people with only two directorships can generate no induced interlocks.

If 179 of the 282 multiple directors had primary interests within the top 250, it follows that 103 did not. These people generated 168 interlocks (28.4 per cent of the total), and it is clearly important to know more about their business background. A number of directors held no full-time executive position but seemed to regard one of the top 250 enterprises as their base company,[7] and others were retired executives or had family connections with a top enterprise. All these could, in fact, be regarded as having a primary interest within the top 250, and adding these people to the 179 executives resulted in 209 'primary directors' – 97 primary financial and 112 primary non-financial. Of the remaining 73 multiple directors, 24 had retired from a top enterprise and no longer sat on its board, 27 had their primary interests in enterprises outside the top 250, and 22 had primary interests outside business. The 22 'outsiders' included 6 past or present politicians and 8 retired civil servants.

The secondary interlocks in the 1976 network, therefore, were carried predominantly by people with some present or past connection with a base company in the top 250. Because they were not current executives the interlocks between their bases and other enterprises (disregarding those induced by them) may be regarded as weaker or less intense than the true primary interlocks but as more intense than those carried by people without such a base. There was a very strong career phenomenon at work. Those who achieved high executive positions over the course of their career, especially those who became chief executives, were likely to accumulate other directorships as their career advanced. On retirement their link to their base company weakened, and in a number of cases was broken completely, and these inner circle members took on an 'elder statesman' role in the business system and joined with the politicians and retired civil servants to generate a significant proportion of the 28.4 per cent of interlocks which have been designated as 'secondary'. It will be shown in the following section that this role in the intercorporate network was associated with their social and political status.

Further examination of the changing structure of the inner circle involves a direct rather than a tangential approach to its structural characteristics. Studies which concentrate on primary interests and other indicators of social background run the risk of reducing the relational features of a network to the individual attributes of the agents who construct it (Burt, 1978b; Friedmann, 1979; Berkowitz, 1980). Referring to career-mobility and recruitment studies, Berkowitz has correctly pointed out that the stages in a person's career (for example, the chief executives in the inner circle described above) can be seen, in part, as a reflection of the temporal transformation of the structure of opportunities available to that person (Berkowitz, 1980, p. 14). As individual agents move through an institutionalised system of positions, those positions and their relations are being continuously restructured. For this reason, the 'attributes' which individuals possess at various stages in their career (primary interests, number of directorships, political affiliations, etc.) are not properties simply of those individuals but are the outcome of the structure of relations between agents – the central concern of social network analysis. The discussion of kinship in the previous chapter showed how the concepts of network analysis can be applied to people as well as to corporate agents, and this can be extended to the internal structure of the inner circle by examining the connections between participants in the network of interlocking directorships.

Bonacich and Domhoff (1981) put forward a method for producing both a network of enterprises and a network of directors, with the directors being classified into a number of 'latent classes', or clusters, on the basis of shared board memberships. This has been investigated in the Company Analysis Project by constructing the 'dual' of the intercorporate network. A dual in network analysis is the logical mirror image of a given network. Because a relation between two enterprises consists of the presence of one person on both boards, it is possible to reverse the picture and see a relation between two people as consisting of their presence on the same board.[8] If the intercorporate network is a network of interlocking directorships, its dual is a network of interpersonal meetings. Two people are connected by a line in this network of meetings if they sit on a board together, though lines of multiplicity one are of limited interest as a large number of such lines are created by enterprises with large boards. The number of lines with multiplicity one in the meetings network is a simple function of board size.[9] The main area in which lines of multiplicity one are important is in determining the relative centrality of people in the network. Table 5.2 lists the most central directors for each of the periods studied. 'Centrality'

Table 5.2   The Most Central Directors, 1904–76

1904		1938		1976	
Director	Adjacency	Director	Adjacency	Director	Adjacency
E. Nettlefold	34	Sir T. Royden	55	Sir J. Partridge	31
C. N. Lawrence	30	Lord Horne	44	Sir F. Sandilands	31
C. J. C. Scott	28	W. K. Whigham	36	Lord Inchcape	31
Lord Rathmore	26	Sir P. Bates	36	Sir R. Clark	30
J. P. Bickersteth	26	R. E. Beckett	35	Lord Caldecote	29
W. T. Brand	24	C. Ker	35	Sir E. Faulkner	29
J. Dennistoun	23	Sir G. Granet	34	Sir R. Geddes	28
Sir T. Brooke	23	C. E. Lloyd	34	Sir A. Hall	27
E. H. Cunard	23	Sir F. L. Joseph	34	Lord Bearsted	27
W. D. Hoare	23	Sir A. G. Anderson	33	Sir P. Matthews	27
C. T. Richie	23				

is measured by the number of other multiple directors which a person meets at board meetings, though all the directors will, of course, meet a large number of other directors who have only one top 250 directorship. Table 5.3 places this in context by showing the distribution of multiple lines in the meetings network.

It can be seen from table 5.2 that the average adjacency for central directors was at its highest in 1938, when Sir Thomas Royden met 55 other multiple directors (16.7 per cent) at the boards on which he sat. The most central director of 1976, Sir John Partridge, met 31 of his fellow multiple directors, just below the 34 met by his counterpart in 1904. The 1938 peak was not, however, the most significant fact about the central directors. Their most important characteristics were the number of boards on which they sat and the spread of their interests. The 11 most central directors of 1904 held 39 directorships on 25 enterprises, the bulk of these being banks and railways. Only two of these people were directors of non-financials. In 1938 the 10 most central held 43 directorships in 25 enterprises – little different from 1904, but their bank directorships accounted for a higher proportion of the total. The data for 1976 show that the 10 most central directors of that year held 41 directorships in 30 enterprises and that almost half of both the directorships and the enterprises were in the financial sector. At the same time, the non-financial directorships held by the top multiple directors in 1976 were predominantly in manufacturing industry rather than transport. It is clear that the top ten of 1976 formed the heart of an inner circle in which financial and manufacturing interests were closely integrated. The banking and commercial interests of the expanding City core of 1904 and 1938 had become the banking and manufacturing interests of the finance capitalists of 1976.

The concept of 'finance capital' refers to the outcome of two parallel processes: the concentration of both banking and industry, and the coalescence of large-scale capital between these two sectors. The trends discussed in chapter 2 produced a transformation of the inner circle of multiple directors. It has been shown that the separation of banking and industry was a product of the late nineteenth century and that the twentieth century has seen a gradual fusion of the two sectors. Finance capital in Britain emerged during the interwar years and was consolidated after the war. The 1976 intercorporate network was the result of these developments and shows evidence of them in the structure of its 'dual'. Hilferding argued that under the aegis of finance capital,

[a] circle of people emerges who, thanks to their own capital resources or to the concentrated power of outside capital which they represent (in the case of bank directors), become members of the boards of directors of numerous corporations. There develops in this way a kind of personal union, on one side among the various corporations themselves, and on the other, between the corporations and the bank; and the common ownership interest which is thus formed among the various companies must necessarily exert a powerful influence upon their policies. (Hilferding, 1910, pp. 119–20)

The inner circle of finance capitalists expresses the fusion of banking, insurance, and manufacturing, and becomes the dominant element in the control and coordination of this 'depersonalised' property.

Further insight into the changing structure of this inner circle can be gained from an analysis of the network of multiple lines, which is summarised in table 5.3. While the number of lines between enterprises generated by each multiple director increased steadily from 1904 to 1976, the number of multiple meetings increased between 1904 and 1938 and then fell back sharply to a 1976 figure lower than that for 1904. At the beginning of the period the 303 multiple directors entered into 176 multiple meetings, while in 1976 the 282 people entered into only 73. This suggests that the internal cohesion of the inner circle was at its highest in 1938: both the density and the intensity of their

Table 5.3   Distribution of Lines in the Network of Meetings, 1904–76

Multiplicity of line	No. of lines		
	1904	*1938*	*1976*
2	166	242	73
3	10	25	—
4	—	11	—
5	—	5	—
Totals	176	283	73

meetings were highest in that year. This is confirmed by the fact that 8 of the 11 most central directors of 1904 participated in these multiple meetings, whereas all 10 of the central directors of 1938 did so.[10] Table 5.4 shows that the largest component in 1904 included 11 people and that of 1976 included just 8; but the largest component of 1938 included 30 people. While the 43 components of 1904 contained 45 per cent of the multiple directors, over one-third of them in pairs, the 42 components of 1938 contained 57 per cent, most of whom were in components of size four or more. In 1938 over half the inner circle participated in multiple meetings, many of them in the very large components, and thus the circle as a whole was highly unified through such intense interaction. By 1976 the emergence of an extensive national network with a less intensive pattern of interlocking had resulted in a less cohesive and less intensive network of multiple

Table 5.4 Components in the Network of Multiple Meetings, 1904–76

Size of Component	No. of components		
	1904	*1938*	*1976*
2	26	17	14
3	6	14	6
4	4	3	2
5	4	2	1
6	—	—	—
7	—	—	1
8	1	—	1
9	—	1	—
10	1	2	—
11	1	1	—
18	—	1	—
30	—	1	—
Number of components:	43	42	25
Proportion of multiple directors:	45%	57%	26%

meetings. Multiple meetings did not involve more than two boards and thus were mainly confined to pairs or other small components based around allied enterprises.

The main conclusion to be drawn about the inner circle is that the move towards finance capital was associated with changes in the network role played by its members. In the earliest period the structure of the inner circle reflected the characteristics of an economy in which economic power was 'personalistic'. Mercantile and banking families constituted a City of London core, a small group of entrepreneurial capitalists united through business and kinship, and this lay at the heart of a network in which the more peripheral areas were dominated by other, provincial entrepreneurs. Entrepreneurial capitalists were the prime movers of economic activity at all levels, whether through their own entrepreneurial firms or through joint stock companies which they collectively managed. The structure of the network was the outcome of the interplay of entrepreneurial interests. Entrepreneurs had limited information about investment opportunities in parts of the economy far removed from their own enterprises and sought to minimise the risk of investment by maximising the intelligence available to them. In doing so, they relied heavily on those other entrepreneurs who were close to them in business, kinship, friendship, and geography (Kennedy and Britton, 1981a–b; Mizruchi, 1982, p. 184). Board recruitment and personal investments tended to be mutually reinforcing and so created clusters of people with intense interpersonal relations and few external relations. The dominant multiple directors owed more to their personal power and wealth than to their position in the intercorporate network. During the interwar years the increased level of interlocking brought these entrepreneurial groups, kine-con groups, and cousinhoods into closer contact and forged them into a large network in which regional and personalistic factors were of diminishing importance. The corporate directorate of 1976 represented a further development of these trends and showed clearly that the coalescence of entrepreneurial capitalists in the City core had given way to the dominance of a group of finance capitalists who acted as 'coordinating controllers' (Barratt Brown, 1968). Central to this process was the system of 'institutional shareholdings' which had gradually superseded the earlier system of personal shareholdings. Insurance companies, pension funds, investment and unit trusts, and bank trustee departments had become all-important in the ownership and financing of both financial and non-financial enterprises. The finance capitalists were the business leaders who played a key role in coordinating this intercorporate network. This role followed not from their personal power and wealth but from the institutional power of the enterprises with which they were associated.

THE INNER CIRCLE AS AN ESTABLISHMENT

It has been shown that the British inner circle cannot strictly be regarded as corresponding to the American model of the money trust. Nevertheless, certain parallels can be drawn between the American inner circle of 1904 and the British inner circle of 1938. The specificity of the British inner circle can best be grasped by seeing it as part of a social and political 'establishment' which dominated British society from the 1870s until at least the Second World War (Scott, 1982b). The leading members of the state apparatus, business leaders, and holders of top positions in such organisations as the Church of England were united with one another through kinship and friendship, through business partnerships, through attendance at the same schools, and through membership of the same 'gentlemen's' clubs (Perkin, 1978; Rubinstein, 1976; Giddens, 1974; Whitley, 1974; Whitley et al., 1981; Fidler, 1981, chapter 4). These links constituted the social and cultural assets which business leaders could draw upon to further their interests and were the basis of the informality and trust which underlay their instrumental transactions. The two most common indicators of establishment membership are education and clubs, and much research has shown that members of the inner circle were drawn disproportionately from the major public schools and tended to be members of the exclusive London clubs (Useem, 1984, pp. 65, 68; Giddens and Stanworth, 1978). Data collected for the Company Analysis Project has extended this concern to two areas which have been particularly under-researched (but see Pumphrey, 1959): the award of social honours and political donations.

Table 5.5   Number of Directorships and Social Honours, 1976

Number of directorships		No. of people			
	Kt/Bt	Life peer	Hereditary peer	Other[a]	Totals
2	42	14	13	9	78
3	26	2	4	2	34
4	6	1	3	—	10
5	4	1	2	—	7
6	1	—	1	—	2
Totals	79	18	23	11	131

Note: [a] Other includes 1 holder of a foreign title and 10 holders of courtesy titles (including Hon.).

Table 5.5 shows that 131 of the 282 multiple directors of 1976 (46.5 per cent) had titles, and that there was a strong association between holding a title and holding a large number of directorships (see also Useem, 1984, p. 69). Less than half of those with 2 directorships were titled, but two-thirds of those with 4 and over three-quarters of those with 5 or more held titles. The accumulation of directorships was associated with being titled. It was not simply that titles were awarded to those with large numbers of directorships in the top 250, though this does seem to have been the case; it was also that those who already had titles were able to accumulate directorships. Just under one-third of the titled multiple directors held hereditary titles or were heirs to titles, and many of the hereditary titleholders were not the first in their line. Most of the hereditary titleholders were barons or heirs, but 10 held higher titles and 4 of these (1 viscount and 3 earls) had 3 or more directorships each. If business achievement was the route to a title, the converse was also the case.

The relationship between titles and business position can be further exemplified through an analysis of those who generated the secondary interlocks. A total of 103 multiple directors had no full-time executive position in the top 250, and the network generated by these people alone contained 110 enterprises in 13 components. The 10 most central enterprises in the largest component (those connected to 6 or more others through secondary interlocks) were connected through the directorships of 26 people. Twenty of these key finance capitalists had titles.[11] The major non-executive directors who tied the 10 enterprises together were much more likely to have titles than were multiple directors as a whole, but this was not because they had large numbers of directorships: only 4 of the 26 were also among the 27 people with 4 or more directorships. Being titled was independently associated with number of directorships and with role in the intercorporate network. The titles of the major non-executive directors reflected their position as the 'elder statesmen' of the business world. Possession of a title was also associated with centrality in the meetings network of directors. All the ten most central directors in 1976 (see table 5.2) had titles. While 7 were among those with the most directorships, none were among the 26 key non-executive directors. Particularly striking was the rise in the number of central directors with titles from 2 in 1904 to 6 in 1938 and 10 in 1976. This reflects the increased routine use of knighthoods in particular as rewards for prominent businessmen. A final feature of titles which is brought out in the data set is the particularly close association between the banks and titled directors. Banks were more likely to have titled directors than were other enterprises, and their titled directors were especially likely to be peers. Titled directors held 44.3 per cent of all clearing bank directorships in 1938 and 47.0 per cent in 1976.[12] Although the proportion of baronets and courtesy-titleholders declined over that period, the proportion of peers remained constant and the proportion of knights increased sharply.

Useem argues that the inner circle comprises the dominant segment of the capitalist class (1982, p. 212). As the planners and coordinators of the system, they are able to formulate generalised corporate interests which transcend the particular interests of specific enterprises. Because of their business experience and their high level of cohesion, they are able to act as the politicised segment of the class and so are able to translate corporate interests into political demands. However, the old institutions of the establishment in Britain weakened to the point at which business leaders could no longer be sure that the state would be especially responsive to their demands. Inner circle members had, therefore, to become increasingly involved in the newer 'corporatist' institutions such as advisory boards and business associations (Useem, 1981b; Useem and McCormack, 1981). The mechanics of this have been thoroughly documented in Useem (1984), and his analysis can be extended into a consideration of the role of political donations.

Koenig (1979) has examined the largest contributors to political party funds in the USA, where contributions must, by law, be made by individuals and not by enterprises. There were 337 large contributors in 1972 and the larger the number of directorships people held, the more likely were they to support Republicans rather than Democrats. That is, finance capitalists were more strongly Republican than were other directors. Furthermore, contributors to the Democrats and those who made no political contributions were more likely to be found in peripheral than in central enterprises. Koenig suggests that the peripheral and isolated enterprises were less likely to have had Nixon contributors on their boards because their peripheral position made it difficult for fund raisers to utilise friendship chains to persuade people to give money. On the other hand, fund raisers could reach central enterprises through multiple channels. However, if the fund raiser did succeed in convincing directors from isolated firms to contribute, then they were likely to make very large contributions because the directors lacked channels of communication through which to determine the standard level of contribution. The key role in the general run of contributions was played by the fund raisers and those finance capitalists to whom they were close and who gave them an entrée to the network (Koenig, 1979).

In Britain, enterprises rather than individuals are the main donors. Useem (1981a, p. 31) argues that companies with a large number of multiple directors tend to be political donors, and that peripheral companies are less likely to support parties with funds. The data collected in the Company Analysis Project makes it possible to identify the mechanisms through which political donations were mobilised. Owing to a lack of information on political contributions in earlier years, analysis has been limited to the 1976 network.[13]

Many companies gave to two or more organisations, but there was little association between the size of their donations to the various organisations. Companies seemed to concentrate the bulk of their funds on favourite organisations, with relatively small donations to any others. Donations also tended to fluctuate from year to year. Nevertheless, two general conclusions can be drawn. First, donations to the Economic League (EL) and British United Industrialists (BUI) were closely related to network properties. EL had solid backing from the big four clearing banks, which provided 22 per cent of its total contributions income. BUI had solid backing from insurance companies. The industrial companies which gave to these two organisations were overwhelmingly drawn from the top 200, and there was some sectoral patterning of donations. Food, drink, and tobacco were especially important sources of income, though the brewers were far less important than conventionally depicted – from the big six brewers, only Allied Breweries and Imperial Group were among the top EL and BUI donors. Donations to both organisations were also systematically associated with structural features of the interlock network: 6 of the top 10 donors to EL and 4 of the top 10 donors to BUI were to be found among the 23 most central companies in the 1976 network (see table 6.2). Measuring centrality in global rather than local terms, 7 EL top donors and 3 BUI top donors were among the 20 most central companies. As only Commercial Union gave large sums to both organisations, a total of 9 of the most central companies were major backers of the two key business pressure groups. There were, of course, other factors at work, primarily the political ideology of dominant entrepreneurial capitalists in the firms they controlled: Tate & Lyle epitomised this among EL donors, as did Marks & Spencer among BUI donors. Nevertheless, the first general conclusion is that major donations to EL and BUI were systematically related to economic sector (banking, insurance, food, drink, tobacco), size, and network centrality.

The second general conclusion is that donations directly to

the Conservative Party were *not* systemic in the above sense. Party contributions were less associated with sector, size, and centrality; and they fluctuated more from year to year, depending on performance in government and opposition. Perhaps most importantly, it was discovered that party funds were very dependent upon the 'middleman' role played by merchant banks. None of the big banks or insurance companies were major donors to the party, and the top 23 donors included only 3 of the 23 most central companies (Hill Samuel, Rank Organization, Lucas). However, 4 of the 23 donors were merchant banks, which seemed to utilise their connections to central companies as ways of gaining access to potential contributors. Although there was no evidence on the intentions of the merchant bank directors, it is significant that they figured as major donors and that 14 of the big party donors were interlocked with the 23 most central companies. Once again, however, the role of ideology in entrepreneurial firms was important – this seemed to have played a role in the donations of Trafalgar House, British & Commonwealth Shipping, Taylor Woodrow, Cadbury Schweppes, S. Pearson, and three of the merchant banks themselves (Barings, Hambros, and Kleinwort Benson). Tate & Lyle was a major donor to both EL and the Conservatives (as well as being prominent in AIMS another business propaganda organisation), while Marks & Spencer was a major donor to both BUI and the Conservatives.

Looking further at the 'middlemen' in Conservative contributions, four merchant banks played a key role: Hill Samuel, Kleinwort Benson, Hambros, and Morgan Grenfell. Hill Samuel was interlocked with one of the other big party donors (Beecham) and was part of a web of connections to those central companies which interlocked with major donors. Kleinwort Benson was interlocked with two large donors (Trafalgar House, Cadbury Schweppes) and was interlocked with Commercial Union, a shareholder in Trafalgar House and a contributor to both EL and BUI. Hambros was interlocked with one major donor (Taylor Woodrow), and Morgan Grenfell with two (GKN, Fisons). The interlocks of these banks tended to be primary interlocks directed from the bank to the donor,[14] with the key executives being Sir Kenneth Keith[15] of Hill Samuel, R. A. Henderson of Kleinwort Benson, C. E. A. Hambro, and Philip Chappell of Morgan Grenfell. An interesting contrast was that the Hill Samuel board had a strong 'corporatist' character, while the boards of the other three banks were much more 'establishment' in character.

The above findings are reflected in the 'interlocks' between donors and political organisations – though these 'interlocks' were not always carried by the same people who carried the intercorporate interlocks. Complete information for 1976 was not available, but the 42-member Central Council of the EL in 1977 included 18 directors from the top 250 companies, 5 multiple directors and 13 single directors. These interlocks tied 27 of the top 250 companies to EL, and the 5 multiple directors included Philip Chappell of Morgan Grenfell.[16]

Three final discoveries, reinforcing the overall picture, concern companies with large numbers of multiple directors, the peripheral companies, and the relationship between donations and titles. A total of 18 of the companies with 7 or more multiple directors were also to be found amongst the 23 most central companies, leaving 6 which were not central. Of these 6, only 1 (S. Pearson) was a major political donor. Clearly, donations were a consequence more of centrality than simply the number of multiple directors. The ten most peripheral companies, as measured by sum distance, included no major donors to either EL or BUI, but did include one large Conservative donor (C. T. Bowring). Peripheral companies, by definition, had no interlocks with the most central companies. Data collected by *Labour Research* analysed donations over the period 1979–82 and the award of titles to directors of donor enterprises in the same period.[17] All 8 peerages and 20 of the 33 knighthoods awarded to directors in the period went to directors of donor enterprises. Although this cannot be directly related to Company Analysis Project data, because of the different time period, it does suggest that inner circle members were associated with donor enterprises and that they were likely to be the recipients of titles.

The relationship between political support and titleholding among the inner circle of the corporate directorate is a matter of considerable interest, as it points not only to their privileged role within the political system but also to a continued commitment to traditional values. Weiner (1981) has documented the way in which such values have inhibited economic development in Britain. The cultural image of rural England and the associated imagery of traditional social status have produced a widespread distaste for industrial management. Although participation in finance was easily reconcilable with 'the gentry ideal' (Weiner,

1981, p. 145), participation in manufacturing industry was not, and this division of social status was reinforced by the separation of banking from industry which emerged in the 1870s. The development of industry was handicapped and distorted, 'and a vicious circle of declining relative profitability was created that continued through the twentieth century' (Weiner, 1981, p. 129; see also Nairn, 1977; Bonnett, 1982). Despite the fusion of banking and industry which has developed during the course of the century, such traditional attitudes have persisted and have official codification in the hierarchy of titles. Whether such attitudes can, in fact, be seen as a major contributor to Britain's economic decline will be taken up in the following chapter.

NOTES

1. The work of Wright (1980) and Wright et al. (1982) is an important attempt to demarcate the boundaries of this class and to distinguish it from those who man the subordinate 'supervisory apparatus'.
2. It should be noted, however, that the total number of multiple directors increased consistently from 260 in 1899 to 347 in 1919. The number of interlocked companies remained virtually constant: 140 in 1899 and 143 in 1919.
3. For a comparison of 1935 and 1965, see also Dooley (1969). On data for 1970, see Smith (1970) and Smith and Desfosses (1972).
4. For a contrary view, see CDE (1980). For studies on Canada, see Clement (1975), Carroll (1982), Carroll et al. (1982), Smith and Tepperman (1974), and Clement (1975).
5. On the general concept of social circles, see Kadushin (1968).
6. The very small number of people with more than six directorships makes it impossible to draw any conclusions from the apparent reversal at this level.
7. In this instance primary interest was operationalised on the basis of the business address given in the *Directory of Directors*.
8. In matrix mathematics the original rectangular incidence matrix (enterprises × directors) can be converted into either an adjacency matrix for its rows (the network of relations between enterprises) or an adjacency matrix for its columns (the network of relations between directors). Thus in the graph theretical representation of the adjacency matrix the original 'points' can be transformed into 'lines' in the dual, and vice versa.
9. Thus, directors with only one directorship will still be involved in the meetings network because they 'meet' all those who sit on the

same board. Measured density would be very low because of the large size of the network.

10. Five of the 1976 most central directors were involved in multiple meetings.

11. Three of the six without titles owed their position in the network solely to the fact that they represented their base bank in the financial consortium FFI, which was jointly run by the clearing banks.

12. This total includes the Bank of England and the Scottish banks, but not merchant banks and discount houses.

13. *Labour Research* publishes regular lists of donors, which were used in the present analysis.

14. The line between Hill Samuel and Beecham had a multiplicity two and was primary in each direction as the chief executive of Beecham was a director of Hill Samuel. The line between Trafalgar House and Kleinwort Benson was induced by Sir Francis Sandilands of the Commercial Union. On Hill Samuel, see Sampson (1979) and also Francis (1968), Beecham (1944), and Lazell (1975).

15. Keith was the son-in-law of a former chairman of the Conservative Party (by his first wife) and sat on numerous public boards. He was knighted by Wilson in 1969 and received a peerage from Thatcher in 1981.

16. The other four were Sir David Barran, Lord Erroll, J. P. R. Glyn, and Sir Gerard Thorley.

17. *Labour Research*, December 1983.

CHAPTER SIX

The Banks:
Problems of Influence and Power

The model of finance capital points to the special role played by the banks and other financial intermediaries, and in works which use the model of bank control, these agents are seen as the most powerful in the corporate system. Indeed, the prevailing view of bank interlocking in much research on intercorporate relations has been that banks are the controlling centres of 'financial groups' or 'interest groups' of associated enterprises. Such a claim involves a number of distinct assertions. First, it requires that there be close connections between financial and non-financial enterprises through commercial, capital, and personal relations. Second, it requires that the network of intercorporate relations be structured into distinct cliques and clusters centred on the large financials. Third, it requires that the central financials subordinate the other members of their cliques to their own interests. This chapter will examine each of these contentions, in order to arrive at an assessment of the actual role played by financial intermediaries in the British intercorporate network.

THE FUSION OF BANKING AND INDUSTRY

The close connections which developed between banking and industry in Britain have been documented at various points in this book. By 1976 the two sectors were closely integrated in both finance and personnel. To this extent, there is considerable evidence to support the first of the claims cited above. Ingham (1984), however, has questioned the claim that finance capital emerged in Britain and argues instead that there is a separation between 'the City' and 'industry'. In arguing this, Ingham is echoing a widely held view of the British economy (see, for example, Aaronovitch, 1961). But Ingham raises certain very important objections to the conventional view of City/industry relations. In particular, he agues that it is based upon an inadequate concept of 'the City'. Banks, and especially the merchant banks, have not been involved in the kind of organisational fusion depicted in Hilferding's (1910) model of finance capital. Ingham argues that they have acted simply as intermediaries and have not become directly involved in production. To this he adds the claim that the merchant banks should not be seen as forms of 'banking capital' but as forms of 'commercial capital'. Their main activities concern the buying and selling of commodities – the money, stocks and shares, raw materials, and services which are necessary to further the international trading activities of the City of London (see Hobson, 1957; Ferris, 1960; McRae and Cairncross, 1973; Spiegelberg, 1973; Clarke, 1979).

Some important points can be raised against Ingham's argument. In concentrating his attention on merchant banks, undoubtedly important enterprises in the City, he underestimates the role of clearing banks and insurance companies in the provision of loan capital. These enterprises are concerned with banking capital as much as, if not more than, they are with commercial capital. They are major agents within the City, and Ingham's concern with the merchant banks is therefore misleading. Perhaps more important is his underestimation of the organisational fusion which has taken place between banking and industry. Large manufacturers, for example, have increasingly become units of finance capital as they have had to enter into stock exchange dealings in the issue of their own shares and, most importantly, as they have used their corporate assets for activities in commerce and banking. Such enterprises have become major currency dealers in the money markets in attempting to safeguard themselves against floating exchange rates. Similarly, an enterprise which manages its own pension fund, rather than delegating this role to a bank, becomes a major dealer on the stock exchange. Organisational fusion can also occur through the uniting of the various form of capital and their associated practices in intercorporate groupings.

Links between banks, insurance companies, and manufacturers may have fallen short of complete merger. The central concern of this book has been to document the variety of intercorporate relations which can exist, and proponents of the model of bank control have seen such intercorporate groupings as basic to their analyses. Finance capital exists in and through such groupings as well as simply in unified enterprises.

To show the contours of finance capital in Britain it is necessary to document the changing composition of the financial sector itself and the nature of the relationships between financial and non-financial enterprises. The top 50 financials comprise a selection of the largest enterprises in each of a number of sectors: clearing banks,[1] merchant banks, insurance and assurance companies, British banks operating overseas, building societies, investment trusts, and property companies. The decision to study the top 50 of each year means that the changing balance between these various sectors was, in part, a reflection of the selection criteria (see Appendix), but certain conclusions can be drawn. A major feature of the period 1904 to 1976 has been the concentration of clearing banking. In 1904 the data set included 17 English clearing banks, while that for 1976 included just 4. Between 1909 and 1918 a spate of mergers created the outlines of the 'big five' and the 'little two' which dominated banking through the interwar period and up to another merger wave in 1968–9. Similarly, the number of Scottish banks declined over the period from 8 to 3, mainly as a result of takeovers by English banks.[2] Alongside this trend, many of the 'private' banks of 1904 – those which had few branches, very wealthy customers, and were not members of the London clearing house – were gradually amalgamated into the big joint stock banks. Those private banks which had merchant banking activities gradually came to specialise around these, just as many 'merchants' become merchant bankers. As a result, the top 50 of 1976 included 10 merchant banks and no private banks. The number of other financial companies also grew over the period, and this was reflected in their appearance in the top 50 in place of the disappearing banks. Building societies and investment trusts had become very important by 1938, and in the postwar period it was necessary to include also property companies (Marriott, 1967), unit trust groups, and various specialist credit banks.

Connections between the top 50 financials and the top 200 non-financials grew over the period studied. In 1904 there were 6 uninterlocked financials, mainly the private and merchant banks, and in 1938 there were 7, the decline in private banking being masked by the inclusion of 6 building societies. By 1976 there were just 3 uninterlocked financials – 2 building societies and

Pearl Assurance. Large deposit and collecting enterprises, therefore, tended to have a low propensity to interlock in both 1938
and 1976. The financial sector of 1976 was highly connected
internally: 43 of the financials were interlocked into a single large
component with a density of 0.096. Table 6.1 shows that a
number of large non-financials had numerous distance two

Table 6.1 Connections Between Non-Financials Through Financial
Interlocks, 1976

	Interlocks with non-financials	*Distance two connections with non-financials*
British Petroleum	14 *Fw 5*	60
Delta Metal	7	59
Imperial Chemical Industries	8	54
General Electric	3	51
Rio Tinto Zinc	4	44
IBM (UK)	4	42
Imperial Group	4	42
Shell	4	41
Dunlop Holdings	4	32
Rothmans International	4	32

connections with other non-financials through their financial
interlocks. BP, for example, was interlocked with 14 industrials
and 5 financials, but its interlocks connected it with 60 non-
financials. Financial enterprises had become all important to the
cohesiveness of the intercorporate network.

The role of financials in intercorporate networks has generally
been studied through the analysis of centrality. Although it has
been shown that there was no real structural 'centre' in the British
network in any of the periods studied, it was nevertheless possible
to identify those enterprises which held individually central
positions. Figure 6.1 presents a schematic view of the two main
concepts of centrality. Local centrality refers to the immediate
connections of an enterprise and is typically measured by its
adjacency. A central enterprise, therefore, has a large number of
distance one neighbours. In figure 6.1, A is the most central
enterprise with a centrality score of five. Global centrality takes
account of the overall connectedness of an enterprise, not simply
its direct interlocks, and is generally measured by the 'sum
distance' of an enterprise. Sum distance is the total distance

Figure 6.1   Types of Centrality

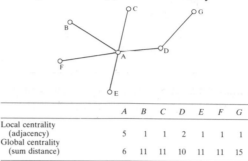

	A	B	C	D	E	F	G
Local centrality (adjacency)	5	1	1	2	1	1	1
Global centrality (sum distance)	6	11	11	10	11	11	15

between an enterprise and all other enterprises, and the most central enterprise in a network is the one with the lowest sum distance score.[3] Referring again to figure 6.1, A is the globally most central enterprise. It can be seen, however, that the measure of global centrality brings out the peripheral position of G. Although G and C each have one interlock, G is much further removed from the core of the network. Both measures are based on raw adjacencies, and the actual scores, therefore, reflect the size of the network. Standardised measures have been investigated by Berkowitz (1982, p. 19) and Bearden et al. (1975), but both studies found a high correlation with the unstandardised scores.[4] In comparing networks of a similar size, therefore, adjacency is an adequate basis for centrality measures.

Centrality is often compared with 'betweenness'. While global centrality expresses the extent to which an enterprise is connected within the network as a whole, betweenness refers to whether or not an enterprise can be considered as an intermediary. A widely used measure of betweenness is the 'rush', which is based on a calculation of the number of times a particular enterprise lies between others. In figure 6.1, for example, D lies between A and G and A lies between 11 pairs, none of the other enterprises acting as an intermediary.[5] In the Company Analysis Project it was found that local centrality, global centrality, and betweenness were closely associated with one another, and this is reflected in the artificial data in figure 6.1.

Table 6.2 lists the ten enterprises with the highest local centrality in each of the periods studied, and table 6.3 puts their centrality scores into context. It can be seen that all 10 of the central enterprises in both 1938 and 1976 had 16 or more interlocks, while only 2 of the 1904 enterprises interlocked at this

Table 6.2 The Ten Most Central Enterprises, 1904–76

1904		1938		1976	
Co.	*Adjacency*	*Co.*	*Adjacency*	*Co.*	*Adjacency*
Nth Br. & Merc.	18	Lloyds Bank	33	Lloyds Bank	28
LNW Railway	17	Midland Bank	27	Bank of England	26
Royal Exchange	14	LMS Railway	26	Midland Bank	21
Bank of England	13	Gt Western Rly	24	BP	19
Nth Eastern Rly	13	Shell	21	Barclays Bank	18
Dunderland Iron	12	Bank of England	21	Commercial Union	18
GKN	11	Sun Insurance	19	National	
Forth Bridge Rly	11	LNE Railway	18	Westminster Bank	18
Union of L & S Bk	11	Westminster Bank	18	Finance For Ind.	17
GN & Piccadilly	11	Venezuelan Oil	17	Delta Metal	16
				Hill Samuel	16

level. The main change in the level of interlocking was an increase between 1904 and 1938 in the proportion with 6 or more interlocks, this being sustained between 1938 and 1976 only for those with 11 or more. Financials gradually became a more significant element among the 10 most central enterprises: 4 in 1904, 5 in 1938, and 8 in 1976. This increase was due mostly to the enhanced importance of clearing and specialist banks at the expense of railways. Despite the large absolute decline in the number of clearing banks, the number of central clearing banks increased from 1 in 1904 to 3 in 1938 and 4 in 1976. The striking feature of the lists is the altered position of railways. Four of the very large number of railways in 1904 were included among the 10 most central enterprises – 2 main-line railways, a bridge consor-

Table 6.3 Distribution of Connections, 1904–76

	No. of companies		
Adjacency	*1904*	*1938*	*1976*
0	53	49	61
1–5	148	116	112
6–10	39	63	54
11–15	8	12	13
16–20	2	4	7
over 20	0	6	3
Totals	250	250	250

tium, and an underground railway. The railway amalgamations which followed the First World War consolidated the position of the main-line railways, but there was a small fall in the total number of railways which were central. By 1976 the one remaining main-line railway did not hold a central position in the network. The position of the railways can be explained by the close association which developed between them and financials to meet the massive capital requirements of the expanding nineteenth-century railway system. The railways were the first enterprises to have to draw on large, anonymous bodies of shareholders on any scale, and the banks were able to provide access to this capital. At the same time, the banks sought representation on the railway boards in order to protect their own interests and to make the railway shares more marketable (Dixon, 1914). This relationship was broken by the nationalisation of the railways, which ceased to hold central network positions. The key to understanding centrality, therefore, is to understand the patterns of bank interlocking.

The overall patterns of bank interlocking have been presented in table 2.9. This shows that the numbers of both financial and non-financial interlocks of the London banks were higher in 1976 than in 1904 and that the average number of interlocks *per* bank increased from 4.4 in 1904 to 15.3 in 1938 and 16.6 in 1976. The City of London core of 1904 had extended its links to the whole of a diffuse national intercorporate network in which financial and non-financial enterprises were closely united. At the heart of the 1904 City core was the Bank of England, which operated *de facto* as a central bank but which was privately owned and recruited its directors from the merchant houses which held the bulk of its shares and comprised its main clients (Thomas, 1931; Clay, 1957; Giuseppi, 1966; Sayers, 1976). Only 2 of the 26 directors were not from a merchant or private banking background, and the 2 exceptions were both brewers. Most directors were merchants rather than bankers, though the boundaries between these two sectors had become very permeable, and families such as Arbuthnot, Campbell, Cunliffe, Gladstone, Lubbock, Baring, and Hambro represented long-standing family lines. The Bank had no executive directors and its interlocks were generated by 14 outsiders. Most of these multiple directors held only 1 other directorship in the top 250 and so the bank interlocked with 13 enterprises: 5 financial interlocks with private banks and insurance companies, and 8 non-financial interlocks with brewers, railways, merchants, and a shipper.[6] The major non-Quaker London clearing banks recruited their directors from a similar pool of merchants, and though they were not interlocked with the Bank of England or with one another they were connected through kinterlocks. The provincial banks generally had a higher proportion of directors from industrials, though many of their board positions were held by provincial merchants. The 'Quaker' banks – Barclays and Lloyds – were less mercantile in character and recruited from their controlling families and from provincial entrepreneurs.[7]

The Bank of England had a long-standing policy of not recruiting any of its directors from the clearing banks and discount houses, and its mercantile base was not altered until 1918, and then only slightly, after an internal inquiry which recommended greater recruitment from British banks operating in India, the colonies, and South America. By 1938, 3 executives had been granted board seats, and the total number of interlocks had increased to 21. Almost one-third of the directors were merchants or merchant bankers and only two directors came from manufacturing or heavy industry. Nevertheless, the Bank had become more widely connected, its 13 non-financial interlocks including 2 from coal, 1 each from textiles and cars, and 2 from public-sector energy and transport undertakings. While 3 of the big 5 clearing banks continued to recruit from their traditional sources, Midland and Lloyds had become overwhelmingly 'industrial' in character. National Provincial and Westminster still recruited from the establishment, the two banks being closely kinterlocked through the intermarried Hogg and Campbell families, and Barclays still recruited from the Quaker cousin-hood.

The Bank of England was nationalised in 1946, which led to some changes in its role, and in its board size and composition. During the 1950s it recruited its first clearing-banker, a director of the Royal Bank of Scotland, but this did not become a precedent for other appointments. In 1976 the Bank had 26 interlocks in the top 250, 20 of these being with non-financials. More than half of the non-financial interlocks were with manufacturers, and a number of others were with enterprises in construction, transport, and mining. It was striking that a number of the industrialists sitting on the Bank of England board were from enterprises subject to family control or influence and were members of the dominant families themselves – this was true of Cadbury, Weir, two (unrelated) Laings, and Pilkington.[8] The prime exception to this generalisation was Lord Robens of Vickers, a former trade-union leader and Labour politician. Clearing-bank interlocks in 1976 showed a majority of non-financial interlocks in all of the big four except Barclays. Lloyds and Midland continued to show a very high proportion of non-financial interlocks.[9]

By 1976 the banks, insurance companies, traders, and manu-facturers had come together in an extensive national network. Finance capital was a reality. Within this organisational fusion of forms of capital, the banks played a key role. They constituted the commanding peaks of the intercorporate network, and the overall structure depended upon them. This supports the first requirement of the model of bank control discussed at the beginning of this chapter, and it is now possible to turn to the second requirement.

THE EMPIRES OF HIGH FINANCE

Supporters of the model of bank control point to two presumed features of the intercorporate network: bank centrality and bank groups. The analysis of centrality presented so far must be extended into a consideration of the forms and causes of centrality and the role of central enterprises in the formation of cliques and clusters. In an attempt to specify the form of modern bank centrality in the USA, Mizruchi (1982) and Mintz and Schwartz (1981b) have employed a distinction between hubs, bridges, and peaks. A 'hub' is a locally central point which has a high proportion of its interlocks with points which are less central than itself. By contrast, a 'bridge' has a high proportion of its interlocks with points which are more central than itself. In figure 6.1, A is a hub and D is a bridge. If G was the hub of an array similar to that of A, then the bridging role of D would be even more marked (see also Mintz and Schwartz, 1979; Mintz, 1977; Berkowitz, 1982, p. 114). A hub might be expected to play an active, coordinating role within a network, while a bridge might be seen as a more passive intermediary. A bridge, therefore, is a 'broker', as it can reduce transaction costs by reducing the number of connections between points. But this role need not be deliberately contrived. Any random variation in interlocking which happens to produce a bridge will thereby produce cost efficiencies. A broker role will tend to persist both through the figurational dynamics of the network and through deliberate emulation (Aldrich, 1982). A 'peak' is a point which is more central than any of the points to which it is connected, but which need not be central in the network as a whole. Thus, point A in figure 6.1 is a central peak, but peaks can also be found towards the periphery of a network.

Mintz and Schwartz argue that American banks and insurance companies can be understood as hubs, but that only banks appear as peaks. Thus, insurance company groupings are interpreted as subordinate to bank groupings. By contrast, they suggest, central non-financials can be seen as bridges connecting the various parts of the network. The British evidence does not show this pattern to the same degree. In 1976 a clear contrast could be drawn between banking peaks and insurance bridges, but non-financials were found among both hubs and bridges. There was, however, a slight tendency for non-financial bridges to be smaller than non-financial hubs. It was further discovered that the hub centrality of the large non-financials was due to their interlocks with banks, as was shown in table 6.1. It can be argued, however, that a clearer understanding of network centrality can be gained from an analysis which disregards loose interlocks and investigates the structure of the network of primary interlocks.

The network of primary interlocks contained 1 large component of 156 enterprises with a density of 0.023, and its 12 most central members are shown in table 6.4. Three-quarters of the

Table 6.4   Centrality in the Network of Primary Interlocks, 1976

Company	*Adjacency*
Lloyds Bank	14
Midland Bank	13
Bank of England	12
Hill Samuel	12
Barclays Bank	11
National Westminster Bank	11
Commercial Union	10
Imperial Chemical Industries	9
Rothmans International	8
Vickers	8
N. M. Rothschild	8
Lazard	8

central enterprises were financials. Although the Bank of England and the London clearing banks appeared as peaks, the merchant banks were important hubs in the network. This can be further illustrated by examining some of the differences between primary financial and primary non-financial interlocks. Those interlocks which were created by inside directors of financials, disregarding those induced, tied 100 companies into a large component,[10] but the network of primary non-financial interlocks was fragmented into 11 components. Table 6.5 shows that merchant banks were especially central in the primary financial network: Hill Samuel had 12 such interlocks, N. M. Rothschild had 8, and Morgan Grenfell and Mercury Securities had 7 each. Bank of England and Lloyds, the two most central enterprises overall, were not especially central in terms of primary financial

Table 6.5   Centrality: Primary Financial and Non-Financial, 1976

Primary financial adjacency		*Primary non-financial adjacency*	
Hill Samuel	12	Vickers	8
National Westminster Bank	10	Imperial Chemical	7
Midland Bank	10	Rothmans	7
Barclays Bank	8	Fisons	6
N. M. Rothschild	8	Delta Metal	5
Commercial Union	7	British Petroleum	5
Morgan Grenfell	7	Assoc. Portland	5
Mercury Securities	7	EMI	5

interlocks. These two banks tended to recruit directors of non-financial enterprises rather more often than they placed their own directors on other boards. The British network of 1976 had a particularly high proportion of primary interlocks (almost half). In the rest of Europe and in the USA many more interlocks were generated by outside directors, and in France and the USA the majority of primary interlocks were generated by non-financial executives. In Britain financial and non-financial executives contributed equally to the network of primary interlocks, though much of its cohesiveness was due to financial insiders (Stokman et al., 1984; Cuyvers and Meeusen, 1976 and 1978; Schönwitz and Weber, 1980).[11]

The network of primary interlocks in 1976 consisted of a number of moderately sized groupings held together by executives of non-financial enterprises, all of these being tied into a large group of 100 enterprises by financial executives. The financial executives came mainly from clearing and merchant banks, and the overall 'peak' centrality of clearing banks reflected their positions in the network of primary financial interlocks, their tendency to recruit non-financial executives to their boards, and the presence of large numbers of outside directors.

Supporters of the model of bank control and the concept of 'financial groups' have searched for the existence of cliques and clusters within which banks play key coordinating roles.[12] A typical view is that of Knowles (1973), which claims that the American economy was organised into a system of pyramid-like centres of power. Within each pyramid a group of wealthy families were represented on the board and among the major stockholders of a bank and pursued their own interests through the links which they were able to establish with other enterprises. Through mutual shareholdings and interlocking directorships, through the use of bank and insurance-company control over credit, and through the use of bank trust departments the allied families were able to control many non-financial enterprises and to influence numerous others.

Attempts to discover such interest groups have generally employed clique and clustering techniques, and it is assumed that these correspond to interest groups. Mizruchi (1982) has correctly pointed out that because the mathematical criterion used for clustering is the determinant of the groups which can be identified in the network, it is necessary to choose a mathematical technique which is appropriate to the model from which we derive the concept of 'interest group'. Typically, he argues, researchers have incorrectly regarded techniques of clique and cluster identification as theoretically neutral ways of identifying interest groups. Against this he argues that the interest groups discovered in many American studies – geographical and regional in character – may be a consequence of the fact that most of the commonly employed techniques search for zones of high density and low centralisation. The implicit model is that the interest groups (i.e., the cliques) are groups of similar corporations; and this implicit model runs counter to the explicit model of bank control. By contrast, the concept employed by Knowles starts out from the presumed inequality of enterprises within an interest group: the bank at its centre is held to dominate the activities of the companies within its group. Mizruchi concludes that any attempt to test for the existence of bank-centred zones must use a technique based upon a centrality measure.

The problem with Mizruchi's position is that it leads to a circularity: the model predicts the existence of bank groups, and so a technique that is designed to optimise the chances of discovering them is used. If no such groups are found, then clearly the model must be reconsidered. But the discovery of bank-centred cliques cannot necessarily be taken as confirming evidence for the model. An alternative strategy, therefore, would be to make the theoretical underpinnings of the techniques explicit, and to use a variety of techniques in the research. This strategy would push the problem of theoretical interpretation to the forefront of the analysis and can be illustrated by considering the question of types of interlock. Use of primary interlocks alone in clique detection involves definite theoretical assumptions about the relative importance of interlocks carried by executives and those carried by non-executives. If a direction is imputed to primary interlocks, then the question of the 'control' which these executives can exercise is raised. The decision as to how to detect cliques is, therefore, a theoretical decision. Numerous other theoretical and technical problems arise in this debate, but they are best considered alongside the empirical evidence produced in studies concerned with interest-group formation.

Drawing on the American data set described in the previous chapter, Mizruchi shows that the 1904 list of central companies in the American network included numerous railways together with insurance companies and large industrials as well as clearing banks. When centrality was recalculated in terms of a modified index for directed lines, then the financials rose in importance relative to the railways and industrials. Within the financial sector itself the recalculation resulted in a marked increase in the centrality of investment banks (Mizruchi, 1982, pp. 62–8). This parallels the British findings on merchant banks in 1976. Mizruchi suggests that the high centrality of railways (and perhaps insurance companies) was due to induced and secondary interlocks. Looking only at primary interlocks, and taking account of direction, the rank order of centrality changed significantly. Mizruchi discovered, however, that the centrality of investment banks was not associated with clique formation in the period 1904 to 1919. The money trust was not sharply divided into distinct interest groups of the classical kind. In 1904 the companies were formed into a single large clique, even in the network of directed primary interlocks. This clique was centred on the investment bank of J. P. Morgan, and Mizruchi argues that this supports the conventional impression of the money trust: an alliance of the personal interests of Harriman, Schiff, Rockefeller, and Stillman under the leadership of Morgan. Morgan had consciously aimed at creating a community of interest in which the rivalries of the various groups could be subordinated to their common interests (Mizruchi, 1982, pp. 145–6). This system of multilateral interlocks within the banking community continued to both 1912 and 1919. The decline in interlocking in this period did not result in a break-up of the trust (Mizruchi, 1982, p. 148).

Much of the research on interest groups has concentrated on the year 1935. Sweezy (1939) identified eight interest groups on the basis of what he termed a significant element of common control. He identified the groups intuitively on the basis of primary interlocks, multiple interlocks, and financial participations. A number of these groups were centred on banks or families such as Morgan, Mellon, and Rockefeller, while others comprised mainly regional links. But the various groups overlapped with one another rather than forming tight, exclusive groupings. This study was replicated by Allen, who used the more systematic procedures of factor analysis and identified ten groups on the basis of interlock data alone (Allen, 1974 and 1978a; see also Galaskiewicz and Wasserman, 1981). The 10 groups identified by Allen were very similar to the 8 identified by Sweezy, but the differences between the two studies show how the identification of interest groups is highly sensitive to differences in methods and procedures. Using his preferred method of 'peak analysis', Mizruchi investigated the structure of the 1935 network of primary lines. The 167 companies were formed into 4 components and 37 isolates, the largest component of 122 companies comprising a major clique with 3 peaks. Mizruchi failed to find any evidence of the sharp cleavages between groups which figured so prominently in the analyses of Allen and Sweezy. He argues that there had simply been a slight break-up of the 1904–19 pattern, corresponding to the decline of Morgan relative to rivals such as Mellon and Rockefeller (Mizruchi, 1982, pp. 152, 170; see also Kotz, 1978, pp. 51–8. It might be suggested that Mizruchi was correct to point to the absence of tight, bank-dominated interest groups, but that Allen was correct in identifying loose regional groups. The high degree of overlap among the cliques identified by Allen and Sweezy is, in fact, indicative of the absence of tight, exclusive groups.

A number of studies have investigated clique formation in the

1960s. Bearden et al. (1975) found evidence of clustering in the network of primary interlocks of 1962, but not in the network of all interlocks. Dooley (1969) postulated the existence of 15 'local interest groups' in 1965, of which some were similar to those identified by Sweezy 30 years before. Once again the groups – identified on the basis of multiple lines – were not sharply distinguished from one another: the New York group, comprising what were formerly the separate Morgan and Rockefeller groups, overlapped with many of the other groups (Dooley, 1969, p. 319). Using multidimensional scaling on part of the Patman data, Levine (1972) found evidence of bank-centred groups in 1966. Similarly, a study for 1970 identified ten geographical groups which were less tightly knit and less associated with financial participations and credit than in 1935 (Allen, 1974, 1978a–b).

The most adequate interpretation of these recent data is undoubtedly that of Bearden et al., who argue that a central, stable group of banks and insurance companies dominated the American money market, with the commercial banks acting as 'hubs' by interlocking with less central companies and with regional banks. The regional groupings identifiable in the net-work of primary interlocks were forged together into a cohesive national system through secondary interlocks (Bearden et al., 1975; Mintz and Schwartz, 1981a, pp. 95, 98–9). Mizruchi's data for 1974 show seven overlapping cliques, and he concludes with a very similar interpretation: 'the concept of separate, specific interest groups is not very relevant for understanding the American corporate system' (Mizruchi, 1982, p. 174). Such cliques as existed were embedded in a more diffuse national structure; interest groups were not, therefore, the main axes of corporate power. New York lay at the heart of a national network, within which loose regional groups were embedded. Regional groups were 'unsegregated areas of relative density in an otherwise integrated network' (Mintz and Schwartz, 1981b, p. 865).

A technique designed specifically to highlight the existence of bank-centred interest groups failed to produce the kind of groups which the model of bank control requires. It would seem that bank control did not exist in the USA. In order to see whether this was also true of Britain a similar clique detection method was applied to the 1976 network of primary interlocks. A search was made for two-cliques of minimum size ten, on the assumption that a bank group would have to include at least ten members to be of any importance. A two-clique is a group within which all members are mutually connected at distance two (the points A, B, C, D, E, and F in figure 6.1 comprise a two-clique). This analysis discovered 8 cliques in the 1976 network, ranging in size from 10 to 15 members (see table 6.6). The cliques were not, however, sharply divided. Although 53 enterprises could be allocated unambiguously to one or another of the 8 cliques, 20 enterprises were members of 2 or more cliques. Nevertheless, an important pattern was discovered. Each clique contained a hub, a focal enterprise around which its exclusive members were connected, and most interlocks ran between the hub and its clique members rather than among the members themselves.[13] Those enterprises which were members of two or more cliques included many of those which appeared as bridges in the overall network. These multi-clique members included 3 banks affiliated to the big four, 1 insurance company, and 8 non-financials. The most important multi-clique members, however, were the 8 hubs, and it can be seen that these comprised the Bank of England, the big four clearers, 1 insurance company, 1 merchant bank, and 1 industrial. All except ICI were among the 10 most central enterprises (table 6.2), and ICI was ranked at number 11. The overlap between the Barclays, ICI, and Commercial Union cliques was particularly great, and they could reasonably be considered as a large cluster in which Barclays took the leading part. Similarly, the Midland and Hill Samuel cliques were allied through the close association of them both with Eagle Star and Shell. The legitimacy of grouping the cliques in this way is apparent from an analysis of triads in the network of primary interlocks. A triad is a set of three points which are mutually connected, and they can be considered the building blocks of complex structures. The large component contained 19 triads, of which 6 contained Barclays and 6 contained Midland Bank. Two of the Barclays triads contained Commerical Union, 2 contained ICI, and 1 contained both of these. Similarly, the Midland Bank triads involved various combinations of Rothmans, Eagle Star, Rank, and Dunlop. There are good grounds, therefore, for considering the primary interlock network to have been organised around 3 cliques and 2 clusters: Lloyds, National Westminster, Bank of England, Midland/Hill Samuel, and Barclays/ICI/Commercial Union.

In order to clarify the roles played by the banks in this structure

Table 6.6   Cliques in the Network, 1976

Clique	Hub	Density	Exclusive members
1.	Lloyds Bank	0.143	Lucas Industries, Fisons, Lead Industries, Ocean Transport, Grindlays Bank, National & Commercial Bank
2.	Midland Bank	0.209	Rank Organisation, Standard Chartered Bank, Rowntree, Clydesdale Bank, English Property, Allied Breweries, UDT, Rothmans
3.	Bank of England	0.167	Pilkington, Laing, United Biscuits, Cadbury Schweppes, Mercury Securities, Rothschild, Hambros, Rio Tinto Zinc
4.	Hill Samuel	0.179	Beecham, Rolls-Royce, British Leyland, Stone-Platt, BPB Industries, Alcan, Marchwiel
5.	Barclays Bank	0.258	Agricultural Mortgage, GKN, Tozer Kemsley, Booker McConnell, Union Discount, R. Fleming
6.	National Westminster Bank	0.167	General Accident, Associated Portland Cement, IBM, Guardian Royal Exchange, Touche Remnant, Redland, Powell Duffryn
7.	Commercial Union	0.218	Debenhams, Trafalgar House, Barings, P & O, Kleinwort Benson, Plessey, British Steel
8.	Imperial Chemical	0.244	National Enterprise Board, Ford, Royal Insurance, Carrington Viyella, Reed International

Note: [a] Measurement of clique density was based on all clique members and not simply on the exclusive members.

a further clique analysis was carried out after deleting all the interlocks generated by directors of the 4 London and 3 Scottish clearing banks.[14] In this way the clearing banks were artificially removed from the primary interlock network. Just under three-quarters of the lines remained in the denuded network, and 165 enterprises were contained in its large component. Deletion of the banks considerably reduced the centrality of Finance For Industry, ICI, and Delta Metal, all of which owed their centrality to those of their directors who sat on bank boards. By contrast, BP, Tube Investments, and P & O owed most of their centrality to directors unconnected with banks. The peculiar network role of the Bank of England is brought out by the fact that its centrality was not at all reduced by the deletion of the banks, because the Bank recruited no clearing bank directors to its own board. The Bank acted as a central forum in the business network, bringing together a number of prominent entre-preneurial capitalists from industry and merchant banking. The denuded network contained only three two-cliques of size ten or more: the Bank of England, Hill Samuel, and Commercial Union cliques, each of which was dependent on its focal enterprise for its structure. The three focal enterprises were 'cut-points', points whose removal would increase the fragmentation of the net-work,[15] and the fact that they only became cut-points after deletion of the banks suggests that some of the cohesion of their spheres was due to interlocks which clique members had to banks. That is to say, the members of a clique tended to have similar patterns of interlocking outside the clique. It was striking that the original ICI clique was almost completely dependent upon bank interlocks, as deletion of the banks led to its disappearance.[16]

The artificial removal of bank directors from the network of primary interlocks made little difference to the number and size of components, but it almost completely disrupted the clique structure. The bank-centred cliques and the industrial-centred clique disappeared, and the remaining cliques became less cohesive. Only the Bank of England clique retained its original size and significance. It can be concluded that the primary interlock network was structured into a Bank of England central forum, 2 bank cliques, and 2 bank clusters, the latter involving alliances between bank cliques and semi-autonomous merchant bank, insurance, and industrial cliques. The Bank of England and the big four clearing banks dominated the network.

The evidence on the second requirement of the model of bank control is not clear-cut. While the network does seem to have been structured into bank-centred groupings, these did not comprise the sharply divided 'empires' required by the model. As in the USA, the bank-centred groups overlapped through numerous bridging enterprises, and the degree of overlap was even greater when secondary interlocks were taken into account. If the banks were all powerful, they did not exercise this power within separate and rival empires of high finance.

BANK CONTROL AND BANK INFLUENCE

The third requirement of the model of the bank control is that banks should actually exercise their power by subordinating clique and cluster members to their interests. The most influential statement of this view has been that of Fitch and Oppenheimer, who extend a critique of Berle and Means (1932) into a general model of bank control in the USA. They argue that the utilities, railways, and industrials of the 1920s which Berle and Means classified as subject to management control were, in fact, characterised by boards dominated by outside banking interests such as J. P. Morgan. The remnants of the money trust constituted the self-perpetuating 'managerial' oligarchies (Fitch and Oppenheimer, 1970a, pp. 79–80). By the 1960s the shareholding and credit base of the financial intermediaries and bank trust departments had created an even more secure basis for bank control, and this was further enhanced by the concentration of banking. The result was a sharp move away from share dispersal (Fitch and Oppenheimer, 1970a, pp. 92–9), and though Fitch and Oppenheimer characterise this as minority control,[17] it is best seen as control through a constellation of interests. This becomes the basis for such mechanisms of bank control as the voting power of the shareholding trust departments, and the external funding of investment (see also Kotz, 1978, pp. 61–3).

Fitch and Oppenheimer argue (1970b, p. 97) that their picture of the American network in the 1960s corresponds to the model of finance capital presented by Hilferding (1910) and Lenin (1916). They seem to suggest that the American network comprised a number of overlapping financial syndicates which created a loose, decentralised network in which rivalry and cooperation coexisted. This image is not, however, made explicit, and Fitch and Oppenheimer concentrate most of their attention on the issue of bank control *per se*, rather than looking at the structure of intercorporate relations within which such control might be exercised. The tenor of their argument is that the 'socialisation of the credit system' enabled the banks to initiate 'an embryonic system of capitalistic planning' (1970c, pp. 75–6). But at this point they depart from the arguments of Hilferding (1910). Rather than postulating the unity of interest between banks and industry which was central to Hilferding's position, Fitch and Oppenheimer claim a fundamental divergence of interest. They argue that bank profits are a subtraction from 'corporate profits' and that, therefore, there is no unity of interest between the two sectors (1970b, p. 85). Entrepreneurial and internal capitalists in industry attempt to fund their investments internally and without making capital issues, in order to keep 'bankers' out of their companies. The interests of 'industrial capital' are to plough back any profits and to secure a low rate of borrowing. The interests of 'banking capital' are to ensure a high dividend pay-out and high lending. Bank dominance reduces the funds available for plough-back and so forces industrials to borrow from them. Banks become crucially important in determining the movement of capital from one area to another because they can force an enterprise to change or diversify its activities where internal management would be unwilling to do this. Banks are also able to force 'reciprocity' trading (preferential purchases and sales) on the enterprises with which they deal, such reciprocities occurring within the bank-centred interest groups.

Although there is much of importance in Fitch and Oppenheimer's analysis, certain of its central tenets must be questioned. Fitch and Oppenheimer fail to distinguish between 'bank capital' and 'finance capital' and so they wrongly assume that the thesis of finance capital involves the dominance of 'banks' over 'industry'. Strictly, bank capital should be regarded as capital invested in enterprises engaged mainly in the making of money loans. On the other hand, finance capital represents the fusion of bank capital and industrial capital (O'Connor, 1971, p. 119). The concept of finance capital does not, of course, preclude a division of function between such institutional forms of finance capital as banks, pension funds, retailers, and manufacturers. But it does require that, at some level, there be an organisational fusion of capital in all its forms. Fitch and

Oppenheimer overlook this by glossing over the distinctions between 'finance', 'financial', and 'banking'. For this reason, Sweezy (1971, p. 31) has argued that the concept of finance capital should be replaced by that of monopoly capital.

Having depicted banks as the dominant enterprises, Fitch and Oppenheimer go on to depict them as parasitic predators upon industrial enterprises. They argue that banks exploit industrials by excluding industrial executives from the effective control of their own enterprises. O'Connor has argued against this by claiming that no capitalist interest can disregard the need to produce profitably. Banks cannot simply drain industrials of resources for there would then be no profits for the banks to appropriate in the future (O'Connor, 1971, pp. 130–31). O'Connor states that 'no financial capitalist group in its right mind would engage in any activity that might have ruinous consequences for the productivity of its profitable enterprises' (O'Connor, 1971, p. 132). This may, of course, occur in particular instances, but it would run counter to the interests of banking capital to pursue it as a general strategy.

The opposition of 'banks' and 'industry' also depends upon a misleading view of corporate management. Fitch and Oppenheimer equate 'managerial capitalists' (i.e., internal capitalists) with 'industrial capital', and so see managers as having different policies from those of the bankers who epitomise finance capital. They suggest, for example, that internal capitalists are less likely to diversify their enterprises because they are recruited from within a particular industry and so see the economic world from that particular standpoint. By contrast, finance capitalists are supposed to move wherever profits are greatest. On empirical grounds the claim that executives are always recruited from within particular industries can be questioned, although it may be true that entrepreneurial capitalists in family firms have failed to diversify (see chapter 4 above). But the general point is that executive management *per se* is not unwilling to diversity: 'modern management has every interest in expanding surplus value in *any* line of business that offers opportunities for maximum profits' (O'Connor, 1971, p. 130).

Fitch and Oppenheimer place great emphasis on the concentration of voting rights represented by the shares held in bank trust departments. But modern trustee business differs markedly from those activities carried out in the heyday of J. P. Morgan. The business of trust departments is to invest money for the beneficiaries of the trusts, and it cannot be used for other purposes (Sweezy, 1971, pp. 3–4). Fitch has countered this by pointing to the change from personal trust business to corporate pension-fund business, claiming that corporate funds can be used as part of a bank's overall investment strategy (Fitch, 1972, p. 115; see also Kotz, 1978, pp. 63–71). This point has been taken seriously by Herman, but he argues that banks are still constrained by the interests of the trust beneficiaries: 'Any bank whose investment policy was dominated by a desire to control would probably do badly as an investment performer, and would soon lose trust department (and other) business as a consequence' (Herman, 1973, p. 21). Herman's study (1981) did conclude that banks have voting discretion in a high proportion of their trust accounts (see also Blumberg, 1975, p. 125), though this conclusion does not seem to hold for Britain. Bank trust companies in Britain act as *custodians* as well as managing trustees, and the custodian or non-voting role was particularly important for pension funds and unit trusts. The majority of the bank 'nominee' holdings ('street names' in the USA) were simply custodian holdings.

The final point to make about Fitch and Oppenheimer's argument is that they use interlock evidence in an indiscriminate way. Interlocking directorships cannot be seen as expressions of bank power unless they are directed from banks to industrials, or they can be shown to vary systematically with other behavioural features. Levine (1978), in a criticism of Mariolis (1975), has argued for bank control on the basis of bank centrality. He argues that if the relative sizes of enterprises are taken into account, then banks interlock more frequently than other enterprises of a comparable size. But, of course, mere frequency of interlocking tells us little directly about bank control, a point made in reply to Levine by Mariolis (1978). In this same tradition Glasberg (1981) supplemented interlock data with behavioural evidence in an attempt to document a particular case of bank control. She shows that a 1967 takeover bid for Chemical Bank from Leasco was beaten off with the help of other banks, and she concluded that banks cooperated in order to fight a common threat. This example is similar to that of Howard Hughes as discussed by Fitch and Oppenheimer, both cases showing indeed that banks tend to put up a common front against 'maverick' entrepreneurs. What the cases do not establish is that this is a routine pattern of behaviour with respect to all non-financials. Furthermore, the evidence on the formation of a united front runs counter to the contention that bank control is exercised within particular interest groups.

Banks cannot be regarded as exercising the kind of power over other enterprises which is required by the model of bank control. Banking and non-financial capital fused to form 'finance capital', banks occupying central positions in the network, and bank-centred cliques were an important feature of intercorporate relations; but the banks were not all-pervasive exploiters of subordinate enterprises. An alternative interpretation of bank interlocking must, therefore, be offered. Banks do, indeed, have the potential for power because of their role in the mobilisation of capital. Enterprises are dependent upon access to capital, and banks occupy a strategic position in the flow of this resource. Through customer accounts, personal trust and executor business, and investment and pension management the clearing banks are able to accumulate surplus wealth and make it available as capital for productive investment. Insurance companies, investment and unit trusts, and enterprises with large pension funds all perform a similar function is converting personal wealth into loan capital, and so can be considered to perform a 'banking' function. But clearing banks and merchant banks play a key role in determining access to these other sources of capital by acting as custodians, advisers, secretaries, and managers to the intermediaries (Gordon, 1945, chapter 9; Herman, 1981). The predominance of control through a constellation of interests has further enhanced the role of banks by giving them a major role in the issuing and underwriting of shares, in organising and syndicating loans, and in corporate advice for expansion and mergers. The banks, therefore, exercise a generalised dominance in the corporate system.

Mintz and Schwartz have introduced the concept of 'hegemonic domination' to describe this situation. In circumstances of hegemony the behaviour of the dominant enterprise alters the conditions in the environment, 'and the altered economic conditions force the complementary response on the part of the subordinate company. Management of the subordinate firm need not agree with or creatively comply . . . they are coerced by the new circumstances to make appropriate changes' (Mintz and Schwartz, 1984, chapter 1.2). Conservely, the dominant enterprise need not act with the intent to coerce compliance: domination is an objective consequence of the relative structural location of the enterprises. Hegemonic domination exists where the influence of one enterprise over others goes beyond the normal interdependence of enterprises within the intercorporate network and becomes the kind of significant, regular, and direct influence which subordinate enterprises cannot counter. Because of their position in the flow of capital, banks have become the hegemonic enterprises of the modern corporate economy. Banks have sought close associations with those enterprises which might be important depositors and customers, and enterprises have sought to move closer to those banks which might ease their access to capital. In Britain and the USA patterns of bank interlocking have resulted in a characteristic structure of loose, bank-centred groupings. The largest non-financials may be powerful enough to interlock with more than one bank, but smaller enterprises tend to ally themselves with one particular bank. The resulting groupings may be termed bank-centred spheres of influence. Banks are not the bases for the exercise of control by bankers. The are central forums within loose spheres of enterprises in which diverse corporate interests come together and are, as a consequence, able to coordinate their own behaviour and to influence wider sections of the economy. Bank-centred spheres of influence are communities of interest within an extensive network of intercorporate relations (Ratcliff, 1980a, p. 567).

It is important to understand why bank hegemony should result in bank-centred spheres of influence in Britain, rather than producing the kind of generalised bank dominance found in Germany.[18] The main explanatory factor is the different banking practices adopted in the two countries. In Germany it was usual for banks to place their own executives on customer and client boards and for two or more banks to participate jointly in the capital and board membership of other enterprises. This resulted in a large number of induced interlocks pulling enterprises together into a large structural centre within which distinct spheres could not be identified. In Britain, bank interlocks were carried by industrial executives and outsiders as well as financial executives, and non-financials did not generally interlock with more than one bank. As a result, induced interlocks were more widely spread in the network, and loose but distinct clusters were formed around the banks.

The big banks in Britain were hegemonic in the network of capital and commercial relations, and this hegemony was expressed in preferential patterns of personal relations. By co-opting industrial and commercial executives to their boards and by placing their own executives on other company boards, they created a pattern of bank-centred spheres of influence. Banks were central to the flow of money, raw materials, and information and so were able to monopolise access to capital and intelligence. Banks were the means through which major capitalist interests could be brought together in such a way that they could cooperate as a community of interest. The bank board, therefore, was not an agency of control by banks; it was a forum for cooperation between banks, insurance companies, retailers, industrials, and other enterprises. The spheres of influence were loose alliances of interest which had their focii on the boards of particular banks. The primary interlocks which constituted the basic structure of the spheres were relatively intense and durable intercorporate relations. The pattern of induced and secondary interlocks reinforced this structure of overlapping spheres and also extended the number of connections between the spheres. The majority of the interlocks which ran between the spheres were not primary, and thus their major significance would seem to have been the facilitation of communication rather than preferential transactions. Channels of communications between enterprises have been claimed to be of particular importance in enhancing the environmental scan of enterprises. The intelligence which enterprises can accumulate, and therefore their ability to reduce the 'uncertainty' in their local environment, depends, to a considerable extent, on their position in the intercorporate network. Bank interlocks were the means through which enterprises attempted to minimise the effects of their resource dependence and thereby to maximise their capacities for autonomous action.

Cooperation between spheres 'occurs at the lowest level necessary for effective functioning' (Aldrich, 1979, p. 326; Granovetter, 1973, pp. 1367–8, and 1982).[19] The spheres had strong ties within themselves, but weaker ties between them. A consequence of this structure is that perturbations could generally be localised to specific parts of the network, and so the stability of the network as a whole was not threatened. For this reason, changes in network structure, as opposed to changes in the structure and composition of particular spheres, tended to be small and incremental. Structural alterations occurred when incremental changes had accumulated to such a degree that a sudden, 'catastrophic' metamorphosis took place (Glassman,

1973, p. 84; Starbuck, 1973; Thom, 1975). Alongside such incrementally generated transformations were radical changes caused by bank mergers. The merging of two banks has implications both for their immediate spheres and for the wider structure, and detailed studies might highlight the ways in which bank mergers are themselves 'catastrophic' consequences of incremental changes.

A high degree of network stability implies an inability to respond to structural economic problems. Such generalised problems in the economy tend to be dealt with as a series of discrete local problems rather than as an expression of system crisis. This can be seen as a major reason for the failure to counteract Britain's economic decline. The broad features of this decline, which has been especially marked in the postwar period, are by now well-known. Annual growth of GDP in 1961–72 was 10.1 per cent in Japan, 5.8 per cent in France, 4.5 per cent in Germany, 4.4 per cent in the United States, but only 2.5 per cent in Britain (Carrington and Edwards, 1979, p. 20). A contributory factor to this decline has been the low level of investment relative to that in other countries, and this was itself due to the practices of the British banking system. Where banks provide long-term direct lending to industry, as in Germany and Japan, there is a highly efficient transfer of funds from savers to borrowers. Bank loans create further credit through the multiplier mechanisms of bank lending, and so an increase in lending leads to an increase in the capacity to lend (Carrington and Edwards, 1979, p. 192). In this way, a small amount of personal saving can generate a high level of industrial investment. When industrial finance is dependent on the mechanisms of the stock exchange, this does not happen. Productive capital is available only in the form of new share issues, and there is no multiplier mechanism involved in this. Britain has a well-developed secondary market in issued shares – which encouraged the takoever boom of the 1960s and the consequent increase in concentration discussed in chapter 2 – and the banks are involved in industrial finance because of their role in the secondary market. Although banks have been important in the management of institutional funds in Britain, only a small proportion of these funds go into new issues (Williams et al., 1983, p. 71). For this reason, the fusion of banking and industry in Britain, expressed in the pattern of overlapping spheres of influence, has been unable to generate a high rate of investment. British banking practices have encouraged cautious expansion plans and low rates of investment by non-financials. Although enterprises interlocked with banks in order to enhance their access to capital and intelligence, the net result has been to reinforce a pattern of low investment.

The conclusion must be that bank interlocking is a reflection of the patterns of capital accumulation which exist in a national economy, and that capital accumulation itself depends upon patterns of bank interlocking. There will be problems of rapid and effective response in an economy which is structured into spheres of influence, and 'intervention' of some kind would be necessary in times of crisis or protracted economic dislocation. This was shown to be the case in the interwar period, when the difficulties facing many sectors of the economy could only be handled when the Bank of England and the government pressurised the banks and major financial intermediaries into co-ordinated action to rescue failing enterprises. This intervention resulted in a restructuring of the intercorporte network and laid the basis for prosperity in the 1950s, but it is clear from the facts of the present decline that this did not constitute a long-term solution. An effective response to economic decline would require a further alteration in the mechanisms of capital mobilisation and network structure, but it would also require action to deal with the other factors recognised as central to the causation of economic decline – factors which distinguish Britain sharply from its major competitors. The inadequacies of the system of capital mobilisation have been reinforced by the Establishment values discussed in chapter 5. They have been exacerbated by the failure of British management to exercise effective control over the labour process and the failure of the state to evolve satisfactory and coherent policies of industrial reorganisation (Williams et al., 1983).

NOTES

1. Clearing banks are strictly those 'retail' banks (commercial banks in the USA) which use a centralised facility for 'clearing' one another's cheques. The term is used throughout this book in the more general sense of those banks which operate domestically through 'high street' outlets and have customer current accounts as a major part of their business. They are therefore distinct from merchant banks (similar to US investment banks), and from overseas and specialist

banks. Studies of recent trends in banking include Channon (1977) and Reid (1980). Particular merchant banks are discussed in Hidy (1949), Morgan Grenfell (1958), and Rosenbaum and Sherman (1979). On insurance, see Supple (1970).

2. The number of Scottish banks included in 1938 and 1976 is artificially high because of the inclusion of some which were subsidiaries of English banks already selected.

3. See note 13 in chapter 2 and note 6 in chapter 1.

4. Mizruchi has shown that a measure of centrality which takes account of the directionality of interlocks correlates less well with a simple adjacency measure. It is, however, no easy matter to assess the directionality of a primary interlock. See Mizruchi (1982, pp. 56–8, 60–62).

5. The rush is defined in Anthonisse (1971). Alternative measures of betweenness are discussed in Freeman (1977) and Wigand (1977). The simplest calculation of the rush is the ratio of the actual to the possible number of shortest paths on which a point is to be found. In practice, the calculation is modified to take account of the assumed proportion of the total 'flow' which passes through a particular point. Although the rush can be calculated on the basis of all shortest paths (geodesics), it is generally more realistic to limit the calculation to geodesics of length two. The calculation can be further complicated by taking account of the multiplicities of lines.

6. Most of the merchant houses themselves were small partnerships outside the top 250. The houses joined in syndicates to form a few large, specialist joint stock trading companies which did appear in the top 250.

7. Scottish banking is discussed in chapter 3; see also Scott and Hughes (1980). Some general trends in bank interlocking can be found in Lisle-Williams (1981). On specific banks, see Crick and Wadsworth (1936), Midland Bank (1979), Chandler (1964), Withers (1933), and Gregory (1936).

8. Lord Nelson of GEC had a long family association with the firm, but the dominant family shareholding was that of Weinstock. See Jones and Marriott (1970).

9. In this context see the conclusion of Overbeek (1980) that Midland and Lloyds could be seen as centres of financial groups in 1976. This contention is discussed below.

10. A further two formed an isolated pair.

11. When direction was assigned from base company to the outside interest it was possible to identify 'strong components'. Where no account is taken of directionality, all components are regarded as 'weak components', and a weak component strictly contains not paths but 'semi-paths' as the actual directionality may vary. In a strong component there is a continuous 'flow' from one point to the

next, all paths running in the same direction. In undirected graphs, strong and weak components cannot be distinguished. Stokman and van Veen (1981) discuss some implications of this. The 1976 directed network contained two strong components, one of size 36 and one of size 2.

12. For the debate in France, see Morin (1974), Sellier (1974), Bleton (1974), Chevalier (1974), Simonnot (1974), Bleton (1976a–b), and Morin (1976).

13. In graph theoretical terminology, the heart of each clique comprised a 'tree'. A tree is a clique which depends upon a focal member whose removal would destroy the clique – as is the case with the clique in figure 6.1. The focal member is termed the 'cut-point', and a clique or component without a cut-point is termed a 'block'. This usage of block must be distinguished from that of White and his colleagues, which is criticised in Levine and Mullins (1978).

14. This involved deletion of all directors and not simply bank executives.

15. See note 13 above.

16. ICI did appear as a cut-point in one of the 31 cliques of minimum size six. Its clique took the form of a tree and included Commercial Union, Carrington Viyella, Reed, Ford, and the National Enterprise Board.

17. They use a 5 per cent cut-off point for identifying minority control.

18. The discussion which follows draws upon Rolf Ziegler's Conclusion in Stokman et al. (1984).

19. For discussions which relate this to the differing viewpoints of central and peripheral agents, see Wellman (1981, pp. 27–9) and Davis (1967, p. 186).

Conclusion

This book is intended not only as a contribution to an understanding of the development of the British economy but also as a statement of a novel perspective on that question. The network analysis of interlocking directorships has rarely been treated as a central perspective on economic power, and the aim of this book is to illustrate its utility. For this reason it is perhaps useful to draw out some of the general conclusions of the book and to state some of their implications.

It has been argued that networks of interlocking directorships can be studied in terms of their cohesiveness and fragmentation. The cohesiveness of a network (its density and centralisation) is a consequence of the number and distribution of directorships, which themselves reflect the recruitment practices adopted by corporate boards. These practices are rooted in the legal requirements of the board system, the role that the board is expected to play in corporate decision-making, and the pattern of capital and commercial relations in which enterprises are involved. It has been argued that in order to analyse the structure of the network it is necessary to distinguish between primary, induced, and secondary interlocks. The number and distribution of primary interlocks reflect most directly the intense and institutionalised capital and commercial relations between enterprises and so give a good picture of the skeletal structure of the whole network. These interlocks are most likely to be involved in any relations of coordination and control which might exist between enterprises, and they tend to be associated with preferential transactions of an instrumental type. Primary interlocks generate a large number of induced interlocks which reinforce the skeletal structure and increase its density. These induced interlocks are consequential upon the establishment of the primary interlocks, but are more likely to be channels of communication than relations of control. Secondary interlocks, often carried by retired executives, tend to have no institutional base in capital and commercial relations, and are therefore of major importance as integrative channels of communication. The overall structure of the network reflects the complex interdependence of each of these types of interlock.

Primary interlocks, which are carried by executives, and those secondary interlocks which are carried by non-executives with a primary interest in one of the top enterprises, together comprise what might be termed 'institutional interlocks', as they are most directly involved with institutionalised capital and commercial relations and are likely to be intense and durable themselves. The purely secondary interlocks, which are carried by outsiders, may be termed 'liaison interlocks', as they generally do not correspond to capital and commercial relations but are involved in the formation of loose liaisons and communities of interest.

Multiple directors are those agents who sit on more than one board and so generate the interlocks. The research has shown that these multiple directors have social characteristics which set them apart from those who sit on only one top board (the 'single directors'), and form them into an 'inner circle' within the corporate directorate of business leaders. In the earliest period studied, the inner circle consisted mainly of entrepreneurial capitalists, a City of London core and provincial entrepreneurs, and formed part of a wider 'establishment' which headed the stratification system. Based in London and county 'Society', this establishment had gradually incorporated provincial business leaders. By the 1930s the City core had become all pervasive through the emerging fusion of banks and industry, and the inner circle, still part of an establishment, comprised a group of proto-finance capitalists. By 1976 an extensive national network had emerged within which the inner circle consisted almost exclusively of finance capitalists (coordinating controllers). Some entrepreneurial and internal capitalists were members of the inner circle, but most were confined to the outer circle. The inner circle still had many of the features which tied it to the establishment, but the decline of the establishment meant that formal participation in political and advisory bodies had become of greater importance than the informal channels which were formerly so important. But other interpersonal connections remained important alongside interlocking directorships. Interlocks generated a pattern of meetings among directors, and this partial network was reinforced by a network of kinship and friendship which generated 'kinterlocks' between enterprises. This whole sphere of interpersonal connections was the basis for cohesion and informality among directors at the level of social integration. People meet as kinsmen, friends, co-directors, and as colleagues of kin and friends, and each relation reinforces the others to produce multiple, and multi-stranded, personal relations. If combined with the looser partial networks of common club memberships and common school or college attendance, a mapping of the structure of the establishment is produced; though the relational features of this have generally been reduced to individual attributes in studies of 'elite social background'.

At the beginning of this book a number of models of intercorporate relations were outlined, and it is now necessary to give a brief assessment of their value in understanding the British intercorporate network. The finance capital model seems to be the most useful for grasping the structure of the network. The primary interlocks produced a network which was structured into recognisable cliques and clusters in which banks held central positions. Banks were central because of their role in the mobilisation of capital, but the loose and shifting spheres of influence did not seem to be as tight and coordinated as the model assumes. For this same reason, the model of bank coordination and control must be regarded as overstating its case. Interlocks were not exclusively directed from banks to non-financials and the spheres did not comprise 'interest groups'. Interest groups certainly did exist within the intercorporate network, but they have never constituted its major organising structures. The position of banks can be understood on the basis of certain of the arguments of the resource dependence model. This model's assumption of a diffuse and unstructured network was not confirmed, but it is clear that capital is a resource upon which all enterprises are dependent and that the position of banks was to be explained in terms of their control over this resource. The model of class cohesion, too, assumed a diffuse network, but its assumptions are particularly relevant to the part played by secondary interlocks. The channels of communication which these open are important aspects of the cohesion of a group which was also united through bonds of kinship and friendship. There is a group of finance capitalists, the inner circle of business leaders, who are simultaneously involved in both banking and industry. Those from an entrepreneurial background and those who have risen through the corporate hierarchy take on a broader system perspective on entry into the inner circle and become incorporated into the prevailing social pattern. The basis of their dominance is the credit system, and those enterprises which are central to the availability of credit – the banks – are their institutional base. From this base the leading members of the inner circle are able to exercise a degree of power and influence over other enterprises and to ensure a certain amount of coordination in business behaviour.

The implication of the research which this book reports is that the managerial theory has the least to offer in studies of corporate power. At the heart of managerialism are two claims: that executive managers are the key decision-makers and that the large enterprise is able to override market mechanisms in the determination of production. In Chandler's succinct statement, the 'invisible hand' of market mechanisms is replaced by the 'visible hand' of corporate planning (1977, p. 1). The market remains important as the generator of demand, but the coordination and allocation of resources to meet that demand is determined by the decisions of corporate management. Managerialists have argued, therefore, that the neoclassical theory of the firm with its model of the entrepreneur subject to competitive market pressures on output and pricing must be replaced by a theory based around the manager and corporate planning. The entrepreneurial capitalist must give up centre stage to the internal capitalist. The problems with the managerialist view of the separation of ownership and control have been discussed at various points in this book (see also Scott, 1979), but problems are also to be found in the concept of the visible hand. It is undoubtedly the case that the large enterprise has a market power unavailable to the classic entrepreneurial firm, and that economic theory must recognise the crucial role of corporate planning. But such theory must also take account of the intercorporate relations in which the enterprise is enmeshed. The intercorporate network comprises a new 'invisible hand' which constrains the options available to corporate management.[1] Internal capitalists must be joined at centre stage by the finance capitalists.

If economic theory could be developed in this direction there would be a much firmer basis for the necessary integration of economics and sociology into a unified social science. It is hoped that the present work and the companion, comparative volume

(Stokman et al., 1984) will contribute to this goal by furthering the reunification of theory and research in the study of corporate power and providing some useful concepts for future research.

Business leaders themselves frequently decry the need for such research. Basing their arguments on an implicit managerialism, they contend that they, as participants, have privileged knowledge of the workings of business and they know that things are not as they have been depicted in this book. Interlocks, they claim, are irrelevant and have no underlying generative mechanisms. Sociologists are used to dealing with such objections from those they study: participation is no guarantee of objectivity and can induce a partial perspective on the structure in which the participant is located. It has been argued in this book that the structures identified are not necessarily the result of deliberate intent and that, therefore, there is no reason to expect agents to be aware of either the structures or their causes. All that is implied is that the normal competences of business practice generate, unintentionally, a structure of social relations which then becomes a constraint upon future courses of action. The recruitment of directors from positions within such a structure will tend to ensure its reproduction over time, whether the participants intend this or not.

But still the objection might be raised that though interlocks may have a structure, they have no consequences for corporate behaviour. Business leaders would be unimpressed by claims that interlocks have implications for the theory of the firm, an understanding of power relations, or the analysis of social stratification, and so perhaps one practical implication should be mentioned. It was argued in chapter 6 that banking practices were a contributory factor to Britain's economic decline, and that the structure of spheres of influence inhibits any significant response to this decline. This is a matter of considerable importance for those active in business, as the future viability of their enterprises is inextricably entwined with the viability of the British economy. For this reason the Bank of England and various representative bodies of manufacturers and financial intermediaries have periodically attempted to encourage the presence of non-executive directors on corporate boards by setting up a clearing house for directors. Any enterprise wishing to recruit an outside director could apply to the clearing house, or be referred by their bankers, and they would be put in contact with suitable candidates. However, if the Bank of England were to operate through the major financial intermediaries, as seems to be proposed, then it will simply be formalising and institutionalising the existing pattern of bank-centred spheres of influence. Far from counteracting economic decline, such a policy may actually contribute to further decline.

The political implications which might be drawn from this argument depend upon one's initial political standpoint. Hardheaded business leaders would no doubt contend that enterprises should be left to their own devices, while corporatist business leaders might argue that the Bank of England should take a firmer *dirigiste* role and not simply rubber-stamp the nominees of the banks. A socialist response might reject both such proposals as inadequate tinkering and argue for a radical reconstruction of the whole system of capital mobilisation. Whatever the implications drawn, it is clear that any strategy which ignores the reality of intercorporate relations is doomed to failure.

NOTES

1. I owe this formulation of the issue to a suggestion made by Michael Mann.

Appendix: Sources and Data Selection

The selection of data for 1976 was based upon the common selection procedures of the international research group on intercorporate structure in order to maximise the chances of international comparison. The 200 largest non-financials by turnover were selected from the lists given in the *Times* 1000 for 1977–8, which approximated to data for the 1976 financial year. The first 200 companies in the main listing were selected, though companies which were wholly owned subsidiaries of other companies in the 200 were excluded. The exceptions to this were: Carrington Viyella, which was majority-controlled by ICI but was not consolidated into the ICI accounts (ICI was in the process of reducing its stake); two unconsolidated subsidiaries of the National Enterprise Board, because of the status of the NEB as a state holding company (the NEB was selected as a nationalised enterprise as described below); and joint ventures. To this list were added any unquoted companies which did not already appear and which had turnover greater than the 200th company on the list. These unquoted companies were identified from lists supplied by the Department of Industry. Nationalised concerns and public boards with a turnover greater than the 200th company were selected from the separate *Times* 1000 list and included in the data set. The total number of companies was then reduced to 200 by selecting the largest. In each case the central parent company was identified and taken as the unit of analysis, except where this was a family trust or private family company. In the latter case, which occurred with two companies, the main public holding company was taken as the unit of analysis.

Financial companies had to be selected on a slightly different basis as no comprehensive ranking of financials exists. It was, in any case, felt that the selection of the top 50 financials had to reflect the fact that the importance of merchant banks and certain other financials was not reflected in their assets or income. The largest financials within each of the main categories were therefore selected. The Clydesdale Bank was included despite being a subsidiary of the Midland Bank because of a wish to study Scottish finance. Where merchant banks were subsidiaries of public holding companies, the latter were selected as the units of analysis.

Selection of companies for 1904 and 1938 could not follow exactly the same procedures because of the absence of comparable lists to the *Times* 1000 for these years. Non-financials in 1904 were selected on the basis of issued share capital, though this is an imperfect measure of size. The largest companies were identified from the Stock Exchange *Official Intelligence* for 1905. This covers the financial year 1904, and it should be noted that the list given in Payne (1967) relates to this same year and not to 1905 as stated. All sections of the *Official Intelligence* were examined in order to find all those companies with a capital of £1m or more and which did not operate purely in the financial sector. Investment and property companies were included if they were holding companies for operating subsidiaries. Sixteen railways with a capital of less than £2m were excluded in order to limit the number of railways on the list – most of those excluded were in fact owned or operated by larger railways. Indian railways were not included. When the information was known, companies which were wholly owned subsidiaries of others on the list were excluded. This selection resulted in 216 companies, and the total was reduced to 200 by eliminating those £1m capital companies with the smallest amount in debentures outstanding. A useful list compiled after the completion of this task is that given for 1907 in Shaw (1983). The 50 major financials were selected in a similar way to the 1976 list, though arbitrary decisions necessarily had to be made.

For 1938 the Stock Exchange *Official Intelligence* for 1939 was used and selection of non-financials was again on the basis of capital. Using a cut-off point of £3m resulted in the selection of 186 companies. Lists produced by Florence for 1936 and Parkinson for 1942 were useful checks for any large companies which fell below the capital cut-off and any which were not on the original list were added. Further additions were made of public corporations to bring the total to 200. Financial companies were again selected by sector. Fuller details and lists of the companies finally selected are contained in a report to the Social Science

Research Council for grant HR6992: 'Interlocking Directorships in Major British Companies, 1904–1976', by John Scott and Catherine Griff, (End of Grant Report lodged at the British Library).

Names of directors were in each case identified from the *Official Intelligence* and cross-checked in the appropriate annual volumes of the *Directory of Directors*. Additional information was gathered from the company records at Companies House and from various specialist directories. The most important such sources were:

Bankers Almanack
Bradshaw's Railway Shareholders Manual
Burke's Peerage, Baronetage, and Knightage
Debrett's Peerage, Baronetage, and Knightage
Fairplay Annual Summary Of British Shipping Finance
Kelly's Directory of Merchants
Kelly's Handbook
List of Members of the Stock Exchange
Manual of Electrical Undertakings
Register of Defunct and Other Companies
Stock Exchange Official Yearbook (successor to the *Intelligence*)
The Syren Financial Yearbook
Who's Who

References

Aaronovitch, S. (1955) *Monopoly*, London, Lawrence and Wishart.

Aaronovitch, S. (1961) *The Ruling Class*, London, Lawrence and Wishart.

Abrams, P. (ed.) (1978) *Work, Urbanism, and Inequality*, London, Weidenfeld and Nicolson.

Addis, J. P. (1957) *The Crawshay Dynasty*, Cardiff, University of Wales Press.

Aldcroft, D. H. (1974) *Studies in British Transport History*, Newton Abbott, David and Charles.

Adrich, H. (1979) *Organizations and Environments*, Englewood Cliffs, New Jersey, Prentice-Hall.

Aldrich, H. (1982) 'The Origins and Persistence of Social Networks: A Comment', in Marsden and Lin (1982).

Aldrich, H. and Fish, D. (1982) 'Origins of Organizational Forms', paper presented to the American Sociological Association, San Francisco.

Aldrich, H. and Mindlin, S. (1977) 'Uncertainty and Dependence: Two Perspectives on the Environment', in Karpik (1977).

Alford, B. W. E. (1973) *W D and H O Wills and the Development of the UK Tobacco Industry*, London, Methuen.

Allard, P, et al. (1978) *Dictionnaire des Groupes industriels et financières en France*, Paris, Editions du Seuil.

Allen, M. P. (1974) 'The Structure of Interorganizational Elite Cooptation,' *American Sociological Review*, 39.

Allen, M. P. (1978a) 'Economic Interest Groups and the Corporate Elite', *Social Science Quarterly*, 58.

Allen, M. P. (1978b) 'Continuity and Change Within the Corporate Elite', *Sociological Quarterly*, 19.

Andrews, J. A. Y. (1982) 'The Interlocking Corporate Director: A Case Study in Conceptual Confusion', MA Dissertation, University of Chicago.

Andrews, P. W. S. and Brunner, E. (1951) *Capital Development in Steel*, Oxford, Basil Blackwell.

Anon. (n.d.) *Burmah Story*, Glasgow, Burmah Oil (?1950s).

Anon. (1908) 'Midland Captains of Industry: LI, Harvey Du Cros', *Birmingham Gazette and Express*, 19 February.

Anon. (1955) *The Master Millers*, London, Harley.

Anthonisse, J. (1971) *The Rush in a Directed Graph*, Amsterdam, University of Amsterdam Mathematical Centre.

Anthonisse J. (1973) *A Graph-Defining Language*, Amsterdam, University of Amsterdam Mathematical Centre.

Aris, S. (1970) *The Jews in Business*, London, Cape.

Armes, R. (1978) *A Critical History of the British Cinema*, London, Secker and Warburg.

Bacon, J. and Brown, J. K. (1977) *The Board of Directors: Perspectives and Practices in Nine Countries*, New York, The Conference Board.

Baglehole, K. C. (1968) *A Century of Service*, London, Cable & Wireless.

Baker, W. J. (1970) *A History of the Marconi Company*, London, Methuen.

Baldwin, E. (1977) 'The Mass Media and the Corporate Elite', *Canadian Journal of Sociology*, 2(1).

Balfour Beatty (1959) *Balfour Beatty: 50 Years*, London, Balfour Beatty.

Baltzell, E. D. (1958) *Philadelphia Gentlemen*, Glencoe, Free Press.

Barclay (1924–34) *A History of the Barclay Family*, Parts I, II, and III, London, St Catherine's Press. Part I by C. W. Barclay, Part II by H. F. Barclay, Part III by H. F. Barclay and A. Wilson-Fox.

Barker, T. C. and Robbins, M. (1963) *A History of London Transport*, Vol. 1, London, George Allen and Unwin.

Barker, T. C. and Robbins, M. (1974) *A History of London Transport*, Vol. 2, London, George Allen and Unwin.

Barnes, J. A. (1954) 'Class and Committees in a Norwegian Island Parish', reprinted in Lienhardt (1977).

Barnes, J. A. (1969) 'Networks and Political Process', in Mitchell (1969).

Barnes J. A. (1972) *Social Networks*, Module in Anthropology, No. 26, Reading, Mass., Addison-Wesley.

Barnes, J. A. (1979) 'Network Analysis: Orienting Notion, Rigorous Technique or Substantive Field of Study?', in Holland and Lienhardt (1979).

Barratt Brown, M. (1968) 'The Controllers of British Industry', in Coates (1968).

Barty-King, H. (1979) *Girdle Round the Earth*, London, Heinemann.

Baumgartner, T., et al. (1977) *Power, Conflict and Exchange in Social Life*, University of Oslo, Institute of Sociology, Working Paper 88.

Bavelas, A. (1950) 'Communication Patterns in Task Orientated Groups', *Journal of the Acoustical Society of America*, 22.

Bearden, J. and Mintz, B. (1984) 'Regionality and Integration in the United States Interlock Network', in Stokman et al. (1984).

Bearden, J., et al. (1975) 'The Nature and Extent of Bank Centrality in Corporate Networks', Paper presented to the American Sociological Association, San Francisco.

Beecham, T. (1944) *A Mingled Chime*, London, Hutchinson, reprinted 1979.

Bellon, B. (1977) Méthodologie de délimitation et de reperage des ensembles financiers', unpublished paper, University of Paris 8.

Ben-Porath, Y. (1980) 'The F-Connection: Families, Friends and Firms and the Organization of Exchange', *Population and Development Review*, 6.

Benson, J. K. (1975) 'The Interorganizational Network as a Political Economy', *Administrative Science Quarterly*, 20.

Benson, J. K. (1977) 'Organisations: a Dialectical View', *Administrative Science Quarterly*, 22.

Benton, T. (1981) 'The Sociology of Power', *Sociology*, 15.

Berkowitz, S. D. (1976) *The Dynamics of Elite Structure*, Ph.D Thesis, Brandeis University.

Berkowitz, S. D. (1980) 'Structural and Non-Structural Models of Elites: A Critique', *Canadian Journal of Sociology*, 5.

Berkowitz, S. D. (1982) *An Introduction to Structural Analysis*, Toronto, Butterworth.

Berkowitz, S. D. and Heil, G. H. (1980) 'Dualities in Methods of Social Network Research', Research Paper No. 18, Structural Analysis Programme, University of Toronto.

Berkowitz, S. D., et al. (1978) 'The Determination of Enterprise Groupings Through Combined Ownership and Directorship Ties', *Social Networks*, 1.

Berkowitz, S. D., et al. (1979) 'Flexible Design for a Large Scale Corporate Data Base', *Social Networks*, 2.

Berle, A. A. and Means, G. C. (1932) *The Modern Corporation and Private Property*, New York, Macmillan.

Bermant, C. (1971) *The Cousinhood*, London, Eyre and Spottiswode.

Bermant, C. (1977) *The Jews*, London, Wiedenfeld and Nicolson.

Berry, W. [Lord Camrose] (1947) *British Newspapers and Their Controllers*, London, Cassell.

Betts, E. (1973) *The Film Industry*, London, George Allen and Unwin.

Beynon, H. and Wainwright, H. (1979) *The Workers Report on Vickers*, London, Pluto.

Bhaskar, R. (1975) *A Realist Theory of Science*, Leeds, Leeds Books.

Bibby, J. B. and Bibby, C. L. (1978) *A Miller's Tale*, Liverpool, J. Bibby & Sons.

Birkhead, E. (1958) 'The Daimler Airway', *Journal of Transport History*, 3.

References 191

Birkhead, E. (1960) 'The Financial Failure of British Air Transport Companies', *Journal of Transport History*, 4.

Blau, P. M. (1982) 'Structural Sociology and Network Analysis', in Marsden and Lin (1982).

Bleton, P. (1974) 'L'Argent: Pourvoir Ambigu', *Economie et Humanisme*, 220

Bleton, P. (1976a) 'Le Capitalisme français à l'ombre de L'Universit', *Economie et Humanisme*, 229.

Bleton, P. (1976b) 'Bons Concepts et mechantes realités', *Economie et Humanisme*, 229.

Blumber, P. I. (1975) *The Megacorporation in American Society*, Englewood Cliffs, New Jersey, Prentice-Hall.

Blumberg, P. M. and Paul, P. W. (1975) 'Continuities and Discontinuities in Upper-Class Marriages', *Journal of Marriage and the Family*, 37.

Boissevain, J. (1974) *Friends of Friends*, Oxford, Basil Blackwell.

Boissevain, J. (1980) 'Network Analysis: A Reappraisal', *Connections*, 3(1).

Boissevain, J. and Mitchell, J. C. (eds) (1973) *Network Analysis*, The Hague, Mouton.

Bonacich, P. and Domhoff, G. W. (1981) 'Latent Classes and Group Membership', *Social Networks*, 3.

Bonavia, M. R. (1980) *The Four Great Railways*, Newton Abbott, David and Charles.

Bonnett, K. (1982) 'Classes, Class Fractions and Monetarism', in Robbins et al. (1982).

Booth, A. (1982) 'Corporatism, Capitalism and Depression in Twentieth-Century Britain', *British Journal of Sociology*, 33.

Bott, E. (1957) *Family and Social Network*, London, Tavistock.

Bourdieu, P. (1971) 'Cultural Reproduction and Social Reproduction', in Brown (1973).

Boyce, G., et al. (eds) (1978) *Newspaper History*, London, Constable.

Bramson, B. and Wain, K. (1979) *The Hambros*, London, Michael Joseph.

Braverman, H. (1974) *Labour and Monopoly Capital*, New York, Monthly Review Press.

Britton, R. E. (1980) *Private Investors in the UK, 1876–1880*, unpublished paper, University of Essex.

Brooks, C. (1933) *The Royal Mail Case*, London, William Hodge & Co.

Brown, R. (ed.) (1973) *Knowledge, Education and Cultural Change*, London, Tavistock.

Bunting, D. (1976a) 'Corporate Interlocking, Part I – The Money Trust', *Directors and Boards*, 1(1).

Bunting, D. (1976b) 'Corporate Interlocking, Part II – The *Modern* Money Trust', *Directors and Boards*, 1(2).

Bunting, D. (1976c) 'Corporate Interlocking, Part III – Interlocks and Return on Investment', *Directors and Boards*, 1(3).

Bunting, D. (1977) 'Corporate Interlocking, Part IV – A New Look at Interlocks and Legislation', *Directors and Boards*, 1(4).

Bunting, D. and Barbour, J. (1971) 'Interlocking Directorates in Large American Corporations, 1896–1964', *Business History Review*, 45.

Burawoy, M. (1979) *Manufacturing Consent*, Chicago, University of Chicago Press.

Burn, D. (1961) *The Economic History of Steel Marking, 1867–1939*, Cambridge, Cambridge University Press.

Burnett, R. G. (1945) *Through the Mill*, London, Epworth Press.

Burt, R. (1978a) 'A Structural Theory of Interlocking Corporate Directorates', *Social Networks*, 1.

Burt, R. (1978b) 'Applied Network Analysis', *Sociological Methods and Research*, 7.

Burt, R. (1980) 'Models of Network Structure', *Annual Review of Sociology*, 6.

Burt, R., et al. (1980) 'Testing a Structural Theory of Corporate Cooptation', *American Sociological Review*, 45.

Byatt, I. C. R. (1979) *The British Electrical Industry*, Oxford, Clarendon Press.

Cable, B. (1937) *A Hundred Years of the P & O*, London, Ivor Nicholson.

Cammell Laird (1959) *Builders of Great Ships*, Sevenoaks, Richard Garrett Services.

Campbell, R. H. (1980) *The Rise and Fall of Scottish Industry, 1707–1939*, Edinburgh, John Donald.

Carchedi, G. (1983) *Problems in Class Analysis*, London, Routledge and Kegan Paul.

Carney, J., et al. (1976) 'Regional Underdevelopment in Late Capitalism', in Masser (1976).

Carney, J., et al. (1977) 'Coal Combines and Inter-Regional Uneven Development in the UK', in Massey and Batey (1977).

Carrington, J. C. and Edwards, G. T. (1979) *Financing Industrial Investment*, London, Macmillan.

Carrington, P. J. (1981) 'Anticompetitive Effects of Directorship Interlocks', Research Paper No. 27, Structural Analysis Programme, University of Toronto.

Carrington, P. J. (1982) 'Comment on Lattin and Wong', *Connections*, 5.

Carroll, W. K. (1982) 'The Canadian Corporate Elite', *Studies in Political Economy*, 8.

Carroll, W. K., et al. (1982) 'The Network of Directorate Links Among the Largest Canadian Firms', *Canadian Review of Sociology and Anthropology*, 19.

CDE (1980) *Banking and Finance: The Hidden Cost*, New York, Corporate Data Exchange.

Chandler, A. D. (1962) *Strategy and Structure*, Cambridge, Mass., MIT Press.

Chandler, A. D. (1977) *The Visible Hand*, Cambridge, Mass., Belknap Press.

Chandler, A. D. and Daems, H. (1974) 'Introduction', in Daems and Van der Wee (1974).

Chandler, A. D. and Redlich, F. (1961) 'Recent Developments in American Business Administration and their Conceptualisation', *Business History Review*, 35.

Chandler, D. and Lacey, A. D. (1949) *The Rise of the Gas Industry in Britain*, London, British Gas Council.

Chandler, G. (1960) *Liverpool Shipping*, London, Phoenix House.

Chandler, G. (1964) *Four Centuries of Banking*, London, Batsford.

Channon, D. (1973) *The Strategy and Structure of British Enterprise*, London, Macmillan.

Channon, D. (1977) *British Banking Strategy and the International Challenge*, London, Macmillan.

Chevalier, J. M. (1974) 'La Domination des firms industrielles par les banques', *Economie et Humanisme*, 220.

Child, J. (1972) 'Organizational Structure, Environment and Performance: the Role of Strategic Choice', *Sociology*, 6.

Child, J. and Kieser, A. (1981) 'Development of Organisations over Time', in Nystrom and Starbuck (1981).

Church, R. (1979) *Herbert Austin*, London, Europa.

Citoleux, Y., et al. (1977) 'Les Groupes de Sociétés en 1974', *Economie et Statistique*, 87.

Clarke, W. M. (1979) *Inside the City*, London, George Allen and Unwin.

Clay, H. (1957) *Lord Norman*, London, Macmillan.

Clement, W. (1975) *The Canadian Corporate Elite*, Toronto, McClelland and Stewart.

Clement, W. (1977) 'Overlap of the Media and Economic Elites', *Canadian Journal of Sociology*, 2(2).

Coates, K. (ed.) (1968) *Can The Workers Run Industry?*, London, Sphere.

Colverd, O. (1972) 'The Early Days of Burmese Oil', *Petroleum Review*, July.

Cook, K. S. (1977) 'Exchange and Power in Networks of Interorganizational Relations', *Sociological Quarterly*, 18.

Cook, K. S. (1982) 'Network Structure From an Exchange Perspective', in Marsden and Lin (1982).

Copeman, F. L. (1971) *The Northern Rhodesia Copperbelt, 1899–1962*, Manchester, Manchester University Press.

Corley, T. A. B. (1982) 'Strategic Factors in the Growth of a Multi-national Enterprise: The Burmah Oil Company, 1886–1928', paper presented to the Association of International Business.

Cottrell, P. L. (1974) *Investment Banking in England 1856–1882*, Ph.D. thesis, University of Hull.

Cottrell, P. L. (1975) *British Overseas Investment in the Nineteenth Century*, London, Macmillan.

Cottrell, P. L. (1980) *Industrial Finance 1830–1914*, London, Methuen.

Cowles, V. (1973) *The Rothschilds*, London, Weidenfeld and Nicolson.

Cowling, K., et al. (1980) *Mergers and Economic Performance*, Cambridge, Cambridge University Press.

Coxon, A. P. M. (1979) 'Perspectives on Social Networks', in Holland Lienhardt (1979).

Crathorne, N. (1973) *Tennant's Stalk: The Story of The Tennants of the Glen*, London, Macmillan.

Craven, P. (1978) 'Canadian Intercorporate Linkages', *Connections*, 1(3).

Crick, W. F. and Wadsworth, J. E. (1936) *A Hundred Years of Joint Stock Banking*, London, Hodder and Stoughton.

Crozier, D. (1965) 'Kinship and Occupational Succession', *Sociological Review*, 13.

Cuyvers, L. and Meeusen, W. (1976) 'The Structure of Personal Influence of the Belgian Holding Companies', *European Economic Review*, 8.

Cuyvers, L. and Meeusen, W. (1978) 'A Time-Series Analysis of Concentration in Belgian Banking and Holding Companies', paper for Planning Session of the European Consortium for Political Research, Grenoble.

Daems, H. and van der Wee, H. (eds) (1974) *The Rise of Managerial Capitalism*, The Hague, Martinus Nijhoff.

Davies, P. N. (1973) *The Trade Makers*, London, George Allen and Unwin.

Davies, P. N. (1981) 'Business Success and the Role of Chance: The Extraordinary Philipps Brothers', *Business History*, 23.

Davies, R. E. G. (1964) *A History of the World's Airlines*, London, Oxford University Press.

Davis, J. (1967) 'Clustering and Structural Balance in Graphs', *Human Relations*, 20.

Deeson, A. F. L. (1971) *Great Swindlers*, London, W. Foulsham.

Deeson, A. F. L. (1972) *Great Company Crashes*, London, W. Foulsham.

Dence, A. H. (1948) *Hovis 1898–1948*, London, Hovis.

Dendy Marshall, C. F. (1963) *A History of the Southern Railway*, London, Ian Allan.

Divine, D. (1960) *These Splendid Ships*, London, Frederick Muller.

Dixon, F. H. (1914) 'The Economic Significance of Interlocking Directorates in Railway Finance', *Journal of Political Economy*, 22.

Domhoff, G. W. (1978) *The Powers that Be*, New York, Random House.

Domhoff, G. W. (ed.) (1980) *Power Structure Research*, London, Sage.

Donnachie, I. (1979) *A History of the Brewing Industry in Scotland*, Edinburgh, John Donald.

Dooley, P. C. (1969) 'The Interlocking Directorate', *American Economic Review*, 59.

Dougan, D. (1968) *A History of North East Shipbuilding*, London, George Allen and Unwin.

Douglas, H. (1963) *The Underground Story*, London, Robert Hale.

Du Cros, A. (1938) *Wheels of Fortune*, London, Chapman and Hall.

Dunlop (1938) *50 Years of Growth*, London, Dunlop.

Dunlop, J. B. (1924) *The History of the Pneumatic Tyre*, Dublin, Alex Thom.

Dunn, M. (1979) *The Penguin Guide to Real Draught Beer*, London, Penguin.

Dunn, M. G. (1980) 'The Family Office: Co-ordinating Mechanism of the Ruling Class', in Domhoff (1980).

Dyas, G. P. and Thanheiser, H. T. (1976) *The Emerging European Enterprise*, London, Macmillan.

Dyos, H. J. and Aldcroft, D. H. (1969) *British Transport*, Leicester, Leicester University Press.

Eastern Associated (1922) *Fifty Years of 'Via Eastern'*, London, Eastern Associated Telegraph Companies.

Edwards, R. (1979) *Contested Terrain*, London, Heinemann.

Eglin, R. and Ritchie, B. (1980) *Fly Me, I'm Freddie*, London, Weidenfeld and Nicolson.

Elias, N. (1970) *What Is Sociology?*, London, Hutchinson, 1978.

Elletson, D. H. (1966) *The Chamberlains*, London, John Murray.

Ellis, H. (1970) *London, Midland and Scottish*, London, Ian Allan.

Emden, P. (1935) *Randlords*, London, Hodder and Stoughton.

Emden, P. H. (1939) *Quakers in Commerce*, London, Sampson Low Marston.

Emery, F. E. and Trist, E. L. (1965) 'The Causal Texture of Organizational Environments', *Human Relations*, 18.

Evely, R. and Little, I. M. D. (1960) *Concentration in British Industry*, Cambridge, Cambridge University Press.

Everard, S. (1949) *The History of the Gas, Light and Coke Company*, London, Ernest Benn.

Everitt, B. (1974) *Cluster Analysis*, London, Heinemann.

Farber, B. (1981) *Conceptions of Kinship*, New York, Elsevier North Holland.

Fennema, M. (1982) *International Networks of Banks and Industry*, The Hague, Nijhof.

Fennema, M. and Schijf, H. (1978) 'Analysing Interlocking Directorates: Theory and Methods', *Social Networks*, 1.

Fennema, M. and Schijf, H. (1984) 'The Transnational Network' in Stokman et al. (1984).

Ferris, P. (1960) *The City*, London, Victor Gollancz.

Fichtner, P. S. (1976) 'Dynastic Marriage in Sixteenth Century Habsburg Diplomacy and Statecraft', *American Historical Review*, 81.

Fidler, J. (1981) *The British Business Elite*, London, Routledge and Kegan Paul.

Firn, J. (1975) 'External Control and Regional Policy', in *The Red Paper on Scotland*, Edinburgh, Edinburgh University Student Publications Board.

Firth, R., et al. (1970) *Families and their Relatives*, London, Routledge and Kegan Paul.

Firth Brown (n.d.) *100 Years in Steel*, Sheffield, Thomas Firth & John Brown.

Fitch, R. (1972) 'Sweezy and Corporate Fetishism', *Socialist Revolution*, 12.

Fitch, R. and Oppenheimer, M. (1970) 'Who Rules the Corporations?', Parts I, II and III, *Socialist Revolution*, 1 (the three parts of this article are referenced as 1970a, 1970b, and 1970c).

Fitzgerald, P. (1927) *Industrial Combination in England*, London, Pitman.

Florence, P. S. (1953) *The Logic of British and American Industry*, London, Routledge and Kegan Paul.

Florence, P. S. (1961) *Ownership, Control and Success of Large Companies*, London, Sweet and Maxwell.

Fox, W. (1931) *The Food Combines*, London, Labour Research Department.

Francis, A. (1968) *A Guinea A Box*, London, Hale.

Francis, A. (1980) 'Families, Firms and Finance Capital', *Sociology*, 14.

Francis, A., et al. (eds) (1983) *Power, Efficiency and Institutions*, London, Heinemann.

Francko, L. G. (1976) *The European Multinationals*, New York, Harper and Row.

Freeman, L. C. (1977) 'A Set of Measures of Centrality Based on Betweenness', *Sociometry*, 40.

Freeman, L. C. (1978) 'Centrality in Social Networks', *Social Networks*, 1.

Freeman, L. C. (1980) 'The Gatekeeper, Pair-Dependency and Structural Centrality', *Quality and Quantity*, 14.

Friedkin, N. E. (1981) 'The Development of Structure in Random Networks', *Social Networks*, 3.

Friedkin, N. E. (1982) 'Information Flow Through Strong and Weak Ties in Intraorganizational Social Networks', *Social Networks*, 3.

Friedmann, H. (1979) 'Are Distributions Really Structures?', *Connections*, 2(2).

Fulford, R. (1946) *Five Decades of BET*, London, BET.

Fulford, R. (1956) *The Sixth Decade*, London, BET.

Galaskiewicz, J. and Wasserman, S. (1981) 'A Dynamic Study of Change in a Regional Corporate Network', *American Sociological Review*, 46.

Garcke, E. (1907) *The Progress of Electrical Enterprise*, London, Electrical Press.

Gardiner, A. G. (n.d.) *The Life of George Cadbury*, London, Cassell (?1925).

Giddens, A. (1974) 'Elites in the British Class Structure', in Stanworth and Giddens (1974).

Giddens, A. (1979) *Central Problems in Social Theory*, London, Macmillan.

Giddens, A. (1981) *A Contemporary Critique of Historical Materialism*, London, Macmillan.

Giddens, A. and Mackenzie, G. (eds) (1982) *Social Class and the Division of Labour*, Cambridge, Cambridge University Press.

Giddens, A. and Stanworth P. (1978) 'Elites and Privilege', in Abrams (1978).

Giuseppi, J. (1966) *The Bank of England*, London, Evans.

Glasberg, D. S. (1981) 'Corporate Power and Control: The Case of Leasco Corporation Versus Chemical Bank', *Social Problems*, 29.

Glasberg, D. S. and Schwartz, M. (1983) 'Ownership and Control of Corporations', *Annual Review of Sociology*, 9.

Glassman, R. B. (1973) 'Persistence and Loose-Coupling in Living Systems', *Behavioural Science*, 18.

Gogel, R. and Koenig, T. (1981) 'Commercial Banks, Interlocking Directorates and Economic Power: An Analysis of the Primary Metals Industry', *Social Problems*, 29.

Gordon, L. (1938) *The Public Corporation in Great Britain*, London, Oxford University Press.

Gordon, R. A. (1936) 'Stockholdings of Officers and Directors in American Industrial Corporations', *Quarterly Journal of Economics*, 50.

Gordon, R. A. (1938) 'Ownership by Management and Control Groups in the Large Corporation', *Quarterly Journal of Economics*, 52.

Gordon, R. A. (1945) *Business Leadership in the Large Corporation*, Berkeley, University of California Press, 1961.

Gospel, H. F. and Littler, C. (eds) (1983) *Managerial Strategies and Industrial Relations*, London, Heinemann.

Gouldner, A. W. (1959) 'Reciprocity and Autonomy in Social Theory', in Gross (1959).

Granick, D. (1962) *The European Executive*, New York, Doubleday.

Granovetter, M. (1973) 'The Strength of Weak Ties', *American Journal of Sociology*, 78.

Granovetter, M. (1979) 'The Theory-Gap in Social Network Analysis', in Holland and Lienhardt (1979).

Granovetter, M. (1982) 'The Strength of Weak Ties: A Network Theory Revisited', in Marsden and Lin (1982).

Grant, A. (1960) *Steel and Ships: The History of John Brown's*, London, Michael Joseph.

Green, E. and Moss, M. (1982) *A Business of National Importance*, London, Methuen.

Gregory, T. E. (1936) *The Westminster Bank*, 2 vols, London, Oxford University Press.

Gregory, T. (1962) *E. Oppenheimer and the Economic Development of Southern Africa*, London, Oxford University Press.

Gross, L. (ed.) (1959) *Symposium on Sociological Theory*, New York, Harper and Row.

Grubb, I. (1930) *Quakerism and Industry Before 1800*, London, Williams and Norgate.

Hadden, T. (1977) *Company Law and Capitalism*, London, Weidenfeld and Nicolson.

Hadfield, C. (1974) *British Canals*, 5th edn, Newton Abbott, David and Charles.

Haigh, K. R. (1968) *Cableships and Submarine Cables*, London, Adlard Coles.

Hamilton, F. E. E. and Linge, G. (eds) (1981) *Spatial Analysis, Industry, and the Industrial Environment*, London, John Wiley.

Hamilton, M. (1976) 'An Analysis and Typology of Social Power (Part I)', *Philosophy of the Social Sciences*, 6.

Hamilton, M. (1977) 'An Analysis and Typology of Social Power (Part II)', *Philosophy of the Social Sciences*, 7.

Hannah, L. (1974) 'Managerial Innovation and the Rise of the Large-Scale Company in Interwar Britain', *Economic History Review*, 27.

Hannah, L. (1976a) *The Rise of the Corporate Economy*, London, Methuen.

Hannah, L. (ed.) (1976b) *Management Strategy and Business Development*, London, Macmillan.

Hannah, L. (1979) *Electricity Before Nationalisation*, London, Macmillan.

Hannah, L. and Kay, J. A. (1977) *Concentration in Modern Industry*, London, Macmillan.

Harrigan, F. J. (1982) 'The Relationship Between Industrial and Geographical Linkages', *Journal of Regional Science*, 22.

Hart, P. E. and Clarke, R. (1980) *Concentration in British Industry, 1935–75*, Cambridge, Cambridge University Press.

Hart, P. E. and Prais, S. J. (1956) 'The Analysis of Business Concentration: A Statistical Approach', *Journal of the Royal Statistical Society*, Series A, 119.

Hart, P. E., et al. (1973) *Mergers and Concentration in British Industry*, Cambridge, Cambridge University Press.

Haslewood, A. (1953) 'The Origin of the State Telephone System in Britain', *Oxford Economic Papers*, 5.

Hatry, C. A. (1939) *The Hatry Case*, London, Nicholls.

Hawkins, K. H. and Pass, C. L. (1979) *The Brewing Industry*, London, Heinemann.

Hedberg, B. (1981) 'How Organisations Learn and Unlearn', in Nystrom and Starbuck (1981).

Heinemann, M. (1944) *Britain's Coal*, London, Gollancz.

Henderson, A. J. (1951) *Under the Furness Flag*, London, Furness Withy.

Henriques, R. (1960) *Marcus Samuel*, London, Barrie and Rockliff.

Herman, E. S. (1973) 'Do Bankers Control Corporations?' *Monthly Review*, 25.

Herman, E. S. (1981) *Corporate Control, Corporate Power*, Cambridge, Cambridge University Press.

Hidy, R. W. (1949) *The House of Baring in American Trade and Finance*, Cambridge, Mass., Harvard University Press.

Hilferding, R. (1910) *Finance Capital*, London, Routledge and Kegan Paul 1981.

Hirsch, P. (1975) 'Organization Efficiency and the Institutional Environment', *Administrative Science Quarterly*, 20.

Hobson, O. (1957) *How the City Works*, London, News Chronicle Book Department.

Hoerning, K. H. (1971) 'Power and Social Stratification', *Sociological Quarterly*, 12.

Hogwood, B. W. (1979) *Government and Shipbuilding*, Farnborough, Saxon House.

Holl, P. (1975) 'Effect of Control Type on the Performance of the Firm in the UK', *Journal of Industrial Economics*, 23.

Holl, P. (1977) 'Control Type and the Market for Corporate Control in Large US Corporations', *Journal of Industrial Economics*, 25.

Holland, P. W. and Lienhardt, S. (eds) (1979) *Perspectives on Social Networks*, New York, Academic Press.

Hood, N. and Young, S. (1976) 'US Investment in Scotland', *Scottish Journal of Political Economy*, 23.

Hooley, E. T. (1929) *Hooley's Confessions*, London, Simpkin Marshall Hamilton Kent.

Hudson, K. (n.d.) *The History of English China Clays*, Newton Abbott, David and Charles (?1969).

Hudson, R. (1981) 'Capital Accumulation and Regional Problems', in Hamilton and Linge (1981).

Hume, J. R. and Moss, M. S. (1979) *Beardmore: The History of a Scottish Industrial Giant*, London, Heinemann.

Hunting, P. (1968) *The Group and I*, London, The Hunting Group.

Hyde, F. E. (1956) *Blue Funnel*, Liverpool, Liverpool University Press.

Hyde, F. E. (1973) *Far Eastern Trade, 1860–1914*, London, Black.

Hyde, F. E. (1975) *Cunard and the North Atlantic*, London, Macmillan.

Hymer, S. (1972) 'The Multinational Corporation and the Law of Uneven Development', in Radice (1975).

Ingham, G. (1982) 'Divisions Within the Dominant Class and British "Exceptionalism"', in Giddens and Mackenzie (1982).

Ingrams, R. (1979) *Goldenballs*, London, Private Eye Productions.

Isichei, E. (1971) *Victorian Quakers*, London, Oxford University Press.

Jackson, A. A. and Croome, D. F. (1962) *Rails Through the Clay*, London, George Allen and Unwin.

Jackson, W. T. (1968) *The Enterprising Scot*, Edinburgh, Edinburgh University Press.

Jenkins, C. (1959) *Power at the Top*, London, MacGibbon and Kee.

Jennings, P. (1961) *Dunlopera*, London, Dunlop.

John, A. H. (1950) *The Industrial Development of South Wales, 1750–1850*, Cardiff, University of Wales Press.

Johnson, P. S. and Apps, R. (1979) 'Interlocking Directorates Among the UK's Largest Companies', *Antitrust Bulletin*, 24.

Jones, A. C. M. (1976–7) *British Independent Airlines Since 1946*, 4 vols Uxbridge, LAAS International.

Jones, R. and Marriott, O. (1970) *Anatomy of a Merger*, London, Jonathan Cape.

Kadushin, C. (1968) 'Power, Influence and Social Circles: A New Methodology for Studying Opinion Makers', *American Sociological Review*, 33.

Kann, R. A. (1973) 'Dynastic Relations and European Power Politics (1848–1918)', *Journal of Modern History*, 45.

Karpik, L. (ed.) (1977) *Organisation and Environment*, Beverley Hills, California, Sage.

Keeling, B. S. and Wright, A. E. G. (1964) *The Development of the Modern British Steel Industry*, London, Longmans.

Keevil, A. (1972) *The Story of Fitch Lovell*, London, Phillimore.

Keir, D. (1951) *The Younger Centuries*, Edinburgh, Wm Younger.

Kennedy, W. P. (1976) 'Institutional Response to Economic Growth: Capital markets in Britain to 1914', in Hannah (1976b).

Kennedy W. P. and Britton, R. E. (1981a) *Portfolio Behaviour and Economic Development*, unpublished paper, University of Essex.

Kennedy W. P. and Britton, R. E. (1981b) *Wealthy Scots 1876–1913*, unpublished paper, University of Essex.

Kieve, J. (1973) *The Electric Telegraph*, Newton Abbot, David and Charles.

Klingender, F. D. and Legg, S. (1937) *Money Behind the Screen*, London, Lawrence and Wishart.

Knightley, P. (1981) *The Vestey Affair*, London, Macdonald.

Knightley, P., et al. [the *Sunday Times* Insight Team] (1979) *Suffer the Children*, London, André Deutsch.

Knoke, D. and Kuklinski, J. H. (eds) (1982) *Network Analysis*, Beverley Hills, California, Sage.

Knowles, J. C. (1973) 'The Rockefeller Financial Group', MSS Modular Publications, Module 343.

Koenig, T. (1979) *Interlocking Directorates Among The Largest American Corporations and Their Significance for Corporate Political Activity*, Ph.D. thesis, University of California at Santa Barbara.

Koenig, T. and Gogel, R. (1981) 'Interlocking Corporate Directorships as a Social Network', *American Journal of Economics and Sociology*, 40.

Koenig, T., et al. (1979) 'Models of The Significance of Interlocking Corporate Directorates', *American Journal of Economics and Sociology*, 38.

Koss, E. (1970) *Sir John Brunner*, Cambridge, Cambridge University Press.

Kotz, D. M. (1978) *Bank Control of Large Corporations in the United States*, Berkeley, University of California Press.

Labour Research Association (1950) *Monopoly Today*, New York, International Publishers.

Lankford, P. M. (1974) 'A Comparative Analysis of Clique Identification Methods', *Sociometry*, 37.

Lanning, G., et al. (1979) *Africa Undermined*, Harmondsworth, Penguin.

Larner, R. J. (1970) *Management Control and the Large Corporation*, New York, Dunellen.

Lattin, J. M. and Wong, M. A. (1982) 'A High-Density Clustering Approach to Exploring the Structure of Social Networks', *Connections*, 5.

Lawford, G. and Nicholson, L. R. (1950) *The Telcon Story*, London, Telegraph Construction and Maintenance.

Layder, D. (1981) *Structure, Interaction and Social Theory*, London, Routledge and Kegan Paul.

Lazell, H. G. (1975) *From Pills to Penicillin*, London, Heinemann.

Leak, H. and Maizels, A. (1945) 'The Structure of British Industry', *Statistical Journal*, CVIII.

Lee, C. (1966) *Sixty Years of the Piccadilly*, London, London Transport.

Lee, C. (1972) *The Metropolitan Line*, London, London Transport.

Leighton-Boyce, J. A. S. L. (1958) *Smiths the Bankers*, London, National Provincial Bank.

Lenin, V. I., (1916) *Imperialism: The Highest Stage of Capitalism*, Moscow, Progress Publishers (1968).

Lenman, B. and Donaldson, K. (1971) 'Partners' Incomes, Investment and Diversification in the Scottish Linen Area, 1850–1921', *Business History*, 13.

Levine, J. H. (1972) 'Spheres of Influence', *American Sociological Review*, 37.

Levine, J. H. (1978) 'The Theory of Bank Control: Comment on Mariolis' Test of the Theory', *Social Science Quarterly*, 58.

Levine, J. and Mullins, N. C. (1978) 'Structuralist Analysis of Data in Sociology', *Connections*, 1(3).

Levine, J. and Roy, W. S. (1979) 'A Study of Interlocking Directorates: Vital Concepts of Organization', in Holland and Lienhardt (1979).

Lienhardt, S. (ed) (1977) *Social Networks*, New York, Academic Press.

Lisle-Williams, M. (1981) 'Continuities in the English Financial Elite 1850–1980', paper presented to BSA/PSA Conference, University of Sheffield.

Lloyd, H. (1975) *The Quaker Lloyds in the Industrial Revolution*, London, Hutchinson.

Lockwood, D. (1956) 'Some Remarks on *The Social System*', *British Journal of Sociology*, 6.

Lockwood, D. (1964) 'Social Integration and System Integration', in Zollschan and Hirsch (1964).

Lukes, S. (1974) *Power: A Radical View*, London, Macmillan.

Lukes, S. (1977) 'Power and Structure', in Lukes, S., *Essays in Social Theory*, London, Macmillan.

Lundberg, F. (1937) *America's Sixty Families*, New York, Vanguard Press.

Lundberg, F. (1968) *The Rich and the Super-Rich*, New York, Bantam Books, 1969.

Lupton, T. and Wilson, C. S. (1959) 'The Social Background and Connections of Top Decision-Makers', *The Manchester School*, 27.

McCord, N. (1979) *North East England*, London, Batsford.

Mace, M. L. (1971) *Directors: Myth and Reality*, Cambridge, Mass., Harvard University Press.

McEachern, D. (1980) *A Class Against Itself*, Cambridge, Cambridge University Press.

Macmillan, D. S. (1967) *Scotland and Australia*, Oxford, Clarendon Press.

McRae, H. and Cairncross, F. (1973) *Capital City*, London, Eyre Methuen.

Macrosty, H. W. (1907) *The Trust Movement in British Industry*, London, Longmans Green.

Mandel, E. (1963) 'The Dialectic of Class and Region in Belgium', *New Left Review*, 20.

Mariolis, P. (1975) 'Interlocking Directorates and Control of Corporations', *Social Science Quarterly*, 56.

Mariolis, P. (1978) 'Type of Corporation, Size of Firm, and Interlocking Directorates: A Reply to Levine', *Social Science Quarterly*, 58.

Mariolis, P. and Jones, M. H. (1982) 'Centrality in Corporate Networks', *Administrative Science Quarterly*, 27.

Marriner, S. and Hyde, F. E. (1967) *The Senior: John S. Swire*, Liverpool, Liverpool University Press.

Marriott, O. (1967) *The Property Boom*, London, Hamish Hamilton.

Marsden, P. V. and Lin, N. (eds) (1982) *Social Structure and Network Analysis*, Beverly Hills, California, Sage.

Masser, I. (ed.) (1976) *Theory and Practice in Regional Science*, London, Pion Books.

Massey, D. B. and Batey, P. W. J. (eds) (1977) *Alternative Frameworks For Analysis*, London, Pion Books.

Mathias, P. (1967) *Retailing Revolution*, London, Longmans Green.

Mathias, P. and Pearsall, A. W. H. (eds) (1971) *Shipping: A Survey of Historical Records*, Newton Abbot, David and Charles.

Mattelart, A. (1976) *Mutlinational Corporations and the Control of Culture*, First English edition, Brighton, Harvester, 1979.

Matthews, P. W. and Tuke, A. W. (1926) *History of Barclays Bank Ltd*, London, Blades East and Blades.

Middlemas, K. (1963) *The Master Builders*, London, Hutchinson.

Middlemas, K. (1979) *Politics in Industrial Society*, London, André Deutsch.

Midland Bank (1979) 'The Origins and Growth of the Midland Bank Group', *Midland Bank Review*, Autumn.

Mills, C. W. (1956) *The Power Elite*, New York, Oxford University Press.

Minchinton, W. (1957) *The British Tinplate Industry*, London, Oxford University Press.

Mintz, B. (1977) 'Managerialism, Stockholding and the Role of Finance Capital', unpublished paper, State University of New York at Stony Brook.

Mintz, B. and Schwartz, M. (1979) 'The Role of Financial Institutions in Interlock Networks', unpublished paper, State University of New York at Stony Brook.

Mintz, B. and Schwartz, M. (1981a) 'The Structure of Intercorporate Unity in American Business', *Social Problems*, 29.

Mintz, B. and Shwartz, M. (1981b) 'Interlocking Directorates and Interest Group Formation', *American Sociological Review*, 46.

Mintz, B. and Schwartz, M. (1984) *Bank Hegemony, Corporate Networks and Intercorporate Power*, Chicago, University of Chicago Press.

Mishra, R. (1982) 'System Integration, Social Action and Change', *Sociological Review*, 30.

Mitchell, J. C. (1969a) 'The Concept and Use of Social Networks', in Mitchell (1969b).

Mitchell, J. C. (ed.) (1969b) *Social Networks in Urban Situations*, Manchester, Manchester University Press.

Mitchell, J. C. (1973) 'Networks, Norms, and Institutions', in Boissevain and Mitchell (1973).

Mitchell, J. C. (1974) 'Social Networks', *Annual Review of Anthropology*, 3.

Mitchell, J. C. (1979) 'Networks, Algorithms, and Analysis', in Holland and Lienhardt (1979).

Mitchell, J. C. (1981) 'Ethnography and Analysis: A Test of some Algorithmic Procedures', *Connections*, 4(3).

Mizruchi, M. S. (1982) *The American Corporate Network, 1904–1974*, London, Sage.

Mizruchi, M. S. and Bunting, D. (1981) 'Influence in Corporate Networks: An Examination of Four Measures', *Administrative Science Quarterly*, 26.

Mokken, R. (1979) 'Cliques, Clubs and Clans', *Quality and Quantity*, 13.

Moreno, J L. (1934) *Who Shall Survive?*, New York, Beacon.

Morgan Grenfell (1958) *Morgan Grenfell & Co 1838–1958*, London, Morgan Grenfell.

Morin, F. (1974) 'Qui détient le pouvoir financier en France?', *Economie et Humanisme*, 220.

Morin, F. (1976) 'Ombres et lumières du capitalisme, français', *Economie et Humanisme*, 229.

Morton, F. (1962) *The Rothschilds*, London, Secker and Warburg.

Mouzelis, N. (1974) 'Social and System Integration', *British Journal of Sociology*, 25.

Muir, A. and Davies, M. (1978) *A Victorian Shipowner*, London, Cayzer Irvine.

Murdock, G. (1977) *Patterns of Ownership; Questions of Control*, Mass Communication and Society, Unit 10, Milton Keynes, Open University.

Murdock, G. and Golding, P. (1973) 'For a Political Economy of Mass Communications', *Socialist Register*.

Murdock, G. and Golding, P. (1978) 'The Structure, Ownership and Control of the Press, 1914–76', in Boyce et al. (1978).

Murray, E. (1927) *The Post Office*, London, G. P. Putnam's Sons.

Murray, M. (1953) *Union-Castle Chronicle*, London, Longmans Green.

Nairn, T. (1977) *The Breakup of Britain*, London, New Left Books.

Neuman, A. (1934) *The Economic Organisation of the British Coal Industry*, London, Routledge.

Niemeijer, R. (1973) 'Some Applications of the Notion of Density', in Boissevain and Mitchell (1973).

Norich, S. (1980) 'Interlocking Directorates, the Control of Large Corporations, and Patterns of Accumulation in the Capitalist Class', in Zeitlin (1980b).

Nyman, S. and Silberston, A. (1978) 'The Ownership and Control of Industry', *Oxford Economic Papers*, 30(1).

Nystrom, P. and Starbuck, W. (eds) (1981) *Handbook of Organizational Design*, Vol. 1, London, Oxford University Press.

O'Connor, J. (1971) 'Who Rules the Corporations?', *Socialist Revolution*, 7.

O'Hagan, H. O. (1929) *Leaves from My Life*, 2 vols, London, John Lane, The Bodley Head.

Ornstein, M. D. (1982) 'Interlocking Directorships in Canada: Evidence from Replacement Patterns', *Social Networks*, 4.

Overbeek, H. (1980) 'Finance Capital and the Crisis in Britain', *Capital and Class*, 11.

Owen, H. (1946) *Steel: The Facts*, London, Lawrence and Wishart.

Pahl, R. E. and Winkler, J. T. (1974) 'The Economic Elite: Theory and Practice', in Stanworth and Giddens (1974).

Palmer, D. (1983) 'Broken Ties: Interlocking Directorates and Intercorporate Coordination', *Administrative Science Quarterly*, 28.

Parkinson, H. R. (1944) 'Who Owns the Railways?', *Financial News*, 31 October, 1, 2, 3 November.

Parkinson, H. R. (1951) *Ownership of Industry*, London, Eyre and Spottiswoode.

Parkinson, J. R. (1960) *The Economics of Shipbuilding in the United Kingdom*, Cambridge, Cambridge University Press.

Parsons, T. (1951) *The Social System*, Glencoe, Free Press.

Payne, P. L. (1967) 'The Emergence of the Large-Scale Company in Great Britain, 1820–1914', *Economic History Review*, 20.

Pennings, J. (1980) *Interlocking Directorates*, San Francisco, Jossey-Bass.

PEP (1936) *Report on the Supply of Electricity in Britain*, London, Political and Economic Planning.

PEP (1938) *Report on the British Press*, London, Political and Economic Planning.

PEP (1939) *Report on the Gas Industry in Great Britain*, London, Political and Economic Planning.

PEP (1958) *The British Film Industry*, London, Political and Economic Planning.

Perkin, H. (1978) 'The Recruitment of Elites in British Society since 1800', *Journal of Social History*, 12.

Perrucci, R. and Pilisuk, M. (1970) 'Leaders and Ruling Elites: The Interorganizational Bases of Community Power', *American Sociological Review*, 35.

Pfeffer, J. (1972a) 'Merger as a Response to Organizational Interdependence', *Administrative Science Quarterly*, 17.

Pfeffer, J. (1972b) 'Size and Composition of Corporate Boards of Directors: The Organisation and its Environment', *Administrative Science Quarterly*, 17.

Pfeffer, J. (1974) 'Cooptation and the Composition of Electric Utility Boards of Directors', *Pacific Sociological Review*, 17.

Pfeffer, J. and Leblebici, H. (1973) 'Executive Recruitment and the Development of Interfirm Organisations', *Administrative Science Quarterly*, 18.

Pfeffer, J. and Salancik, G. R. (1978) *The External Control of Organisations*, New York, Harper and Row.

Phillips, A. (1960) 'A Theory of Interfirm Organization', *Quarterly Journal of Economics*, 74.

Plummer, A. (1937) *New British Industries in the Twentieth Century*, London, Pitman.

Poensgen, O. H. (1980) 'Between Market and Hierarchy: The Role of Interlocking Directorates', *Zeitschrift für die Gesamte Staatswissenschaft*, 136.

Pollard, S. (1962) *The Development of the British Economy*, London, Edward Arnold.

Pollard, S. and Robertson, P. (1979) *The British Shipbuilding Industry, 1870–1914*, Cambridge, Mass., Harvard University Press.

Prais, S. J. (1976) *The Evolution of Giant Firms in Britain*, Cambridge, Cambridge University Press.

Price, F. V. (1981) 'Only Connect: Issues in Charting Social Networks', *Sociological Review*, 29.

Protz, R. (1978) *Pulling A Fast One*, London, Pluto.

Pudney, J. (1971) *A Draught of Contentment*, London, New English Library.

Pudney, J. (1975) *London's Docks*, London, Thames and Hudson.

Pugh, D. S. and Hickson, D. J. (1976) *Organizational Structure in its Context*, Farnborough, Saxon House.

Pumphrey, R. E. (1959) 'The Introduction of Industrialists into the British Peerage', *American Historical Review*, 65.

Radice, H. (ed.) (1975) *International Firms and Modern Imperialism*, Harmondsworth, Penguin.

Raistrick, A. (1950) *Quakers in Science and Industry*, London, Bannisdale Press.

Ratcliff, R. E. (1980a) 'Banks and Corporate Lending: An Analysis of the Impact of the Internal Structure of the Capitalist Class on the Lending Behaviour of Banks', *American Sociological Review*, 45.

Reader, W. J. (1960) *Unilever: A Short History*, London, George Allen and Unwin.

Reader, W. J. (1970) *Imperial Chemical Industries*, 2 vols, London, Oxford University Press.

Reader, W. J. (1980) *Fifty Years of Unilever*, London, Heinemann.

Reckitt, B. N. (1952) *The History of Reckitt and Sons*, London, A. Brown.

Rees, G. (1973) *St. Michael: A History of Marks and Spencer*, London, Pan.

Rees, J. M. (1922) *Trusts in British Industry*, London, P. S. King.

Reid, J. M. (1964) *James Lithgow: Master of Work*, London, Hutchinson.

Reid, M. (1980) *The Secondary Banking Crisis*, London, Macmillan.

Robbins, D., et al. (eds) (1982) *Rethinking Social Inequality*, Aldershot, Gower.

Rochester, A. (1936) *Rulers of America*, New York, International Publishers.

Rosenbaum, E. and Sherman, A. J. (1979) *M M Warburg & Co.*, London, C. Hurst.

Ross, W. D., et al. (1949) *Royal Commission on the Press, 1947–9*, CMND 7700, London, HMSO.

Roy, W. G. (1983) 'The Unfolding of the Interlocking Directorate Structure of the United States', *American Sociological Review*, 48.

Rubinstein, W. B. (1976) 'Wealth, Elites and the Class Structure of Modern Britain', *Past and Present*, 70.

Rytina, S. (1982) 'Structural Constraint on Intergroup Contact', in Marsden and Lin (1982).

Sampson, A. (1975) *The Seven Sisters*, London, Hodder and Stoughton.

Sampson, A. (1979) 'Musical Chairs for Beecham Brigade', *Observer*, 18 November.

Savage, D. (1979) *Founders, Heirs and Managers*, London, Sage.

Sayers, R. S. (1957) *Lloyds Bank in the History of English Banking*, Oxford, Clarendon Press.

Sayers, R. S. (1976) *The Bank of England*, Cambridge, Cambridge University Press.

Schlesinger, P. (1978) *Putting 'Reality' Together*, London, Constable.

Schönwitz, D. and Weber, H. J. (1980) 'Personelle Verflechtungen Zwishchen Unternehmen', *Zeitschrift für die Gesamte Staatswissenschaft*, 136.

Scott, J. D. (1958) *Siemens Brothers*, London, Weidenfeld and Nicolson.

Scott, J. D. (1962) *Vickers*, London, Weidenfeld and Nicolson.

Scott, J. D. (1978) *Vickers Against the Odds*, London, Hodder and Stoughton.

Scott, J. P. (1979) *Corporations, Classes, and Captialism*, London, Hutchinson.

Scott, J. P. (1982a) 'Property and Control: Some Remarks on the British Propertied Class', in Giddens and Mackenzie (1982).

Scott, J. P. (1982b) *The Upper Classes*, London, Macmillan.

Scott, J. P. (1983) 'Declining Autonomy: Recent Trends in the Scottish Economy', in *Scottish Government Yearbook*.

Scott, J. P. and Hughes, M. D. (1975) 'Finance Capital and the Upper Classes', in *The Red Paper on Scotland*, Edinburgh, Edinburgh University Student Publications Board.

Scott, J. P. and Hughes, M. D. (1980) *The Anatomy of Scottish Capital*, London, Croom Helm.

Sellier, F. (1974) 'Les Banques et l'industrie américaine', *Economie et Humanisme*, 220.

Sessions, W. K. and Sessions, E. M. (n.d.) *The Tukes of York*, London, Friends House Service Committee.

Shaw, C. (1983) 'The Large Manufacturing Employers of 1907', *Business History*, 25.

Simmons, J. (1978) *The Railway in England and Wales, 1830–1914*, Leicester, Leicester University Press.

Simonnot, P. (1974) 'Du pouvoir bancaire en France', *Economie et Humanisme*, 220.

Smith, D. and Tepperman, L. (1974) 'Changes in the Canadian Business and Legal Elites, 1870–1970', *Canadian Review of Sociology and Anthropology*, 11.

Smith, E. P. (1970) 'Interlocking Directorates Among the "Fortune 500"', *Antitrust Law and Economics Review*, 3.

Smith, E. P. and Desfosses, L. R. (1972) 'Interlocking Directorates: A Study of Influence', *Mississippi Valley Journal of Business and Economics*, 7.

Snijders, T. A. B. (1981) 'The Degree Variance', *Social Networks*, 3.

Sonquist, J. A. (1980) 'Concepts and Tactics in Analysing Social Network Data', *Connections*, 3(1).

Soref, M. (1979) 'Research on Interlocking Directorates: An Introduction and a Bibliography of North American Sources', *Connections*, 2(2).

Soref, M. (1980) 'The Finance Capitalists', in Zeitlin (1980b).

South Metropolitan Gas (1924) *A Century of Gas in South London*, London, South Metropolitan Gas Company.

Spencer, A. and McAuley, J. (1980) 'The Role of the Non-Executive Director: A *Verstehen* Approach', *Journal of Management Studies*, 17.

Spender, J. A. (1930) *Weetman Pearson*, London, Cassell.

Spiegelberg, R. (1973) *The City*, London, Quartet.

Stacey, M. (1960) *Tradition and Change: A Study of Banbury*, London, Oxford University Press.

Stacey, M., et al. (1975) *Power, Persistence and Change: A Second Study of Banbury*, London, Routledge and Kegan Paul.

Stanworth, P. and (1974) Giddens, A. (eds) (1974) *Elites and Power in British Society*, Cambridge, Cambridge University Press.

Stanworth, P. and Giddens, A. (1975) 'The Modern Corporate Economy', *Sociological Review*, 23(1).

Starbuck, W. (1973) 'Tadpoles into Armageddon and Chrysler into Butterflies', *Social Science Research*, 2.

Stewarts & Lloyds (1953) *Stewarts & Lloyds Ltd*, Glasgow, Stewarts & Lloyds.

Stokman, F. N. and Van Veen, F. J. A. M. (eds) (1981) *GRADAP User's Manual*, Amsterdam, University of Amsterdam Technical Centre.

Stokman, F. N., Ziegler, R. and Scott, J. (eds) (1984) *Networks of Corporate Power*, Cambridge, Polity Press.

Sturmey, S. G. (1958) *The Economic Development of Radio*, London, Duckworth.

Supple, B. (1970) *The Royal Exchange Assurance*, Cambridge, Cambridge University Press.

Sweezy, P. M. (1939) 'Interest Groups in the American Economy', in Sweezy (1953).

Sweezy, P. M. (1951) 'The American Ruling Class', in Sweezy (1953).

Sweezy, P. M. (1953) *The Present as History*, New York, Monthly Review Press.

Sweezy, P. M. (1971) 'The Resurgence of Financial Control: Fact or Fancy?', *Monthly Review*, 23.

Taylor, J. (1976) *Ellermans*, London, Wilton House Gentry.

Tepperman, L. (1972) 'The Natural Disruption of Dynasties', *Canadian Review of Sociology and Anthropology*, 9.

Tepperman, L. (1981) Factors Aiding the Persistence of Dynasties', Research Paper No 29, Structural Analysis Programme, University of Toronto.

Terreberry, S. (1968) 'The Evolution of Organizational Environments', *Administrative Science Quarterly*, 12.

Thom, R. (1975) *Structural Stability and Morphogenesis*, Reading, Mass., W. A. Benjamin.

Thomas, S. E. (1931) *British Banks and the Finance of Industry*, London, P. S. King.

Tilling, J. (1957) *Kings of the Highway*, London, Hutchinson.

Time and Tide (1969) Various articles on Cadbury dated 6–12 February, 13–19 February, 20–26 February, and 27 February-5 March.

Tracey, M. (1978) *The Production of Political Television*, London, Routledge and Kegan Paul.

Trebilcock, C. (1977) *The Vickers Brothers*, London, Europa.

Truex, G. F. (1981) 'Kinship and Network: A Cognitive Model of Interaction', *Social Networks*, 3.

Tuke, A. W. and Gillman, R. J. H. (1972) *Barclays Bank Ltd.*, London, Barclays Bank.

Useem, M. (1979) 'Studying the Corporation and the Corporate Elite', *American Sociologist*, 14.

Useem, M. (1980) 'Corporations and the Corporate Elite', *Annual Review of Sociology*, 6.

Useem, M. (1981a) 'Business Segments and Corporate Relations with US Universities', *Social Problems*, 29.

Useem, M. (1981b) 'Blue Chip Guide to the Inner Circle', *Guardian*, 5 August.

Useem, M. (1982) 'Classwide Rationality in the Politics of Managers and Directors of Large Corporations in the United States and Great Britain', *Administrative Science Quarterly*, 27.

Useem, M. (1984) *The Inner Circle*, New York, Oxford University Press.

Useem, M. and McCormack, A. (1981) 'The Dominant Segment of the British Business Elite', *Sociology*, 15.

Utton, M. A. (1970) *Industrial Concentration*, Harmondsworth, Penguin.

Utton, M. A. (1982) *The Political Economy of Big Business*, Oxford, Martin Robertson.

Vaizey, T. (1960) *The Brewing Industry 1886–1951*, London, Pitman.

Vaizey, J. (1974) *The History of British Steel*, London, Weidenfeld and Nicolson.

van Poucke, W. (1979) 'Network Constraints on Social Action', *Social Networks*, 2.

Verdon, M. (1981) 'Kinship, Marriage and the Family', *American Journal of Sociology*, 86.

Vernon, A. (1958) *A Quaker Business Man*, London, George Allen and Unwin.

Watts, H. D. (1981) *The Branch Plant Economy: A Study of External Control*, London, Longman.

Weiner, M. J. (1981) *English Culture and the Decline of the Entrepreneurial Spirit*, Cambridge, Cambridge University Press.

Wellman, B. (1981) 'Network Analysis From Method and Metaphor to Theory and Substance', Working Paper 1B, Structural Analysis Programme, University of Toronto.

Whitbread (1964) *The Story of Whitbreads*, London, Whitbread.

White, H. P. (1963) *The Regional History of the Railways of Great Britain*, Vol. 3: *Greater London*, Newton Abbott, David and Charles.

Whitley, R. (1973) 'Commonalities and Connections among Directors of Large Financial Institutions', *Sociological Review*, 21(4).

Whitley, R. (1974) 'The City and Industry', in Stanworth and Giddens (1974).

Whitley, R., et al. (1981) *Masters of Business*, London, Tavistock.

Whitt, J. A. (1981) 'Is Oil Different? A Comparison of the Social Backgrounds and Organizational Affliations of Oil and Non-oil Directors', *Social Problems*, 29.

Wigand, R. T. (1977) 'Some Recent Developments in Organisational Communication', *Communications*, 3.

Wilkinson, E. (1939) *The Town That Was Murdered*, London, Gollancz.

Williams, K., et al. (1983) *Why are the British Bad at Manufacturing?*, London, Routledge and Kegan Paul.

Williamson, O. E. (1970) *Corporate Control and Business Behaviour*, Englewood Cliffs, New Jersey, Prentice-Hall.

Williamson, O. E. (1975) *Markets and Hierarchies*, New York, Free Press.

Wilson, C. (1954) *The History of Unilever*, 2 vols, London, Cassell.

Wilson, C. (1968) *Unilever, 1945–65*, London, Cassell.

Windsor, D. B. (1980) *The Quaker Enterprise*, London, Frederick Muller.

Withers, H. (1933) *National Provincial Bank*, London, National Provincial Bank.

Wood, A. (1952) *Mr Rank*, London, Hodder and Stoughton.

Wright, E. O. (1980) 'Varieties of Marxist Conceptions of Class Structure', *Politics and Society*, 9.

Wright, E. O. et al. (1982) *The American Class Structure*, Working Paper No. 3, Comparative Project on Class Structure and Class Consciousness, University of Wisconsin.

Wrong, D. (1968) 'Some Problems in Defining Social Power', *American Journal of Sociology*, 73.

Young, D. A. (1966) *Member for Mexico*, London, Cassell.

Zald, M. (1969) 'The Power and Function of Boards of Directors: A Theoretical Synthesis', *American Journal of Sociology*, 75.

Zeitlin, M. (1974) 'Corporate Ownership and Control: The Large Corporation and the Capitalist Class', *American Journal of Sociology*, 79.

Zeitlin, M. (1980a) 'On Classes, Class Conflict and the State: An Introductory Note', in Zeitlin (1980b).

Zeitlin, M. (ed.) (1980b) *Class, Class Conflict and the State*, Cambridge, Mass., Winthrop.

Zeitlin, M. and Norich, S. (1979) 'Management Control, Exploitation, and Profit Maximization in the Large Corporation', *Research in Political Economy*, 2.

Zeitlin, M. and Ratcliff, R. E. (1975) 'Research Methods for the Analysis of the Internal Structure of Dominant Classes', *Latin American Research Review*, 10.

Zeitlin, M., et al. (1975) '"New Princes" for Old? The Large Corporation and the Capitalist Class in Chile', *American Journal of Sociology*, 80.

Ziegler, R. (1978) 'Editorial', *Social Networks*, 1.

Ziegler, R., et al. (1981) 'Market Structure and Cooptation', working paper for the project 'Personnel – und Kapitalverbindungen', München, Ludwig-Maximilians-universität.

Zijlstra, G. J. (1979) 'Networks in Public Policy: Nuclear Energy in the Netherlands', *Social Networks*, 1.

Zollschan, G. K. and (1964) Hirsch, W. (eds) (1964) *Explorations in Social Change*, London, Routledge and Kegan Paul.

Index

SUBJECTS AND AUTHORS